LICHTENBERG'S COMMENTARIES ON HOGARTH'S ENGRAVINGS

Georg Christoph Lichtenberg

Lichtenberg's Commentaries on Hogarth's Engravings

TRANSLATED FROM THE GERMAN
AND WITH
AN INTRODUCTION BY
INNES AND GUSTAV HERDAN

LONDON: THE CRESSET PRESS

Contents

———————

List of Plates

Introduction

I

BETWEEN the years 1784 and 1796 there appeared in a German literary journal, the *Göttinger Taschenkalender*, a series of commentaries on Hogarth's engravings by G. Ch. Lichtenberg. They were so successful with the public that an enlarged and revised version was published separately in instalments between 1794 and 1799, comprising two single engravings ('Strolling Actresses' and 'A Midnight Modern Conversation') and five series of pictures ('Marriage-à-la-Mode', 'A Rake's Progress', 'A Harlot's Progress', 'The Four Times of the Day', and six plates of 'Industry and Idleness'). This is the version which is translated here, except for the series 'Industry and Idleness', which Lichtenberg did not complete.

It was an age of literary journals. In the first decades of the century the English public had already been delighted by *The Tatler* and *The Spectator*, with their varied and faithful portrayal of the social scene, and which were succeeded by Johnson's *Rambler* and *Idler*. In the Germany of those times it was even harder for an author to make a living by his pen than in England, so that many turned to literary magazines, which multiplied and gained in popularity as the century went on. The *Göttinger Taschenkalender* was one out of more than 500 such publications, and contained fashion notes as well as literary articles and polemical writings. Its circulation was wide and the Hogarth commentaries when they appeared caused the greatest sensation, as we learn from Goethe's *Tag- und Jahrbuch*, 1795.

A German elector was then on the English throne, and the special bond

ix

between England and Hanover created a lively interest in English life and manners among the readers of the *Göttinger Taschenkalender*; Hogarth's paintings with their pungent criticism and sharp illumination of English society were ideally suited to their tastes, and it is from this point of view that the Commentaries should be read. The eagerness with which they were received was well justified, for they succeeded to an amazing degree in transforming the two-dimensional pictorial representation of a certain section of English life into a three-dimensional dramatic one. Not only do we *see* what before we had only *looked* at, but by providing us with a sort of recollection of what preceded the pictured situation, and with a sort of presentiment of what is to follow, the commentary turns the picture into a dramatic scene. One recalls Lamb's delightful testimony to that dramatic quality in Hogarth, which has been so brilliantly re-created in the Commentaries.

'I was pleased,' he says, 'with the reply of a gentleman who on being asked which book he esteemed most in his library answered "Shakespeare", and being asked which he esteemed next best, replied "Hogarth". His graphic representations are indeed books; they have the teeming, fruitful, suggestive meaning of *words*. Other pictures we look at—his prints we read.'[1]

Considering this remark of Lamb's, it is a remarkable coincidence that the work through which Lamb has endeared himself perhaps most with the English-speaking world, his *Tales from Shakespeare*, should have its counterpart in Lichtenberg's commentaries on Hogarth, which might truly be described as *Tales from Hogarth*, for this is what they are.

In accordance with this dynamic quality of Hogarth's art, the Commentaries present the pictured event of a gesture or movement as the differential of the motion in time. That is to say, the fleeting moment which Hogarth has fixed by his stylus is conceived as the turning, or at least the transition, point between what went before and what is to follow. This gives the engravings the curious property which certain Japanese colour-prints are said to possess, and from which their name derives—'the living art'; namely, that if looked at in the proper way, the figures actually move before the eye of the observer. Without claiming so much for Hogarth's pictures when seen by themselves, they certainly acquired that property in

---

[1] 'On the Genius and Character of Hogarth.' *Works of Charles Lamb*, Vol. I, p. 70. 1818.

the mind of the observer when seen in the light of the Commentaries.[1]

What steps forward from the picture under the pen which wrote the Commentaries as if under a magic wand is another version of Gay's *Beggar's Opera* with both light and darkness intensified, its social bearings amplified and its treatment immensely diversified. The persons become the characters in a play; we see them act and hear them talk, and both the tying of the dramatic knot and its severance become visible to our inner eye.

That Hogarth's work lent itself to such treatment there can be no doubt. Hogarth is often described as a 'comic writer', a 'dramatist', a 'moralist', by men like Lamb, Hazlitt and Thackeray, who understood and appreciated his peculiar genius. And just because Hogarth's themes and the cross-section of human life which he chose for their presentation were the sort which according to Lessing's 'Laokoon' theory of the border line between poetry and art were not really fit subjects for pictorial presentation, they are brought so much nearer to us through the addition of Commentaries like these. All this is perhaps readily understandable. What is more difficult to understand is that the Commentaries should have been written by one whose background was so entirely different from what we might have expected. In a time of over-specialization like ours, the lesson we can derive from this curious phenomenon of literature is particularly valuable.

The author of the Commentaries was Georg Christoph Lichtenberg, Professor of Physics in the University of Göttingen. He was born on July 1, 1742, in the little village of Oberramstadt, near Darmstadt, the eighteenth child of the village pastor. Through the negligence of his nurse, the young Georg Christoph had an unfortunate fall whose consequences he had to carry for the rest of his life. From his eighth year his spine began to curve, he became hunch-backed, and throughout his life was in poor health. Of his mother we know little, hardly more than her son has told us in his letters and notes, but we gather that she was gay,

<hr>

[1] cf. Hazlitt in his essay *On Hogarth's Marriage-à-la-Mode* in *The Round Table*, London, 1877, p. 27 ff.

'Everything in his pictures has life and motion in it. Not only does the business of the scene never stand still, but every feature and muscle is put into full play; the exact feeling of the moment is brought out, and carried to its utmost height, and then instantly seized and stamped on the canvas for ever. The expression is always taken *en passant*, in a state of progress or change and, as it were, at the salient point.'

active, and sympathetic, and that her temperament helped him to rise above his physical disability. In his inner life she played a much more important role than did his father.

Lichtenberg's father was a man of considerable theological learning who in 1749 became General Superintendent at Darmstadt, and thus the highest church dignitary in the district, but he also had tastes for natural science which he delighted to expound in his sermons, and it was this bent of mind which the young Lichtenberg inherited. His early interest in science developed into his life's work; the quiet piety of his mother and the atmosphere of the parsonage clung to him too, despite his rationalistic outlook, and manifests itself in his writings in quite unexpected places. He tells us that as a child he once wrote on a piece of paper, 'What is the Aurora Borealis?', addressed it to an angel and put it in the attic, an early example of how he managed to combine credulity with scientific curiosity.

On his father's death in 1751, Lichtenberg was sent to the Gymnasium at Darmstadt where his scientific bent soon became apparent, and in 1763 a grant of 400 florins from the Landgraf of Hessen enabled him—who otherwise would have been without the means of further study—to enrol at the University of Göttingen, then one of the best in Europe, and to study physics and mathematics under Kästner, a famous physicist and writer of epigrams, who became his lifelong friend.

When only 25, he was offered by the Hessian Ministry of Education the post of Professor of Mathematics at the University of Giessen, which Lichtenberg, however, did not accept, probably because he already had his eye upon a similar post in the far more renowned University of Göttingen, where at the age of 28 he was in fact installed as Professor Extraordinarius in Physics; five years later he became Ordinarius. His lectures enjoyed immense popularity, and to his influence as a teacher we have many testimonials from his students. His lectures were sparkling with wit and good humour, and the students frequented them not only in order to have the subjects of geophysics, astronomy and electricity explained to them in a clear and masterly fashion, but also to benefit from the perpetual good humour of the little hunch-backed professor whose face was always ready to give way to a smile.

Göttingen remained his home for almost all the rest of his life, but it was England which offered him perhaps the greatest intellectual stimulus and became the dominating influence on his general character. In this we find a partial answer to the question which must have been on the reader's lips: how did a Professor of Mathematics and Physics come to write an interpretation of Hogarth, and was this not an amateurish work?

It may truthfully be said that not only was it far from being that, but that probably no one was ever better suited to write such a commentary than Lichtenberg. With an early mastery of the English language, he was well versed in the writings of the great English poets and novelists of the eighteenth century, especially Pope, Swift, Fielding and Sterne, on the beauties of which, and on those of Shakespeare, he never tired of expatiating. He loved their good sense, their patient study of mankind, their close observation of human nature, contrasting them favourably with what he regarded as the inflated or exaggerated writings of the German novelists and philosophers of his day with 'their torrents of Olympian prose'.

He made two visits to England, in 1770–71 and again in 1774–5, and the time he spent there he always counted among the happiest of his life. A meticulous observer in any circumstances, this faculty of observation was intensified when he came to live in what he considered the paradise for cultured human beings—the England of his time, in contrast to the Germany of his time. Everything worthy of remembering, everything in which England differed from Germany, was stored in his mind and thus was formed the rich background on to which to project Hogarth's pictures when talking about them to Germans.

The letters which he wrote from England to Heinrich Christian Boie, editor of the *Deutches Museum*, to his devoted friend Dieterich, also a publisher, to his former Professor Kästner, and others of his friends, were published, some before and some after his death, and throw an interesting light on Lichtenberg as the future interpreter of Hogarth. As a distinguished representative of Göttingen University and a friend of Lord Boston, whose sons he had tutored in Germany and now escorted to England, Lichtenberg was welcomed in court circles, and even enjoyed a remarkable degree of friendship with George III himself, and with Queen

Charlotte; yet it cannot be said that we learn very much from these letters about life at the English Court or the habits of the aristocracy. What gleams from their pages in colour and vigour is the teeming life of the London streets, the jollity, the ugliness, the charm, the exuberance of the rabble in eighteenth-century London. That is what fascinated Lichtenberg.

The confectioners dazzle your eyes with their candelabra and tickle your nose with their wares, for no more trouble and expense than that of taking both into their establishments. In these hang festoons of Spanish grapes, alternating with pineapples and pyramids of apples and oranges, among which hover attendant white-armed nymphs with silk caps and little silk trains, who are often (here's the devil to pay) too little attended. Their masters wisely associate them with the cakes and tarts, to make the mouth of even the most replete water, and to strip the poor purse of its last shilling but one; for to entice the hungry and rich, the cakes and their brilliant surroundings would suffice. All this appears like an enchantment to the unaccustomed eye; there is, therefore, all the more need for circumspection in viewing all discreetly; for scarcely do you stop than, crash! a porter runs you down crying 'By your leave', when you are lying on the ground. In the middle of the street roll chaises, carriages, and drays in an unending stream. Above this din and the hum and clatter of thousands of tongues and feet one hears the chimes from church towers, the bells of the postmen, the organs, fiddles, hurdy-gurdies, and tambourines of English mounte-banks, and the cries of those who sell hot and cold viands in the open at the street corners. Then you will see a bonfire of shavings flaring up as high as the upper floors of the houses in a circle of merrily shouting beggar boys, sailors and rogues. Suddenly a man whose handkerchief has been stolen will cry 'Stop thief!' and everyone will begin running and pushing and shoving—many of them not with any desire of catching the thief, but of prigging for themselves, perhaps, a watch or purse. Before you know where you are, a pretty, nicely dressed miss will take you by the hand: 'Come, my lord, come along, let us drink a glass together', or 'I'll go with you if you please'. Then there is an accident forty paces from you: 'God bless me', cries one; 'Poor creature', another. Then one stops and must put one's hand into one's pocket, for all appear to sympathize with the misfortunes of the wretched creature;

but all of a sudden they are laughing again, because someone has lain down by mistake in the gutter: 'Look there, damn me', says a third—and then the procession moves on. . . . That is Cheapside and Fleet Street on a December evening.[1]

Is that not completely in the spirit of Hogarth? And would it not have served almost as a description of his pictures 'Noon' and 'Night', in 'The Times of the Day'?

Another element which emerges from the Letters is Lichtenberg's admiration for the English theatre, and especially for the acting of Garrick in Shakespeare. The first series of Letters, addressed to Boie and intended for publication in the *Deutches Museum*, is devoted entirely to this subject, and seldom, if ever, has an actor been so marvellously interpreted as was Garrick there by Lichtenberg. His figure, his expression, his movement, the flick of his eye, the way he takes snuff, wears his hat or carries his cane, the significance of each is revealed with a rare penetration. 'I admit,' he writes, 'that thousands cannot see all that Garrick has to show them, for in this respect he is not a whit more fortunate than those congenial spirits, Shakespeare and Hogarth. In order to miss nothing of their art, one must bring one's own little light to eke out the usual illumination.' What he did then for Garrick he was later to do for Hogarth, and the reader of the Commentaries will discover how brilliant was the 'little light' with which he illuminated them.

Lichtenberg had recognized a common quality in Shakespeare, Garrick and Hogarth, and one which he himself shared, namely an inexhaustible interest in human nature. He writes of Garrick:

Man was his study, from the cultured and artificial denizens of the salons of St James's down to the savage creatures in the eating houses of St Giles. He attended the same school as Shakespeare and like the latter, did not wait for inspiration but worked hard (for in England all is not left to genius as in Germany); by this school I mean London, where a man with such a talent for observation can learn as much by experience in a year as in a whole lifetime spent in some little town.

Although this was written of Garrick, it reads like a description of

<hr />

[1] Letter to Ernst Gottfried Baldinger, Professor at Göttingen, dated January 10, 1775. (*Lichtenberg's Visit to England*, Clarendon Press, 1938.)

Hogarth, and as a comment on Lichtenberg himself during his visits to England it could hardly be bettered.

What Lichtenberg and Hogarth had in common was their interest in human nature, especially in its lower specimens. As in pathology, it was the aberrations from the norm which helped to exhibit the latter. Lichtenberg's interest in physiognomy which found expression in his pamphlet, *Ueber Physiognomik*, predestined him to become Hogarth's commentator. The following entry in his diary shows that as far as human heads went, he was a Raphael without hands.

> In the year 1769 I hit upon the idea of drawing all kinds of faces upon a sheet of paper one after the other, which mostly had something funny about them. Few of the people to whom I showed the paper could refrain from laughing. After I had drawn about forty such heads, I felt already exhausted and new heads were added only with difficulty. In the following year, I was laid up with a feverish disease. My bed had a sloping canopy through whose not-too-thick material one could see the white wall. Here now I saw a countless number of the queerest and funniest faces. In an area hardly the size of a quarto sheet, I could produce more than a hundred, and each had more expression and peculiarity than one usually finds in drawings of faces, excepting the inimitable heads by Hogarth, with most of whom they had much in common.

III

But these two factors alone—familiarity with English life, and a knowledge of the human heart, as it was then called—would not have enabled Lichtenberg to do more than give a meticulous description of the pictures in the pedestrian way others had trod before and after him. To give his Commentaries their distinctive characteristic, something more was needed. 'There are two ways of interpreting Hogarth,' says Lichtenberg in the Preface to the Commentaries, 'the "prosaic" and the "poetic". According to the first, one would explain in brief and dry terms the meaning of the items in the inventory of these pictures and specially draw attention to such objects as might be overlooked, or at least misunderstood by someone unfamiliar with either the genius of the artist or his country. In the second way of interpretation, on the other hand, one's aim would be to express in words everything the artist has shown pictorially, in such a way as he, Hogarth, would have said it had he been as expert with the pen as he was with the stylus.'

According to one critic[1] Lichtenberg has fallen short of this goal of verbally re-creating the pictures, although, in the main, his presentation of their content had been the 'poetic' one. The main objection to Lichtenberg's claim to re-creation is that he has rendered his subject in the mood which it produced in him, whereas he ought to have reproduced the mood of his subject. It was thus himself he expressed, and not the pictures.

But was Lichtenberg's description of the 'poetic' way of comment to be taken quite so literally? Is not the deviation observed by the critic not only inevitable, but even the very characteristic, the stamp of any original work, be it artistic creation or criticism? We shall have to answer that question in the affirmative, and, what is more, recognize in the manner in which Lichtenberg has succeeded in expressing himself while commenting on Hogarth the most valuable characteristic of the Commentaries. Lichtenberg himself says:

> Part of the pleasure provided by the immortal work of our artist depends, just as with the works of Nature, upon the exercise of one's own ingenuity, which must play its own part. I at least have been fascinated for many years not so much by the wholly unmistakable in the artist's wit and mood, but by the easily mistakable and the actually mistaken. Who would seek will always find something. Perhaps it was precisely that feature, so favourable to the artist, which prevented him from writing a commentary to the work himself, although he had often been asked to do so by his friends, and had promised to do it, too. It certainly would not have been to his advantage. In order that something should be thought very deep, it should never be known how deep it is.

Man's mind is not a mirror of the outer world; it is the intellect of man which creates that world under the stimulus of experience. We do not *see* colours, for instance, but *make* them when the retina is excited by electromagnetic vibrations. On a higher plane, it has been rightly said that the Book of Nature is not given us to read but has to be written by us.

The mind of an observer, say of pictures, is not a *tabula rasa* upon which

[1] F. H. Mautner in *Modern Language Quarterly*, Vol. 13, 1952.

the pictures just impress themselves 'as they are'; they can only serve as stimuli to make the observer re-create them according to the materials at his disposal, that is, by means of the intellectual devices and with the stock of relevant observations which he is capable of bringing to bear upon the subject. Even the 'mere' description of a picture requires this kind of 'apperception' or 'appropriation' on the part of the observer, since there is no hard and fast rule as to where to begin and what to include in such a description. Still more when it comes to the point of where to put the accents, what to select and what to suppress from the continuous manifold of observation.

IV

What is it that Lichtenberg has done to the pictures? It would be very difficult to treat the matter in abstract terms and yet with sufficient concreteness so as to recognize Lichtenberg's hand in any given instance, were it not for the knowledge we possess of a certain trait in Lichtenberg's character, or rather his intellectual make-up, which furnishes a key to our problem. He once said of himself:

> One of the most remarkable traits of my character is a curious super-stition which makes everything into an omen and interprets hundreds of things every day as oracles. Every creeping of an insect serves me as the answer to a question about my fate. Is that not strange for a Professor of Physics? But is it not also deeply rooted in human nature, and only grown to monstrous dimensions in my own case, extended beyond the proportion of the normal dosage, when it is justified and wholesome?

Thus Lichtenberg recognized clearly that the trait which in his later years, after a severe illness in 1789, made his life, intermittently at least, a misery, was deeply rooted in his own intellectual make-up and was natural as long as it kept within certain limits, and he rightly saw in it one of the sources of the originality of his thinking.

From this stems his preference for analogies:

> If I possess strength in anything, it is certainly in the finding of analogies, and through it in making clear what I myself understand thoroughly.

Thus a picture by Hogarth becomes for him an occasion for displaying that trait, and upon the scene is superimposed the network of cross-relations which has made Lichtenberg's brain spin forth. Lichtenberg has himself drawn the line between over-explanation and animated explanation of the kind which he called 'poetic'. The former imputes to the author of the picture intentions which he never had; the latter, on the other hand, while preserving the spirit of the whole, superimposes a net-work of relations which makes the picture infinitely more interesting to us, since it renders it properly our own. The work of art thus acquires a life of its own in the mind of the observer. Since Lichtenberg's head was one of the finest of his time, and his heart one of the gentlest, we are justified in expecting much from his absorption of Hogarth's pictures into his mind, and their re-emergence in the form of the Commentaries.

One of Lichtenberg's favourite expressions is the 'brain-fold' (*Gehirn-falte*) which he uses as the physical equivalent for inveterate habits of thought—'I do not wish to break the fold in your head differently, Sir, but I can only tell you it is not true'. We might thus in his language speak of such a network of brain-folds of his own, which overlays Hogarth's pictures, and which, like an orientation grid, or like the co-ordinate system of longitude and latitude, helps us to find our bearings. And this function is admirably fulfilled by Lichtenberg's thought-nets. What he has wished for himself—'If I could only draw channels in my head so as to facilitate the inner traffic between my stores of thought!'—he has achieved for the spectator of Hogarth's pictures. By the lightning quickness of his intellect, he has drawn such channels which enable the onlooker to incorporate the often diffuse aggregate of little traits into a consciousness of the whole.

If the present writer may apply Lichtenberg's method and draw channels between the various details in Lichtenberg's intellectual life, with a view to fixing the person and his work as one organic whole in the reader's mind, he would like to point to the phenomenon which bears the name of Lichtenberg as its discoverer. In 1777 Lichtenberg found that the discharge of the electric spark produces on the surface of certain kinds of powder and plastic material regular star-like figures. Such effects had, of course, been *looked at* many times before—just as were Hogarth's pictures—but it was left to Lichtenberg to *see* them as a subtle, orderly arrangement of matter taking place on such occasions, and thus to recognize the regularity of shape which so far had escaped attention. This is on the same plane with his recognizing and strengthening the relations between apparently unrelated parts of Hogarth's scenes, hereby fixing the whole in our mind. He had the rare gift of raising into consciousness what before was only looked on, by means of a network of relations, like a fisherman who explores and exhibits the contents of the sea by means of a fishing net. In Lichtenberg's case, that net was of his own making and has served to disclose even the most recondite of Hogarth's allusions, and so to make his pictures truly our own.

V

All this contributed to raising Lichtenberg's Commentaries high above those of his predecessors, Nichols and Irving. Beside his, they seem very pedestrian indeed, and for once it was the German and not the Englishman who had the sparkling wit congenial with Hogarth's. But his Commentaries will survive through yet another feature, and that is their style. Not 'Style' with a capital 'S' in the sense in which we would say that Macaulay or Ruskin had style, but as the term would apply to La Rochefoucauld, to Samuel Butler (who said of himself that he had no style) or to the best of Somerset Maugham's work.

Lichtenberg has made it easy for us to understand the secret of his style: in his *Aphorisms* he has given all the clues we need. His main thesis is this:

> Through a strict attention to our own ideas and sensations, and through the most forcefully individualized expression of them, by carefully selected words which are written down immediately, one can in a short time obtain a store of observations which can be put to good use in many ways. We come to know ourselves, we give our system of ideas firmness and continuity; what we speak in company obtains a certain individuality like that of faces, which is a recommendation to the discerning and whose absence produces a bad effect. One builds up a store which could be used in future work, forms at the same time one's style and strengthens the inner sense and one's capacity for attentiveness to everything. Not all who are rich have become so through luck, but many through thrift. In this way can attentiveness, economy of thought and practice compensate for lack of genius.

And again:

Oh, if we could only see the notebooks out of which have often grown immortal works . . . it would certainly give comfort to thousands. Since this is not so easy to do, one must learn through oneself to understand others. One should never believe anybody too great, and should firmly believe that all works have always been the fruit of industriousness and of intense application.

One cannot easily think too much, but one can easily read too much. The more objects I am thinking about, that is the more I try to build them into my system of ideas, the more power do I gain. With reading it is the opposite. I spread myself without strengthening myself.

His Commentaries may be regarded as an application of these maxims. In them he has 'brought to book' what might be vaguely floating in the mind of the spectator of Hogarth's pictures, but so very vaguely as hardly to admit even of the most sober description. Nobody knew this better than Lichtenberg:

In every human being there lie a great many correct observations, but the art of expressing them appropriately is very difficult, at least much more difficult than many believe.

And:

If a witty thought is to be striking, the appositeness must not only be obvious, although this is indispensable, but it must not yet have been found by others, and yet everything pertaining to it must be so evident to everybody that they should find it surprising not to have thought of it themselves. This is essential . . . People see many things every day from which they could learn, but without avail. They do not 'bring them to book', and this is the proper mine of wit.

And again:

The commonest people, although they do not think it worth while to write down what they see and feel, yet see and feel all that would have been worth while recording in writing; and the difference between the common and the educated people often consists merely in the art of apperception, the art of how to 'bring to book'.

Just as he was one of the neatest craftsmen in the expression of ideas, not leaving unfinished bits of thought lying about, but sweeping the corners of his brain for the expression of even a trivial thought, so did he deal with Hogarth's pictures. He is not out to create a *Knalleffekt* by describing only the main action or that which is most obvious, but closely examines every corner of the scene, every object put there by Hogarth, trying to discover—and in most cases succeeding—Hogarth's intention. He inspects the portraits on the walls to see how they fit into the tapestry of action depicted here, and by using them as a running commentary to the main action of the picture shows the uncanny penetration of his mind.

We read his Commentaries as his students listened to his lectures. Again we delight in seeing the little professor conjuring up in his Puckish way the most recondite relations between the various parts of the Universe. Whether he interprets tombstones as IOU's of stone with which Mother Earth as the recipient of the body acknowledges, mostly in over-enthusiastic terms, the goods received by her; whether he shows the actress dressing to be intended by Hogarth for an inverted Diana, being covered just where Diana is bare and vice versa; whether he sees in the attitude of a pair of dogs a replica of a human pair of lovers; whether he tells us in all detail what preceded the scene of the husband's murder in the fifth picture of 'Marriage-à-la-Mode', or traces back the villain of this piece to what seems quite a harmless conversation in the fourth picture; whether he shows us all the topsy-turvy comedy of the 'Strolling Actresses', puts every little utensil hidden away in corners and every picture on the walls in relation to the scene enacted; whether he calls the hangman's rope a legal collar, or tells us of the man who always found it remarkable that the cat had two holes cut in her skin just where she had her eyes, he makes us dwell upon these scenes until they become part of our living experience.

And these are only a few specimens taken at random from the multitude of such ideas which Lichtenberg scattered over his Commentaries, true to his maxim:

No work of art, and especially no work of literature, should betray the labour that went into its making. A writer who wishes to be read by posterity must not be averse to putting hints which might give rise to whole books, or ideas for learned discussions, in some corner of a chapter so that one should think he can afford to throw them away by the thousand.

This is true of Lichtenberg if it ever was of a writer.

As we read his Commentaries, Lichtenberg's own personality communicates itself to us, and we begin to understand and love him as a human being with rare qualities of head and heart, who has said of himself:

His body is such that even an indifferent draftsman would draw it better in the dark, and if it were in his power to change it he would give some parts less prominence. With his health, although not of the best, he is quite content, and he has the gift of utilizing his good days in a very high degree. He has loved only once or twice, the first time not unhappily, the second happily. He has won a good wife simply through cheerfulness and lightheartedness, and though now he often forgets both over the complications of married life, he will always revere cheerfulness and lightheartedness as the characteristics of his soul to which he owes the best hours of his life, and could he choose one more life and one more soul, I do not know whether he would choose others if he could have his own again.

What Lichtenberg had before him when writing the Commentaries was a set of engravings by the German engraver E. Riepenhausen, in which left and right had been restored to what they were in the original paintings. This Lichtenberg regarded as a point in favour of Riepenhausen's reproductions and often stresses the difference between them and the other type, with left and right reversed. Our Plates are reproduced from the original Hogarth engravings in the British Museum, some of which had to be reversed in order that the left and right should be as in the original paintings, so that the reader of the Commentaries should see the engravings exactly as Lichtenberg did, and the reproductions tally with the text. This entails, of course, that writing on such Plates would also appear reversed, e.g. 'Marriage-à-la-Mode', plates I and II; 'A Rake's Progress', plate VIII; and 'Morning' and 'Evening' (see pp. 276, 288). The reader who wishes to check Lichtenberg's remarks on the writing can easily do so by reading it in a mirror. Footnotes other than Lichtenberg's own are marked Ed.

Our thanks are due to Mr John R. Freeman for permission to use his photographs of Hogarth's engravings in the British Museum for the 26 Plates.

INNES AND GUSTAV HERDAN

A Harlot's Progress

A Harlot's Progress

I

I⊤ was mainly through these six Plates that Hogarth first laid the foundation of his widespread fame, which, despite all opposition by people now forgotten, he has enjoyed ever since, till this very hour. They were received with indescribable applause. He obtained 1,200 subscribers for them; they were reproduced on coffee cups as an admonition, and painted on fans to be looked at on hot days, and looked past, too, if need be. The wittiest heads of the time have quoted the dramatis personae of these scenes in support of their immortal ideas. Theophilus Cibber introduced them on the stage in pantomime, and others have spun out single events from them into operettas.[1] They found it easier to delineate man from that infallible *camera obscura* than from nature. Very naturally. It is unfortunately very much the prerogative of this Paper Age of the world that, since the Universe has become the subject of the book and picture trades, thousands of writers and artists have grown blind to the direct rays of Nature, but see quite satisfactorily if this ray is reflected from a sheet of paper. It is fortunate if the reflection is always at first hand, and if the page itself is always as clear, as neat, and as mirror-bright as that which our great artist holds up to us here.

The work is entitled 'A Harlot's Progress'. It is not her whole life which Hogarth gives us, but only scenes from various periods of it, each of which is distinguished by a striking decline from the preceding one. He begins with the pure, even tender innocence of his heroine, and ends with the deepest corruption. This is a harlot's progress—here at least!

[1] Nichols speaks of a ballad opera entitled *The Jew Decoyed* or *The Harlot's Progress*.

The heroine of the piece is the daughter of a poor village parson[1] from Yorkshire. We see both father and daughter in the first Plate. The girl, standing in the foreground, has just got down from the wretched cart which, as appears from its superscription, has brought her from the country; the father in the background is not so much riding as merely straddling his horse. How the girl stands there! Of course she is not a great beauty—one can see that. Hogarth was no painter of beauty; as far as I know, only two people in his whole life have claimed this for him: one was Hogarth himself and the other his good wife. But what the girl lacks in refinement is more than compensated by good health, childish simplicity, and gentle innocence. Her manner is that of a sturdy, clean, well-behaved village girl, who could be made into something—and that is just what happens.

Her figure seems to have developed somewhat on the broad side, in the rough service of Ceres and Pomona. Had she been gathering forget-me-nots, daisies, violets and all the rest of the sentimental love-posies, she would perhaps have been cast in a finer mould. However, she is still in her middle teens, and still growing, and doubtless much of the angularity in her appearance must be put to the account of the village tailor.

In her attire, so simple and countrified, like her whole person, there is not a trace of falsehood; nothing is built up too high or spread too wide. Hat, corsage, and neckerchief guard and protect what has been entrusted to them faithfully, without bragging, and with the least possible display, like honeycombs. There are no unoccupied storeys in the former, and in the latter no empty galleries. Her face which reposes under the former speaks for itself in eloquent silence, is understandable to all and open to all, and needs no interpretation; to what is beneath the latter, on the other hand, where only conjectures are permitted, Flora has given an almost superfluous security by fixing a little rose there: innocence with the bloom of youth. From here the fortification proceeds downwards in the usual manner with three- or four-fold wall right to the little feet, standing

---

[1] More properly a so-called curate, one of the miserable creatures whom Johnson defines as being hired by others to do service for them. The souls of the parishioners do not suffer thereby as a rule (and this keeps the custom alive) whereas the person of the curate would suffer if that institution did not exist. Complaints about the institution are very general in England, and Hogarth is quite justified in his satire.

A Harlot's Progress Plate I

parallel. If the commander is not susceptible to bribery, then, as far as that quarter is concerned, the campaign looks promising. At her side hangs a needle-case and a little pair of scissors, and from her right arm a small bundle: they were probably put there by the poor weeping mother when she said goodbye, for occupation and refreshment on the journey. Much of the utter resignation in the attitude of her arms and the shyness in her glance are due, however, to the fascination exercised by the elegant watch of the great lady with whom the good child is here put *en rapport.* The reader will hear about Her Ladyship in due course. As yet we have to deal only with innocence, and therefore proceed immediately to the poor father.

There he sits upon the faithful family chattel, a miserable grey who has probably done his best for sixteen years already to support (though, of course, some other of God's creatures could have done it better) the poor equestrian with a wife and ten children living on an income of 150 thalers net in the rich countryside where they all belong.[1] A sorry figure to be sure! The skin on his knees has been kneed through in heavy service, and but perfunctorily patched up again by Nature. The shape of the neck and the position of the legs which have something of the cow about them and something of the lathe, do nothing to improve matters. Nor can one say that the horse, as might sometimes happen, is in the least ennobled by the figure of its rider. In the service of Holy Church the latter is in rather the same position as his loyal quadruped would be in any princely stable. He too is old, stiff, tottering, and in heavy service—bless us!—he too has worn out his knees, and like his friend is now without hope of a softer bed. Just look at his parched mouth and the highlights on the joints of his shrivelled hands! One would sooner expect to see in them the scythe of the general friend of living nature, than the reins. He sits there in his clerical garb, the only suit left in his wardrobe which could command such respect on the road as would certainly have been denied to the state of innocence underneath; the same applies to the breeches. They are certainly kneed through, and the high shovel hat serves not only for ornament

---

[1] Roucquet says: 'English clergymen usually ride greys. That is, black on white.' Since Roucquet knew Hogarth personally and Hogarth evidently knew that remark, it is very probable that the mischievous Englishman wantonly persuaded the credulous Frenchman to believe it. This in a way shows what Hogarth's commentary on his own work would have been like, had he left us one.

but is at the same time a protection against mockery and moths. Every ornament in the world ought to be of that sort: *decus et tutamen*. The bleached, washed out and thinned out wig is of great significance here. It was not very thoughtful of the Reformation to allow the tonsure, which after all can be undone by Nature, to be covered by a wig, and yet to deprive a tonsured wig, which is much more difficult to restore, of the covering of the monk's hood, which would have concealed all deficiency. In Germany we have not the least idea of what the English clergyman's wig is like. Haven't we really?—No! And if anyone tries to contradict me, I shall say outright that in Germany we simply do not know at all what a wig is. Ours are mere anatomical specimens of wigs. In short: as regards dignity and impressiveness they are the exact counterpart of the beard of the ancients, with this difference only, that the hair is fixed on the other side of the face. And the form of it? Very well, I will describe the clergy-man's wig, in its flowering time of course, in the manner of Linnaeus. Everyone knows how onions blossom. The little flowers form together a sort of sphere which is set high and firmly at the end of a long stem, as if on a spit. Now imagine the hollow stem to be the neck, and imagine from that sphere as many little flowers cut away in front as would be needful to accommodate a mask, and from the top as many as needful to accommo-date a hat, but with no mask or hat there, and you have exactly the shape and even the colour of the English clergyman's wig. I do not know whether it is a deranged imagination or some other metastasis of the poetic gift in me, but often on fine summer evenings, when I could no longer clearly discern the thin, hollow stems, I could not help comparing a field of onions in flower with an English Church Convention. Now let us cast a final glance at that washed-out sheepskin of a poor man there upon the grey. Hogarth speaks here to our hearts, and Heaven forbid that we should add the smallest touch which would lead in a different direction. He speaks, I say, straight to the heart of those in this world who know what an amount of brushing and rubbing and combing it must have cost the honest man before he arrived at the point, through no fault of his own, of being no longer able to display in public the miserable insignia of his state and order; the order to which, in the eyes of the eternal Judge, he will often do more honour than his temporal Superior. I am in earnest here, my dear reader, and therefore I beg your attention for another moment. Oh, if this figure of death would but once ride as if alive, like

Lenore's Wilhelm,[1] over the ceiling of the Hall where the Bishop or the Rector are at their *Te Deum*—by feasting, or if he rode his screw across the path on which they gallop in coach and four, and if they were to recognize in that image a man of their own flesh and blood and calling (of their wig, one might almost say) who despite his greater merit had made his *Te Deum*—by hungering all his life, it would be better for the poor clergy in rich England. But that is poetry: away with it—in times like these.

Away with poetry, that is; for we must still linger a moment with the poor parson and his daughter. The old man has accompanied her to town, the first of his children to attain by Nature a sort of currency value in the world, she in the cart and he upon the poor grey. He had had to choose between two shock machines, and chose for himself the cheaper, not the more comfortable one. They have just arrived at the Bell Inn in Wood Street, a well-known public house. The old man is reading the address on a letter of introduction: 'To the Right Reverend Bishop—London'. A testimonial which might hit its mark, provided it was loaded with a bullet. He has not got his spectacles with him and is laboriously studying the address. The grey takes advantage of this moment to make up for what he has missed on the way, and snatches greedily at the packing straw of some earthenware which is here displayed for sale. As a result, flower pots, dishes and pans and what-not, all empty, are tumbling around the famished animal. Very ominous. In all probability, if it comes to an argument, the bill for these empty dishes will far exceed the price of many a full one which the poor man has denied himself on the journey, and all that had been saved through the use of the shock-machine, and (deducting the hopes) the whole value of the letter to the Right Reverend! But we must leave this woeful scene, for much still lies before us.

Farewell then, unhappy pair; we shall not meet again so soon. Endure in patience a little longer the few blows of your common fate which may still lie in store until the great knock-out blow of Nature falls, which makes an end of all. It will save you at the same time, my good old man, from witnessing the unspeakable misery which awaits your beloved Mary. As yet you do not know that the procession which you and your faithful

---

[1] A reference to *Lenore*, the famous ballad by the German poet Gottfried August Bürger (1747–94), in which Lenore's dead lover comes to her door at night and carries her off on horseback. Ed.

servant led here from York was a funeral procession in which the virtue and, therefore, the happiness of your daughter, were conducted to a most terrible grave! And you, faithful grey, in whose side I discern, just behind your rider's spur, a little spot of reality which has cost the artist but a slight pressure of his stylus, but has cost you precious blood; believe me, the discovery has made me feel for you three times more keenly. I was sorry to discover, so shortly before our parting, this sign of conjunction between you and your master. But be comforted! The similarity between the two of you is even greater than you imagine: he too all his life long has carried just such a merciless rider as you have, and it would have cost the artist more than a single stroke to depict the scars which the poor victim covers here with the clerical *Copri-miseria*.[1]

Our heroine, the good, honest, village girl from Yorkshire, thus alights at the Bell Inn in London. The healthy, country flower is transplanted from its native soil into this boundless garden amidst fertilizers and insects in a thousand forms, unknown in Yorkshire; unfortunately, she just chances to light on one of the most infamous flower-beds for miles around. Before she has time to strike root, an insect (I mean here Her Ladyship with the dainty watch) fastens in its sting, which is to ruin her straight growth for ever, at least upon this earth. The explanation is as follows:

Hogarth makes the girl come from Yorkshire. Why from Yorkshire? The artist and writer for posterity makes no stroke without meaning. Yorkshire produces (I speak here as a statistician) the prettiest girls; that it breeds the finest horses is already well known. And a cart laden with the poorest, though by no means the plainest, of these creatures puts up every week at the Bell Inn in Wood Street, or at least calls there. This is the scene here. To paint it yet clearer, still a few more words. Above the front door we see the chessboard sign: its meaning has often been a subject of controversy in English journals, and still is. The dispute however seems now to be resolved. It is the sign which all houses selling strong spirits are obliged to display. The Warren family, whose coat-of-arms bears such a chessboard, has in fact up to the present day the exclusive right of distributing licences to such retailers, and it is customary, for the convenience of the tax-collector, to have that chessboard painted over the doorway and on the door posts, so that the houses can

[1] *Copri-miseria*, Misery-cover—the significant name given to a kind of overcoat in Italy.

be recognized from a distance.[1] It turns up in various places in the work of our artist, just like the people who are usually found in such houses. The courtyard of the Inn is situated, as one sees, in a miserable quarter. Although there may be houses in the neighbourhood which have their good side, so much is certain, they are not turning their more respectable one to us here. For instance, in the house to the left, on the veranda, which incidentally is partly propped on posts and partly suspended from poles, we see two inverted chamber-pots. This seems to be their customary residence during the day, to get some fresh air; at night they retire dutifully to the service of the family, whose size is thus indicated by the number of these objects. On the line hangs the washing, or at least something that was in the water that morning, whether destined for future use on the human frame or merely for the limbo of the paper mill would be difficult to decide, from one piece at least. The girl who peers down is holding either a pair of boots or a pair of stiff stockings which seem to have a generous admixture of water. Evidently some of it is meant to run off, and she seems to contemplate a bath of drips for some passers-by with good hope of success.

Into that wretched hedge-alehouse, disregarding all the misery around, has ventured the man with the somewhat ungainly calves whom we now see standing in the doorway. That there is a servant with hair-bag, evidently a most devoted one, standing behind him, leads us to expect something high-class. He has come here expressly to wait for the cart with the Yorkshire girls so as to have first pick when it was unloaded. Apart from the satellite with the hair-bag behind him, there is also the great lady with the *cul-de-Paris* who has evidently come with him. Who can the man be? This the reader will now hear in detail.

The man who stands here with one foot in the courtyard and the other still in the doorway, with the left hand resting on a stick, and the right engaged in some private business, is the notorious Colonel Charters. Those who know how readily Hogarth could hit off a face and figure must be gratified to see preserved upon this Plate the physiognomy and form of one of the greatest scoundrels the stylus has ever rendered immortal. Two of the actors in our drama die on the gallows, but that man is not one of them, though he deserved it just as much. He only

[1] The latest information about this is to be found in the *Gentleman's Magazine*, September 1794.

escaped hanging because in addition to the numerous fraudulent practices which lead to the gallows, in all of which he was a past master, he had been clever enough to study that one by which the gallows themselves are deprived of their due. Never, perhaps, had the gallows been so cheated as on the day when that beast died in his bed. For those of our readers who are familiar with Pope, Swift, Arbuthnot, and in general with the English classical writers of that time, or who have found pleasure in studying the spirit and character of that nation great even in its monstrosities, as they annually come before its Criminal Courts, we are not recording anything new here. Felon, scoundrel, whoremonger, are so many descriptions of Colonel Charters. Pope, to put it in a nutshell, once spoke of 'Charters and the Devil'.[1]

Charters and the Devil. That sounds almost like a Trading Company. They had indeed a sort of traffic with one another just as the French Charters has nowadays with those hotter regions.[2] And it would not, I think, have shamed the Devil to sign some of his newest bills on Nantes and Bordeaux with 'Charters, Bros. & Co.'

Now to a more detailed description of the creature. We shall begin with Pope's own note on the passage we mentioned; in cold-blooded prose.

Francis Charters, a man infamous for all manner of vices. When he was an ensign in the army he was drummed out of the regiment for a cheat; he was next banished Brussels and drummed out of Ghent on the same account. After a hundred tricks at the gaming tables he took to lending money at exorbitant interest and on great penalties, accumulating premium, interest, and capital into a new capital, and seizing to a minute when the payments became due; in a word, by a constant attention to the vices, wants and follies of mankind, he acquired an immense fortune. His house was a perpetual bawdy-house. He was twice condemned for rapes, and pardoned; but the last time not without imprisonment in Newgate, and large confiscations. He died in Scotland in 1731, aged 62. The populace at his funeral raised a great riot, almost tore the body out of the coffin, and cast dead dogs, etc., into the grave along with it.

[1] *Moral Essays*, Ep. III, v. 20, 'Of the use of riches'.
        'Giv'n to the Fool, the Mad, the Vain, the Evil,
        To Ward, to Waters, Chatres [*sic*], and the Devil.' Ed.
[2] The Duc d'Orléans, formerly the Duc de Chartres—*nomen est omen*. He called himself a roué, but he died 'ruable' (fit to be thrashed), just as his namesake in England died 'pendable' (fit to be hung).

The following Epitaph contains his character very justly drawn by Dr Arbuthnot:

HERE continueth to rot
The Body of FRANCIS CHARTRES,
Who with an INFLEXIBLE CONSTANCY,
and INIMITABLE UNIFORMITY of Life,
PERSISTED,
In spite of AGE and INFIRMITIES,
In the Practice of EVERY HUMAN VICE,
Excepting PRODIGALITY and HYPOCRISY:
His insatiable AVARICE exempted him from the first,
His matchless IMPUDENCE from the second.
Nor was he more singular in the undeviating *Pravity* of his *Manners*
Than successful in *Accumulating* WEALTH.
For, without TRADE OR PROFESSION,
Without TRUST of PUBLIC MONEY,
And without BRIBE-WORTHY Service,
He acquired, or more properly created,
A MINISTERIAL ESTATE.
He was the only Person of his Time,
Who could CHEAT without the Mask of HONESTY,
Retain his Primeval MEANNESS
When possess'd of TEN THOUSAND a YEAR,
And having daily deserved the GIBBET for what he *did*,
Was at last condemn'd to it for what he *could* not *do*.
Oh Indignant Reader!
Think not his Life useless to Mankind!
PROVIDENCE conniv'd at his execrable Designs,
To give to After-ages
A conspicuous PROOF and EXAMPLE,
Of how small Estimation is EXORBITANT WEALTH
in the Sight of GOD,
By his bestowing it on the most UNWORTHY of
ALL MORTALS.

Now that is what I call an epitaph. *Sit tibi terra levis*, Charters, with thy dead dogs!

11

There is some drumming here, it is true. If, however, we consider the high and solid character of Dr Arbuthnot, the certificate loses through its poetic form nothing of its force and has the weight of prose.

Why do we never read such epitaphs in churchyards? Indeed, when we walk through a churchyard and read the stone receipts which our common mother draws up in exchange for the nailed-up boxes deposited with her, one cannot help thinking that she must either be a very rich and kindly mother who intends one day to make good the defects out of her own means, or a very foolish one who lets herself be taken in quite lamentably by some of those bereaved families. I must confess that when I read the inscriptions on tombstones I am often at a loss to know which is really the side of glory. For there could surely be no happier world than one where the graves gave up without the smallest rebate everything which according to the tombstone inscriptions they had received; or one in which all those who escaped hanging really were such paragons as are said to have been delivered here.

Now only a few lines more on behalf of the *Tout comme chez nous*: a few days after Charters' death the following touching article is said to have appeared on the back page of an Edinburgh newspaper among the writs of arrest issued for thieves, and the advertisements of new books and patent medicines which encourage the reader partly to catch and partly to be caught:

Stenninghill near Edinburgh, the 22nd of May, 1732.[1] Yesterday evening between 5 and 6 o'clock our dearest husband and father, Colonel[2] Francis Charters of Amsfield in his sixty-second year peacefully exchanged his toilsome but successful life for eternity. Religion and Country mourn in him a courageous defender, the orphan a gracious father, and poverty an untiring benefactor. This heavy blow which brings sorrow to the whole county is felt by none more deeply than by us, his deeply stricken family. Convinced of the part which not only our friends but the whole world takes in this our loss, we decline all condolences

HELENA CHARTERS

N. CHARTERS, COUNTESS OF WEEMS.

[1] This is the place and date of death given in the *Gentleman's Magazine* of that year, and not as previously, 1731.

[2] That a drummed-out Ensign could have died a Colonel is comprehensible only in the case of a miracle-worker like him.

This Charters, with an income of 60,000 thalers, comes now to that dirty hovel simply to wait for the consignment of girls from Yorkshire. The fellow behind him is a certain John Gourlay, who usually accompanied Charters, especially when something was to be acquired for the household, a sort of blood-hound. About the lips of that noble pair there hovers an expression, not so much ingratiating as actually of savouring something, which has such an abominable effect that it might tempt the hand of any honest and honour-loving fellow to apply itself thereto in the form of a fist, and with accelerated motion, without any more ado. They have, however, no confidence in their own appearance when confronting innocence and have found it necessary to interpose between themselves and the poor inexperienced village girl a little object of attraction. This is Her Ladyship, an old cunning decoy-bird, who as a rule sings only bawdy songs, but on occasions like these still knows how to pipe her woodland airs and to lure the free flight of the little birds of heaven towards the cages of London. A notorious woman who, though not hanged, met a death which in shamefulness was only a few degrees removed from death on the gallows, and which in every other respect was much more painful. It is in fact a portrait of a Madam Needham, commonly known as Mother Needham, a notorious and generally despised character of those times. She kept a bawdy house in Park Place, a *cul-de-sac*, if I am not mistaken, off St James's Street, one of the main thoroughfares of the City. She was called 'Mother', no doubt, because she had the virtue and honour of her pupils just as much at heart as her own. Pope has immortalized her too. He calls her 'pious Needham'.[1] To call a go-between and procuress 'pious' merely in irony would have been a far too commonplace joke for so witty a man. No; she really was pious, and exercised her piety, as it is exercised by thousands, regularly, according to the clock. She washed herself morning and evening with her prayers, according to the best prescriptions, and every Sunday she had a grand washing day; the remaining time she spent in her office or was otherwise occupied. One might perhaps imagine she was a religious hypocrite. That sort of thing would depreciate Pope's remark still more, for what is more common than procuresses who are also hypocrites? No; she is said to have really *thought* sometimes when she prayed, which is *differentia specifica,* and thus Pope's comment acquires significance. It was expressly remembered of her that she often implored

[1] Dunciad, I, 323.

Heaven with tears for a blessing on her occupation, so that she might one day, freed from shame, serve Heaven fully in spirit and in truth. Was this a pious fraud? Heaven declined to grant that well-meant request. She was arrested, put in the pillory, and on the second occasion (she was to undergo the operation three times) was so badly mauled by the rabble on the maxim: 'I love treason but hate the traitor', that she died before it came to the third ordeal. This was indeed worse than a hanging.

Here she stands, albeit rather weathered; the facing begins to crumble just like the wall of the alehouse which serves as a significant background to her head. In order, however, to impede as far as possible the flight of her remaining charms, she has stuck little plasters over the main avenues of escape, through which they usually disappear, while the faded ones have evidently been freshened up. I may be mistaken, but whenever I look at that nose I cannot help thinking of snuff and spectacle marks. Besides, one can very well see how the face, especially that delightful mouth, is doing everything it can to mask the repellent traces which the habits of fifty years have left in some of its regions. To bring her heart close to the poor girl's through her finger tips, she has taken off her glove, for the theatrical gesture which she is performing would not penetrate through calf skin. And so the poor little bird sinks into a charmed sleep while being put into the cage of a seemingly great lady, a cage however which has a little back gate through Charters' hedge, and so—everything is lost! And all this is happening while our good old man in poring over an address forgets to alight from his horse. Thus here is another case of fragile goods—tumbling down, to the detriment of the poor devil, which no bishopric will ever restore. So much for a letter of introduction!

So much for the essential features of this first scene. Now a little more about the decorations. In the lower right-hand corner stands quite a sizeable trunk with M.H. painted on the lid. It contains the girl's trousseau for this marriage of hers with—shame and destruction. With a sort of prophetic foresight which nothing in the world can justify, Hogarth has given his heroine the name of Mary Hackabout, thus not so much expressing her character as her future fate. This would have been better left undone. The English word 'to hack', if used of a woman, denotes every possible shame which could be put to her account. Mamselle Maria Everybody's would be the most literal translation, and this is at least free of the ugly associations from which the English word can only with difficulty be separated, including even saddle and reins. Why this in such a work of art? And if the girl's name was Hackabout, what was then the name of the poor innocent father? It is to the credit of the Germans that they do not permit, or only reluctantly, such treason of writers against their heroes. Woe to the author who has to give his hero a label in order to draw attention to him. Hogarth was least of all in need of such a device. He sets forth the girl's story in such a way, and describes her life so clearly, that in the end one would have to regard her as a Hackabout even if the saddler had nailed 'Susannah' upon the trunk. And this, I think, is the right way. In Greek or Hebrew such names may perhaps pass; one has grown accustomed to them, just as one is used to 'Doctor' and 'Magister' which nowadays begin to acquire the character of Christian names. The love of God of some Theophilus is of about the same degree as the blessed state of some aetheist Benedict, like Spinoza. Little Pandemos would have been perhaps the most suitable name if Hogarth had wanted to indicate his intentions.[1] So far as I know the name does not appear in any calendar, unless perhaps in a ladies' calendar, and those I do not read. Close to the trunk lies a poor goose almost strangled by the address label round its neck (in a way, like the poor parson on horseback through his). It reads: 'te my lofing Cosen in Tems-street in London.' New orthography with old-time folly in sisterly conjunction as usual. Where now is little Pandemos to go? For in Thames Street, one of the most roaring and crowded thoroughfares in London, live lofing Cosens by the thousand who are only too willing to accept unlabelled geese with their heart in their mouth. The poor animal is addressed, just like you, my good little Mary, and like your poor Yorkshire travelling companions in the cart who are going on farther and who will not lack lofing Cosens, either! Lying on the ground is a packed case also with an address. We mention this merely to tell the reader that the address upon the original is intentionally just as unreadable as here. It is merely something typical which is always happening, a box waiting patiently for the fulfilment of its *cite citissime* until in the end an honest carrier who cannot read, or a sly thief who does not want to, takes charge of it.

[1] From the Greek πανδγμος, belonging to Everyman. Even those whom the name fits will find their fate more tolerable when they hear that the Greeks had a Venus Pandemos as well as a Venus Urania.

15

II

HIGHER than this, little Pandemos will never climb; it is her Silver Age. Tea-table, tea-pot, and what have you, are all of this metal. Her Golden Age was spent in Yorkshire—without money; her Silver Age in London, with silver, and that is of much more value—to a young girl. And are there many men who think otherwise? Oh! beloved Golden Age, your credit would stand so much higher in the world if you would only once reward your followers with something to jingle in their pockets, instead of paper money and cheques upon philosophy. Alas! the lions no longer care to lie down with your moral lambs, and your moral gold, if you but knew it, has changed into mere counters.

Thrown away, no doubt, by Charters (for with him girls shared the fate of playing cards in great Faro banks; he was soon done with them, but they passed on to others like new), she has now been acquired by a wealthy Old Testament sinner. She appears here as the mistress of a Portuguese Jew. He keeps her, as one sees, with Jewish splendour; all is somewhat rich, somewhat heavy; also sometimes, like the girl, somewhat second-hand but always of good value in the fraternity. But more about that later. Honour to whom honour is due. First Molly Hackabout.

In Heaven's name, just compare this figure with that piece of carved wood on the first Plate. How quickly its feet could acquire pretty ankles upon the slippery ice of London! There she stood like a slow, honest, good and clumsy animal, a plump pug-dog, everything parallel, indifferent to rest or motion. Here, though seated, is she not the living image of mobility? A whippet like a china ornament, poised rather than standing upon

16

A Harlot's Progress Plate II

its three little legs, and the energy which it cannot expend on running is expressed at least by trembling; ever divided between Heaven and Earth. And her face! Is that caricature? Do you really think so? Ah, my good Hogarth, they still call you—you the painter of souls—a caricaturist, but take comfort. Those who so mistake you are very commonplace people. How to scrape laboriously together from little pots of paint a Greek stone-face with blind eyeballs cribbed from some concealed original, that you understand just as well as they did, and as well as hundreds of your countrymen all of whom are forgotten, whereas you live on, and always will.

I have drawn attention to the face. To understand it thoroughly we must now explain the whole scene, in rough outline first and then in detail. The girl is the mistress of this Israelite who has rented a room for her far away from his office and, perhaps, from his honest wife, where he can visit her at his convenience, at any hour of the day, counting the day as twenty-four hours. This morning he has driven up for breakfast. He must have come by coach, for such a wig, such coat sleeves, and such a *chapeau bas* the London urchins of the New Testament would certainly not have tolerated in a pedestrian. Anyone parading on foot through London like that exposes himself as if in the Pillory, especially in the busy part of the City. But the deceived deceiver comes too soon. Payment on sight, if not demanded, was at least expected, and so this presentation ends with a protest. The funds are in an awful state. The lover with whom we spent the night is still on the premises and must first be disposed of before we can undertake even to speak of payment. There he slinks away at the back, only just not without his trousers, towards the door which, as fate would have it, opens on the wrong side, under the protection of the chamber-maid, who, to judge by her expression, has not had much experience yet of such a situation. To cover this retreat (an art which the greatest strategists have considered twice as difficult as achieving a victory) Molly fires off all her guns, and even explodes a mine. She has evidently led the discussion into the region of debt and credit, and at the moment when the Jew reaches the undermined spot, the mine explodes, she lifts her right leg and overturns the silver table with tea-pot and cups and every-thing that was on it, and throws it all down topsy-turvy. Everything jingles and clatters and crashes; even the *Zona torrida*, the Moor, trembles and stands petrified, while his compatriot, the monkey, makes off. Only

17

imagine what will happen when the table falls, and fall it certainly will! No Homeric shield, when its bearer fell, ever made such a crash as that upon the Trojan heath. And so the retreat is covered, and the lover has escaped from the Portuguese sanctuary.

Now for the little face.

Greater impertinence in the eyes of a girl still in her teens, greater familiarity with all the practices of harlotry, combined with the knowledge of a still greater unused stock in reserve, could hardly be better expressed in so few strokes. In the whole face no line and no contrasting shadow, and yet how eloquent! 'See, fellow, not so much do I care for you and your wretched plunder; a fig for it!', and with a snap of her finger she indicates exactly how much she thinks of the plunder. It is half a finger joint and a little sound that she brings to his notice. The right eye has something indescribably scornful. But the fellow has money and that is an important item which the left eye clearly recognizes. The feint is, I think, quite unmistakable. On her whole right wing, war is declared, while the left is at peace, or at least, some admission is made there of guilt. On the right wing the knee is raised at least a few hands above the line of modesty, and in an ugly way, so that the tip of the foot is turned inwards; and the arm stretched out so that in the Quart[1] she brings the snap of her fingers as close beneath the enemy's nose as if it were a pinch of snuff. The bracelet is missing. Where could it have been left last night? I have searched the departing lover for it more than once, but in vain. The upper part of the body leans over to support the lunge with its weight, and the head is drawn back to support it with contempt. The bosom presses forward, not as an offensive measure, of course, but the impertinence of the right side is palpably increased thereby. I have also read somewhere that a besieged enemy was once harassed, not only by cannon balls, but also in a most grievous manner by roast geese and wheaten bread which were displayed to him on a turnspit from afar. It is said that this form of attack was much more painful than the other because there was nothing with which to counter it, and every shot was a hit. On the left flank all is much more compliant, even the pretty arm speaks only of affability. I have seen them sometimes like that, when there was no enemy about, but merely an innocent neighbour.

We still cannot get away from that little head. If the whole scene had

[1] A fencing term. Ed.

18

not been a surprise attack, but merely an early breakfast, which the suspicious Jew has made into a too-early one, I would regard the girl's hair style as a product of art. Why is it that an unruly coiffure suits a pretty face so much better than one from which the scaffolding has just been removed? The source of this charm must lie very deep and be rooted in human nature. For even the humblest members of the female sex feel that it is at least more to their advantage to shake the hair sometimes off the face, than to pin it neatly back. The Roman ladies felt that long ago. Indeed, what did they not feel?

> *Et neglecta decet multas coma. Saepe jacere*
> *Hesternam credas*; *illa repexa modo est.*[1]

'What suits the girl so charmingly you take for the ruins of yesterday's hair-do? You silly ass! She has just finished arranging it like that.'

In English gardens ruins are newly erected to improve the scenery. There they are meant to evoke meditations on the vanity of all human beauty and greatness, with the passage of the centuries. Here the momentary effect is also chronological, but points only to the possibility of a mysterious destruction in one night. It must appear, however, that such pre-arrangement was highly unlikely, otherwise everything is lost and the warmest enthusiasm congeals at the sight of an unlovely, cold, hair-dresser's model. I feel the utmost pity for the good young wives who have announced in the newspapers their decision not to mourn for their—dear—husbands (this is not a question of spirit and truth, but only weeds and black). For Heaven's sake and your own, take back that vow! Otherwise it may not come true. Weeds and black on young widows have always been regarded as a sort of solemn illumination of the burnt down part of a beautiful building, of which just the finest wing has remained standing, and who would not, thinks everyone, try to save the best and most beautiful in a conflagration? If they cease to mourn, nobody will feel sorry for them any longer, and all the great arrangements in the world for catching and letting oneself be caught will lose their force, and young widows dwindle down to mere youngish spinsters. This is a sad transformation, and at least one that is not advantageous to the ruins. So much for charming—ruins.

[1] Ovid. *Art. am.* III, 153.

19

We have no language to describe what Molly's mouth is saying or has said. Only musical notes could do that in a range of at least four octaves. She has absolutely no ear, as on all such occasions. Instead her mouth has become two-tongued—Bilinguis—Billings—Billings-gate—Billingsgate-language.[1] Ten invectives a second with a snap of the fingers to beat time. Save us!—and protect us! from such a storm and such porcelain hail-stones! How does the Jew comport himself? He accompanies the four-octave descant of his beauty in deep, slow, nasal bass, and he is well advised to do so. The first violin would burst if he had responded in still faster rhythm. He does not care to risk that. He has her on a life-and-love annuity. The interest, of course, for this morning, has gone, but the capital must be preserved. If anyone cannot follow the meaning of Kleist's

One sees the voice but hears it not,

he would be well advised to listen to that mouth and its neighbour, the reverberating nose, and he will surely *see* what sound they make. All is terror, astonishment, and apprehension in that noble head. His not very closely cropped hair seems to stand on end under its artificial load, so that Cupid wins time to push forward a little wisp of oriental hue over his brow which could not be more charming. *Hesternam credas.* The poor fellow! One really cannot look at him without smiling. For terror itself becomes ridiculous if its cause is the loss of unlicensed goods or forbidden fruit; and this is the case here. How mechanically he grips with all five fingers (it might very well have been six),[2] upon one of which visibly rests Ephraim's blessing. I mean, a Berlin jeweller's. What he wants to catch hold of is silver, but the table will surely fall, because it cannot put a leg forward like its owner, who through this prerogative of all living things is by means of his legs only just able to keep himself in his seat. A

[1] To the Englishman, or anybody who knows England, this climax is clear. On behalf of the German reader I must explain that Billingsgate is the London fishmarket, which is served mostly by women-fishwives, people of incredible volubility. Better representatives of the mute genus of fishes could not have been obtained in a world where it is absolutely necessary to speak.

[2] In his youth when he still engraved billheads for tradespeople and artists, Hogarth really drew a figure, which was to represent the Patron of Trade, with six fingers on one hand. At the time it was said to have been an error, but I do not quite trust the fox, even when he was still a youngster. Moreover, I cannot see that it would be so absurd, provided the sum total of ten was preserved and the other hand had four fingers. The former would then be the take-hand and the latter the give-hand, and all would fit quite nicely.

solitary teacup is also saved, being perilously balanced in his right hand. But the others! One can hardly bear to look at it. Confusion and distress on every side. Everything is taking flight before the raised knee and tries to save itself. The sugar bowl and the little dish, and what appears to be a milk jug, venture first to spring overboard—and are no more! A little lid jumps after them and while still in the air sees the same fate approaching. Another lid appears to make a running start upon deck so as to jump over the others—with a like result. Calmest of all seems the teapot. Before risking the fatal jump it rids itself not only of its lid, which it has thrown a good way in advance, but also of its boiling ballast, and that straight into its master's stockings, and thence still farther, into his shoes. To judge from the hasty flight of the lid, and because this way of softening human skin is rather slow, the pot is going to turn topsy-turvy before it has finished, to accelerate the process. If one could reason with teapots, I know what I should tell this one—'This,' I would say, 'was a perfidious prank of yours, and the more perfidious the more it looks like a Last Will. Provided you get away without complete destruction, take care that as a reward for your pranks you do not become a badly glued-together, or even a mutilated laughing-stock, for the servants, in all your future services.'

That what the girl has just said must have been far weightier than what she indicates with her finger tips, may be seen from the petrifaction of the man, from which even the boiling tea, served at the utterly unsuitable end, is not capable of rousing him. Hogarth has done all that very well. For indeed, if he has not made us feel that, we should not hear either the creaking of the door, or the footsteps of the sly and lucky rival who even has his shoes carried after him.

The Europeans in this picture seem to pay little attention to the clatter of the falling tea-table with all its appurtenances. Three of them are not losing anything by it, and the fourth ignores it because he is losing so much. All the stronger, however, do the two directing gods of love from the torrid zone, monkey and Moor, feel the sad movements of the two hearts which they keep in trust, and which are now at variance. Looking at the monkey beside a pair of lovers like that, it is almost impossible not to think of him with bow and arrow. He is in flight, the poor devil; just now he was playing peacefully with mother's cap, just as in former days the Greek ideal whom he is aping disported himself with the helmet of

Mars, when he came to mother with fatherly intentions. And now the swarthy god of love! His woolly hair seems to stand on end. Perhaps while sorrowing over the fate of his West Indian brothers, he sees with horror that here too he will have to—clear up the mess. The figure is striking and the expression has become almost proverbial. Garrick, whose stature tended more to the graceful than the majestic type, and whose whole soul found expression above all in his face, once undertook to act the part of Shakespeare's Moor of Venice, the strong, passionate and thundering Othello, a part which the most versatile soul could not have acted without physical weight. The consequence was that every make-up he put on was a failure, and especially that of the chimney sweep, which simply made night out of his day. When he appeared thus, Quinn, a comic actor of the first rank, notorious for his loose, biting humour, called out: 'Here's Pompey,[1]—where's the tea-kettle?' Only once more, it is said, did Garrick ever dare to appear in that role, and then never again.

The escaping lover we shall allow to escape. To look at him is enough; it needs no comment. Only a single incidental remark on the sentimental side of his appointment. There is no Cupid to be seen fluttering over that Adonis to cover his retreat with delicate wings and in the end smile contemptuously back into the room. Instead, and this is far safer, he has cudgel and rapier under his arm. Whoever creeps into such a hen-house must always expect that the first person he meets will be just such another cock. One cannot miss the cockade on his hat. Thus he was here merely on duty.

Immediately in front of the monkey stands a toilet table, and his flight is evidently directed thither. He wants to crawl underneath where at least he will no longer see the danger, and this, as is well known, is as good as security itself for monkeys and children and whatever else belongs to that category. A mirror stands on the table, and a little packet of visiting cards and a mask are lying there. Perhaps Molly returned last night from a Masked Ball and brought with her the new recruit who is about to desert in the background. What lies in the right-hand corner there looks very much like a discarded domino. To be sure there could be no greater warning against masquerades, at least the London ones. Hussies like her brought together with honest people into one and the same game on a perfectly equal footing merely through a flimsy disguise!

[1] A name sometimes given to Moors in England.

Nothing good can come from that. We all hope for equality in the next world. To look for it here already is dangerous in any case, and especially in a domino; for it does not always cease when the mask is thrown down, and upon such a cessation depends after all the whole charm of the short illusion.

On the back wall hang two pictures, which may even be woven into the tapestry, for the corner of one of them is under the frame of the door. However, strict perspective was never Hogarth's strong point. The one nearest the door represents the prophet Jonah facing the city of Nineveh, and as if boxing with a cluster of sunrays which the worm-eaten water-melon is no longer capable of warding off. Such fists have the weight of words in England. The other represents King David, not in his glory, but when he dances before the Ark of the Covenant and is despised by Micah, Saul's daughter, who looks out of a window. The Ark of the Covenant is drawn by oxen who upset it, as it is written in the Bible, and the Ark falls, or is about to fall. A certain Uzzah tries to support it, and for that service a man in a Bishop's mitre runs a knife into his breast, from behind. The Bible only says, 'and the anger of the Lord was kindled against Uzzah, and he smote him for his error and there he died by the Ark of God'. I am sorry to find that Hogarth wants to interpret the ancient Bible in a modern way. Take care, good friend, I thought to myself, there you are upon the dangerous bridge which is to connect Sunday faith with week-day reason! Of what avail are your pictures against folios of which you do not understand a syllable, and which, had they ever so little force would still remain respectable through their mass alone. Take care! Though nobody is likely to murder you from behind, as they did your Uzzah before the Ark of God, but I don't mind betting that before you know where you are something very hot may be poured into your shoes, as happened to our Jew at the tea-table. 'Stick to your last' is a proverb upon which the earth itself rests. It is this true saying which restrains us here and compels us to pass over the second picture completely. Since the interpretation of straightforward prophecies of even the minor prophets offers such difficulties to the most profound scholars, how much more difficult is it for an insignificant writer to interpret the artificial misuse which a sly fox makes of them. One word only on the subject: Jonah complains about a misfortune which has not materialized, and is afraid of sunstroke. Here too there is at least an indication that the two diamonds in the Jew's head might blaze up and prove deadly; a misfortune which though conjectured by almost every reader does not materialize either. No more now about these pictures, though a more courageous interpreter could and would perhaps say more. If anyone would like to venture an interpretation of his own he may look up the fourth Chapter of the prophet Jonah and 2 Samuel, Chapter 6. On the same wall hang two engravings of characters from the New Testament, with wigs and *chapeau-bas*; thus scholars. In the first copies of the engraving the higher one was a portrait of the famous Dr Clark,[1] and the one beneath of Mr Woolston.[2] The latter has written an apologia for the Christian religion against the Jews, and the former on a number of topics which would here provide more material for conjecture. This must, however, be left undone because Hogarth by eradicating their names in later copies has expressly shown his wish that it should be left undone.

[1] Probably Sir Thomas Clarke (1703–1764), Master of the Rolls, referred to in 'The Causidicade, a panegyrici-satiri-serio-comic dramatical poem', 1743. Or Lichtenberg may have meant Samuel Clarke (1675–1729) who came to occupy a leading position in English philosophy and theology. Ed.

[2] Thomas Woolston (1670–1737), enthusiast and free thinker. He tried to interpret the Scriptures as allegories and was imprisoned for his irreverent jocularity. Ed.

III

MOLLY is falling—falling faster and faster! This is only the third station in her journey out of the six which our artist has represented, and two-thirds of the journey are already over. After the second station, there were still some Summer by-ways with agreeable meanderings, though of course not for every equipage. The *Chronique Scandaleuse* speaks of women, even wives, who started out like that and yet arrived quite safely! Only the *Chronique Scandaleuse*?—Oh! the venerable annals of history itself, and not very far back, tell of Vice-Queens who set out from this post house for the last station.

But here all is lost! She has, as Basedow[1] once said of himself jokingly and in a manner of speaking, arrived at her destination in earnest and married herself to the public. She appears here as the central figure in a small establishment of the third rank, for the quenching of hearts aflame. How low she has fallen! *Fuimus*, everywhere!

In other pictures, we left the description of the furnishings to the end. They were of secondary importance. It was the human figures who explained the significance of the furniture. Here it is the furniture which has to illuminate the human beings. A young female body, not without charms, is soon adorned. What does not grace it will be graced by it, and what may be lacking here or there in person or attire will not be noticed by young people of the opposite sex, or it can easily be made good by something of which another part has been deprived, and which it is perfectly willing to do without *in majoram gloriam* of the whole. In this way

[1] J. B. Basedow (1727–90), writer on theology, education and philosophy. Ed.

such a creature can go far, always patching up the visible garment at the expense of the invisible, and the decay in beauty at the expense of honesty, until the whole, patched and repatched for the last time, attains its resurrection after a brief death, and what decayed as Hackabout rises again as Mother Needham. But for the lodging and its furniture, patching up is not so easy in London where money is so cheap and, consequently, everything else so terribly expensive; nor is it so necessary. For when someone goes out into the street from a room like that, he will no longer remember what it looked like, and the eyes coming in from the street will certainly have some degree of blindness and intoxication.

The scene is Drury Lane,[1] as we can tell from the Pewter jar which stands on the ground in the right-hand corner.[2] The little room must be rather high up, for to see so much sky through the door as we see here would be possible in Drury Lane only in the vicinity of the chimney stacks. This is also indicated by the windows opposite where no light enters even through the sections where the glass is missing, and where they have *ad interim* replaced the glass by mere air. The light comes mainly from the side from which we are looking and Hogarth leaves it to our architectonic intuition to imagine the hole through which it might come. What a transformation! Here, too, tea is being drunk, but in what style? Were it not for the cups and the teapot, one would almost expect to see shoes being repaired here! The silver table with its delicate legs is gone, and in its place is another with a pair of legs that could support an ox. Evidently the service it is now performing is not the only one it has to do. To judge from its strong and somewhat thick-set shape, it seems likely that it is sometimes used for pounding meat on, or even as a stand for the washtub, or for tired guests who cannot find accommodation elsewhere. The same little foot and the same knee which overturned the silver table are again in evidence, but no longer for the purpose of upsetting the table; on the contrary the foot seems to find support on its structure. The silver teapot, too, has gone, yielding place to a miserable tin affair, just as the long-tailed monkey has been replaced by a long-tailed cat and the chamber-

---

[1] A long, narrow London street which contains not only the world-famous theatre, but also establishments like the one represented in this Plate, by the hundred. Upon these stages are enacted, year in year out, scenes which usually end in the illness of the hero, the so-called Drury Lane Ague, and not uncommonly with murder and manslaughter, as do so many other plays in the neighbourhood—in the world-famous theatre.

[2] The words of the inscription are 'John Dry [?] in Drurylane.'

A Harlot's Progress Plate III

maid and negro by a hybrid creature who is a cross between a chamber-maid, a negress and a long-tailed monkey. On the little table we see only one cup and saucer, and an odd cup, probably containing sugar, a small loaf of bread, a knife and a little butter for which a literary production has provided the plate. For the sheet of paper on which it lies is part of the Pastoral Letter of Bishop Gibson, Bishop of London, which that honest man had with the best intentions despatched to his parishioners. It is said that despite the address clearly written on them, they did not reach their destination until the grocers co-operated and undertook the delivery.

Beside the bed stands a miserable cane chair, the only one in the room however, if the little table has to serve for breakfast or washing. The chair now in its turn is serving as a sort of table and carries a bottle which has been elevated to the rank of a candlestick, and a soup plate which last night was so far degraded that from now on it could only serve with honour under the bed. Over the chairback she has thrown her last night's jacket, probably of red material with imitation gold trimmings, which would look splendid especially by the light of a street lamp of the fourth magnitude, inducing curiosity and fancies. When a garment like that is on show, Londoners of all ranks will be caught in the snare like larks in reflected sunlight.

Opposite this chair, near the empty porter mugs, stands the toilet table, also on elephant rather than goat legs. It is really a gate-legged table which, like everything else in this room, performs multiple service. Against a punch bowl with an indenture which is newer than the bowl leans a triangular fragment of a mirror, which is newer than the whole. Neither the cut-out nor the cut-off portions are the work of art, but of chance. In front of the mirror there lies here too an ivory weapon[1] for waging war against bites from outside; against those from inside from which people might sometimes suffer here, there stands the armoury next to the mirror—a little brandy glass and a brandy measure. The former, we observe, has also by chance suffered a terrible amputation whereby it is forced to stand upon its head when empty, and to let itself be held up when full. It is usually just the opposite with the men whom it serves and who do homage to it. The other objects standing there are apparently cosmetic paraphernalia intended to transform, for a little while, into deceptive wax fruit the face decayed too soon, which in Yorkshire would no doubt have

[1] See p. 161.

remained a sound and natural fruit. A little note, to 'Md. Hackabout', peeps out of the drawer, evidently a little love sigh which vents itself in writing.

On the back wall next to the door we see a length of string with loops from which to hang anything and everything, but from which nothing at all is hanging at present. It appears to be the wardrobe. Also a *fuimus*. Perhaps its previous contents have been taken in custody by the pawn-broker, or have been distributed all over the room, or else it serves for hanging up temporarily what was only borrowed for the moment.

So much for the furnishings as far as they throw light upon the economic circumstances of the lady. Everything else which is standing there, or lying about or hanging up, serves to interpret other circumstances which touch our heroine one degree closer, and their meaning is therefore best explained together with the history of the *dramatis personae* themselves, which we fear we have already withheld too long for our readers' curiosity.

It is a quarter to twelve in the morning according to the sun, but since breakfast is only just being served, it is still very early, about seven o'clock according to the fashionable time they keep here. Our heroine has roused herself and is supporting herself somewhat wearily and heavily upon her right arm; in her left hand she dangles a watch at the end of a ribbon, her head in a listening attitude. Evidently the watch is a repeater and is striking the hour. The hour? Alas! it is nothing but a meaningless 'eleven'. What help are all the repeater watches in the world to you? A pair of repeater ears through which the warning of your honest father would again resound in your soul would be of infinitely more value. But listen —the hour has struck! Much is lost, but not yet everything. Justice is awake and holds back the final stroke which already hovers over your head. The door opens and Sir John Gonson[1] with his retinue enters the room

---

[1] Not Gonston, as Mr Ireland always writes. Sir John Gonson was a magistrate who made it his business to exterminate houses of ill repute. He filled the important post which the famous Fielding held for a short time, and after him his half-brother, Sir John Fielding, for a long time, and, although he had lost his sight, carried out his duties with great distinction. The main occupation of these important persons is to send their officials to visit criminals of all kinds or to cross-question them and according to circumstances either release them or remand them in custody for trial at the Old Bailey. Sir John Gonson's activity and zeal were praised in several poems, as for example in the Sapphic Ode, 'Ad Joannem Gonsonem Equitem', by a Mr Loveling. It begins:

and our heroine is arrested. Evidently the watch is a small item of booty from last night, and the loser has perhaps complained to the authorities. The charming creature whose upper half appears to be supported by a rag-heap of petticoats is evidently the president of the establishment. Her nose seems to have suffered, whether in an affair of the heart through internal inflammation, or in an *affaire d'honneur*, where she assisted with eyes and teeth, we do not know. At this point we must ask our readers to shed a few tears on behalf of a poor devil who has given them much pleasure, but who now is no longer: the gay, droll, latinizing Partridge in Fielding's *Tom Jones*. For as Fielding himself assures us, the notorious better half of that martyr was the very spit of this turbot![1] But let us avert our eyes from thy boundless suffering, poor devil, for I seem to hear thee whisper thy favourite refrain with which thou didst crown so many reflections, and which thou didst ever find apt since thou didst not understand it:

Infandum, Regina, jubes renovare dolorem.

We proceed to the remaining ornaments on the Plate, which will now be better understood. At the head of the bed, or rather of the recess under which the bed frame stands, there hovers between canopy and earth a comet with a terrific tail—the broom of education—the birch. We have been rather slow to mention it although among all the inanimate objects on the Plate this is usually the first, after the watch, that is, to attract the eye of the spectator. We have called it terrible, but merely in accordance with linguistic custom; for these comets on the firmament of morals do just as little harm to that system as those in the sky to the system of the physical world. Just as Newton has assumed that the latter might perhaps with their tails fan an invigorating atmosphere into the system, so it might not

---

Pellicum, Gonsone, animosus hostis,
Per minus castas Druriae tabernas
Lenis incedens abeas Diones
    Aequus alumnus.

It is worth remarking that it was this Plate which roused the first great applause for our artist. The day on which it appeared, the House of Lords was in session. One of the noble Lords bought it on his way to the House and took it with him. The others were so struck by the great resemblance to Sir John Gonson that after the Session they all went out and bought a copy of the Plate, and thereby was Hogarth's name established.

[1] *Tom Jones*, Book II, Chapter 3.

only be supposed but could be geometrically demonstrated that the former actually sweep a great deal of evil out of the world with theirs. If, however, we see them not as birches but merely as bundles of faggots, then their use is really limitless; one might well ask, for example, what would become of the rushing stream of instruction and learning which in school pours through both our ears, if they were not in due course to build a dam at the other end out of such faggots to prevent its escaping there helter-skelter. But how does the pedagogic faggot or rod of philanthropy come to be here, and just on the head-board of the bed? The problem, I must admit, is really not an easy one. I wish it were even more difficult, or so difficult that it simply could not be solved. Oh! that sort of problem makes the most wonderful material for authors who are paid by the page, like bricklayers by the cubic foot. But alas! the problem is not an easy one, and that is just what makes it so difficult. However, we will try. A small introduction to start with. For the first time in the work of our artist we are here at a point to which we shall often have to return, and twice in this series of pictures alone. It is namely the point where morals themselves prohibit moralizing, and the most eloquent interpretation grows dumb or at least pretends to be dumb and makes only signs to the passer-by, or if it is ultimately compelled to speak, will say nothing more than 'I am dumb'.

Philosophers have observed long ago that blindness is partial death, and indeed Nature seems to subscribe to that opinion, which is not always so with the remarks of philosophers. But I doubt whether against any evil in this vale of misery there are more remedies than against the inability to see. If the sun will not come out, all right, we can put the light on. That is only a small thing. If cataract shuts the window, again no harm; the ophthalmic surgeon will open it again. If a man becomes myopic, and sees no more of the Universe than the tip of his own nose, or if he becomes a Presbyterian (or should I say presbytopic?) and sees the church steeple clearly but not his neighbour who stands before him, the whole matter can be put right with twelve shillings paid to the optician. With the help of that great Triple Alliance, candle-maker, ophthalmic surgeon, and spectacle maker, man has successfully fought absolute as well as relative blindness, defensively at least, so that its encroachment which may still take place here and there is hardly noticeable. Indeed, we have even taken the offensive, and there is hope one day of seeing the mote in a brother's eye as far away as the moon. Is it not queer with vision? Have we not already a sort of telegraphy with the moon so that by exact calculation we can find out, in one and a half seconds, when a *monte nuovo* has emerged up there, or a Lissabon or Messina come to an end? But alas! if only there were a telegraph for the remaining five senses, too! But with these it is rather a sad story! There the Presbyterian grows more and more myopic; long sight becomes short sight, and soon ends in complete blindness. Oh, that someone could kindle a light in that quarter or operate for cataract or make a pair of spectacles! Oh! that would be the alchemist's stone, I mean of old age, without which no wisdom is possible. It has been tried a thousand times, but with what success? But we were speaking I believe of the educational birch at the bed-head. Is this then a pair of spectacles—for Presbyterians? To tell the truth, I am not quite sure myself; I only know this, that if it is such a thing, it will not be worn on the nose. I think I have done my duty now, in having commented on a ticklish passage in my author at such length that I do not understand myself any more, and that is all an honest commentator can do. What, however, this locus lacks in clarification, we promise our readers to make good tenfold in other places where it might not be half so necessary, and this again is all an honest commentator can do.

On the canopy of the bed, as if it were quite at home there, lies the wig-box of a notorious street robber, James Dalton. If it is not already a legacy, it will surely become one soon since the fellow was hanged about that time. How low our heroine has fallen! Street robbers are criminals of the third rank, altogether without professional honour. In a nation of highwaymen, who count their ancestors right back to Alexander, they would just be hanged. To his honour and the girl's we will assume that he was no sly pickpocket but that he robbed honestly and took risks, heart against heart, or at least pistol or knife against cudgel; but still only as a foot-pad and not on horseback. The horse elevates and ennobles even rogues—in England. It has been said that the robber who sticks to the ground is something of a Yahoo, while the one on horseback is always a

---

[1] 'James Dalton his Wigg-box' runs the inscription. It should of course read 'wig-box'. Evidently the lapse in orthography is not due to James Dalton, but to Hogarth. His pictures are full of such mistakes. There are two more in this Plate: under one of the portraits should stand 'Mac' instead of 'Mack', and under the other 'Sacheverel' instead of 'Sacheverall'. We have, however, carefully preserved all these mistakes, since a whimsical fellow like Hogarth may have had some intention with them. The address round the goose's neck on the first Plate is an undoubted example of this.

bit of a Houyhnhnm.[1] It is no trifle that Dalton has entrusted there to the girl. Wigs of every condition, form and hue are important items in a robber's inventory. He might change his appearance, like the hares and partridges of some regions, who in summertime look like ploughed land or stubble fields, and in winter like snow. Or if he has plundered in one wig as a caterpillar, he may change through another into a chrysalis, and in a third he may evade the arm of justice as a butterfly. It is on record that some rascals before being brought to their Examination and Promotion have in the course of eight days made the round of all Four Faculties with their wigs. In the end, of course, these masks of the back of the head become witnesses against the head itself, and this renders the pawn on the canopy here still more important.

On the wall there hangs *in effigie* Mac Heath, one of the greatest men in his profession. His name is sometimes spelled M'Heath with M in front, whereas many of his kind had the M behind. Even the famous Gay counted it an honour to have become the Curtius to that Macedonian of the heath.[2] At his death a monument was erected in his honour, but curiously enough without a pedestal. Its support came from above, evidently because his M stood in front of his name. Moreover he did not hang there in marble or bronze, but in order to save the expense of a sculptor or iron-founder, and also to obtain the greatest possible likeness, the man was used *in persona*. Never have I wished for more space than here. There is so much to say. But only a brief outline can be given. We have *statuas pedestres* and *equestres*, just as we have foot-pads and highwaymen. But it seems to me that in the classification of statues in this world, an important type has been left out, which neither Greece nor Rome has reckoned with, and which seems to have been left to our time; that is, the *Statua pensilis*. A small *contradictio in adjecto* between standing and hanging will, I hope, be disregarded by the critic; it is only a grammatical contradiction, and in the usual run of our statues we have more occasion to swallow contradictions that go much deeper. I cannot see why people who have, *cum grano salis*, served the human race should not be suspended in bronze and by chains of bronze, with a hymn book in hand, and even on a

---

[1] If anyone is yet unacquainted with the history of these remarkable people, or is acquainted with it and now feels some inclination to join them, he will find the necessary information in the Travels of the famous surgeon and ship's captain, Lemuel Gulliver, Part 4.

[2] MacHeath is the hero of *The Beggar's Opera*.

gallows of bronze in the backyard of the Pantheon for instance. Should perhaps the secret foundries of Meudon[1] go in for that sort of thing? They could always work in advance. For it would be an easy matter for French wit and French artistry to create a monument with movable limbs so that it could be erected in the wind month (Ventose), and in the heat month (Fervidor) hang suspended in the backyard of the Pantheon.

Next the M'Heath hangs another man with S.T.P. after his name, meaning Sanctae Theologiae Professor, Dr Sacheverel.[2] It is a very good thing for an interpreter of these Plates that the name Sacheverel undoes ten times over what the letters S.T.P. may for a short time have bestowed on him. He disported himself upon the highway to Heaven just like his counterpart on the road from London to Oxford. Hogarth deserves praise for stringing him up like that. The trial of that fanatic has been compared in some German newspapers recently to that of the cobbler Hardy.[3] To whose credit I hardly know. The uproar which accompanied the trials had, of course, some similarity. Equality of that sort is easy to establish in London. Tumult in the depths is there always the effect of movement from above, whatever the movement may be. Dr Sacheverel and Hardy both caused a commotion, but, it seems to me, with the important difference that people considered that caused by the Doctor as too high, and that by the cobbler as perhaps too low. Dr Sacheverel was one of the Watchers of Zion of whom Lessing has said that whenever they see something glimmer in the dark they immediately cry 'fire!' without first making sure whether it might not be only a little streak of the Northern Lights. But, strictly speaking, the Doctor lit his pipe in a place and at a time when he ought not to have done so. He proceeded so incautiously that, in the end, Zion and the City very nearly suffered the damage which the Doctor had been paid to prevent. Sacheverel was an extremely Tory-minded preacher at a time (1709) when the Government, as is well known, was Whig. But it seemed to him, and that was his little pipe, as if all dissenters were not only tolerated, but favoured. After some strong pulls at the pipe in the dark, and being perhaps a little giddy or otherwise not quite himself, he fancied he smelt the flame licking towards Zion and

---

[1] A town in northern France, $2\frac{1}{2}$ miles south-west of Paris, not far from Versailles. Ed.

[2] 1674?–1724, a political Divine who preached violently against Dissenters and Whigs. Ed.

[3] Thomas Hardy (1752–1832), a bootmaker of Piccadilly who turned political agitator. He founded 'The London Corresponding Society', meeting at the Bell Inn, Strand, to promote parliamentary reform. He was arrested for treason but acquitted. Ed.

shouted for help. He preached, not in a small chapel, but in Saint Paul's Cathedral itself, on the words of the Apostle about the danger of false brethren; attacked the Ministry and its laws, not even in allegories but with outspoken words in the most violent manner; referred in the pulpit to the then Lord Chancellor under the name of Volpone, and commanded the people to put on the armour and the sword of God, and to rise against the false brethren. The day chosen by that true brother for his sermon was the 5th of November. As is well known, this is the anniversary not only of the Gunpowder Plot, but also of the famous landing which brought about the Bloodless Revolution.

It is also known how on that day the protestant heresy of the London crowd, having rested quietly on the yeast the whole year through, starts to ferment, just like some wines when the vine begins to blossom anew. In the name of the Gospel, sacred fires are kindled in the streets, and the Pope is burned in effigy as a warning to false brethren. Sacheverel's sermon had the effect that not only window frames, shop windows, cellar doors, booths and similar inflammable material were brought to feed the fire, but also the church pews of the false brethren, and almost the false brethren themselves. Wasn't that terrible? But surely, some reader will perhaps join me in asking, there must have been a fire hose near at hand to direct upon the mouth, from which that glowing sulphur was issuing, an arm-thick jet of water, and consecrate the head with a baptism of water? Perhaps the people at the sight of such a contest of the elements might have put on the garment of mirth and the mien of mockery and the whole matter would have been extinguished. But alas! it did not end like that. The Lord Mayor at that time, probably also a sulphur-saint, had the righteous one's sermon printed, and now there was fire everywhere; it was extolled to Heaven by his followers. The wiser heads in Parliament advised against making the matter more important than it really was by drawing attention to it, but in vain. Sacheverel was arraigned before the Bar of the House of Lords as a major law-breaker. That was just what he wanted. Things grew worse and worse; his carriage was escorted daily by a huge crowd of jubilant people on its way from Westminster Hall to Temple Bar. The houses of the dissentient community were looted, chapels hitherto tolerated were pulled down, and even the houses of the Lord Chancellor Lord Wharton, and the Bishop of Sarum, were threatened with destruction. And what was the final outcome of all this tumult? Sacheverel was found guilty of a misdemeanour, which means anything between a crime deserving capital punishment, and nothing at all, and on which English Courts make no definite pronouncement. Had the Doctor stolen a seal he would have been hanged. As it was, however, he was suspended from preaching for three whole years, and his Opus was publicly burned. Was it all over now? Far from it. The affair spread higher and higher, farther and farther, and, one must admit, from now on with good reason. The trivial punishment was regarded as the equivalent of a discharge, just a face-saving device, and the culprit, while still alive, was regarded thenceforth as a saint and a martyr at the same time. In his honour England blazed at night from one end to the other with sacrificial fires and sacrificial illuminations. Now the martyr began to enjoy his position with a vengeance. He drove in triumph through the land. The University of Oxford came to greet him with pomp and a ceremonial procession, and they caroused all day long for the sake of the Gospel. A large part of the English aristocracy entertained him with magnificence and pious debauchery, and the municipal magistrates came to meet him with music, mounted soldiery and *in pontificalibus*. The bushes by the wayside where he passed were decorated with garlands, while pennants and flags fluttered from the steeples, and the whole air reverberated with 'Sacheverel and the Church'.[1] That is how things stood then. Posterity, we see, has revised the case and quashed the sentence, and Hogarth who, when it came to the execution of sinners whose neck was too strong for ordinary justice, possessed an inimitable strength, has here hanged the saint next to MacHeath. *Sic pagina jungit amicos.* And the MacHeaths and the Daltons are indeed said to have played a major part in Sacheverel's transfiguration. While he sowed his spiritual blessing, they carried the necessary agricultural tools with which to till the ground in a temporal way, if need be, should it prove too stubborn to receive it.

There are two more pictures hanging on the same wall. Immediately below MacHeath a little half-length portrait with a halo and, above the uneven windows, Isaac's sacrifice. The interpreters, if they mention the first at all, simply say it is the Virgin Mary. This is, however, to say the least, a very poor idea of theirs. For one thing, the figure is obviously of

[1] One of the most recent publications where this history is briefly and well described is the *Memoirs of the King of Great Britain, of the House of Brunswick-Luneburg*, by W. Belsham, London, 1793. II vol. 18 vo., Vol. I, p. 60 ff.

the male sex, and that puts an end to their interpretation. But even if it were not so, the idea in itself is somewhat repellent to a certain sentiment which Hogarth, despite his roguery, never offends as far as I know. Nor would it be a good sign in him. Of course, here or there in the Christian world the image of that holy figure may be hung in some private temple wherein God is served as badly as in this one. But such an explanation is much too far-fetched, and one's immediate revulsion would blunt all feeling for the feeble attraction of such a commonplace joke. In a word, it is not true. The thing is surely a Calendar Saint. Think only of their number, 365. In that considerable flock, should there not have been a single mangy specimen like Sacheverel or MacHeath? About Isaac's sacrifice the interpreters either say nothing at all, or something which is just about as valuable. This is the interpreter's way with tricky passages. Apparently the picture is a relic from the Portuguese establishment and what we said earlier (p. 28) quite ingenuously contains perhaps the best explanation. It is really there that the girl's history takes a turn which, for one in her position, could still be called fortunate. The sword that was raised above her is halted, and the place where Isaac was to be sacrificed merely signified: the Lord sees. What more? Hogarth evidently did not see very deeply here, and thought merely of salvation from violent death, or of withholding a blow from the sword of strict justice in special cases through the intervention of a higher grace endowed with the power to do this. That is how thousands who see nothing deeper in it understand the story of Isaac. Had Hogarth been also a philologist and a divine, the explanation would of course have been forced. But is this not often true of Bible interpretations by people who are everything that Hogarth was not? How much more readily then should we not forgive in a Christian way a man from whose character a little light-hearted frivolousness cannot be completely explained away.

Having examined the main features of this remarkable Plate, we shall now with a few strokes of the pen gather together what here and there has so far escaped our attention.

Just above the man with the clerical collar stand a couple of medicine bottles with their doctor's frills, looking out of the window through which hardly anybody ever looks in, and on the other side, if I am not mistaken, stands an ointment jar. Good, since it stands there it is our duty to let it stand. It rings a bell already and needs no further interpretation.

The cat! It is supposed to be after a mouse that has just escaped, a sign of the poverty and dirt in that apartment. Rats and mice rarely go begging from well-to-do people, and in this, I think, they are not far wrong. But the cat's posture is not that of an animal stealthily stalking with intent to pounce. So we shall leave that where it is, too. On the back curtain of the bed there still hangs a winged head-gear from the previous evening, having evidently escaped there in haste during the attack, so that the pleats should not be crumpled. The hat seems to have escaped before that and while the parties were still upright. Now a few words about the knot in the bed curtain. Mr Ireland sees a face in it, and even a resemblance to the Mother Superior, the Turbot. I have so little against this hypothesis that I even find that Mr Ireland has seldom seen with such Hogarthian eyes as here. It certainly is not out of keeping with Hogarth's character as poet and artist to give the knot in a curtain around the altar of Venus Pandemos the form of a miserable face which, with averted eyes, weeps for the sacrifices which are offered up there. The knot appears to be tied with care and certainly not without meaning; apparently to admit the necessary light and also allow free falling space for the comet when it approaches the sun. Whether in addition the face resembles that of the High Priestess, the Turbot, we shall not decide, but we cannot help winding up at this juncture with an incidental observation about the golden rule: *Ne quid nimis*. It is true we have to deal here with a very whimsical and original humorist, but this should not make us ruin our own healthy eyesight, nor should we believe we see things in the picture which in fact only exist this side of the tip of our own noses. This is reminiscent of our modern prophetesses who with the point of a needle trace out Mamselle's fortune from the coffee grounds in her cup, and hold forth something like this: 'Do you see, my charming young lady, the little circle here; it is as clear as can be, it is a carriage wheel; and these little dots here, 4, 8, 12, 16, 20, 24, those are the footsteps of—wait a moment my dear child— yes, that's right, of six horses. Oh, would you breathe on it once more? Now, do you see? That's clearly a star. Count the points yourself. So my dear young lady, a carriage and six, and a star as well, and now this here, ah! what could that be!' . . . but *ne quid nimis*. This, however, is not an attack upon the small sallies of wit, be they true or assumed, which a commentator allows himself, obviously at his own expense. These are the stamped property of the commentator, which we may or may not accept.

What concerns me here is only the deeply sensed meaning of the whole. The meaning of the whole Hogarth has never concealed; he could have done so only to his own disadvantage. His general aim is apparent at the first glance, and this is essential. Without it, a work of art of this kind cannot succeed. Once, however, that meaning is established, the desire to elucidate small subordinate obscurities will increase the pleasure of the onlooker, which would be completely destroyed by obscurity in the whole. We should throw the picture away. Thus the picture of the Strolling Actresses is simply a representation of the disorder and ridiculous contrasts which must necessarily arise when strolling actresses are dressing in a small room; to make the contrast still more striking, he chooses an opera about the gods, in which, in the theatre, Diana hunts the stag, and behind the scenes, the stag often chases Diana. To present that disorder as a whole in a single picture was the richest possible subject for the talent of our artist. Here his genius was at home. Had he been compelled to have his wings clipped in accordance with some conventional rule or particular theme, he certainly would not have risen from the earth. This, for instance, very likely happened to him in the Hudibras pictures.[1] Whoever, therefore, looks for a plan in that Plate and a particular mythological play, certainly does not know Hogarth's genius too well. It would, of course, have been more in accordance with the Proclamation of Aesthetics if he had, despite all his self-assurance and confidence in his inner strength, subordinated himself to the contract which crude barbarity must necessarily conclude with refined humanity if it wishes to sell its wares in our philosophical markets. But that he could not do; he could only produce the shape, we others might do the finer work. To give just one example: this very picture of the Actresses has been interpreted, confidently and with an air of superiority, as representing the love affair between Diana and Endymion. One of my friends has countered that ridiculous explanation not only with the attitude but with the confidence of true superiority, by an interpretation of the same picture which I should have liked to relate here in full. He has explained it by reference to the French Revolution, and with a wittiness which is immensely superior to that other trivial invention. I can only briefly outline it here. But I, as well as my friend, are compelled to suppress some of the strongest touches because of feelings

---

[1] A series of engravings by Hogarth illustrating Samuel Butler's famous satirical poem of that name. Ed.

of a higher kind which persuade us that a joke like that, expressed in public, could easily be misunderstood, since it concerns persons who have a right to our compassion, the more so the less we know today what our own fate may be tomorrow. Thus the two devils at the altar with the bass viol and the head of the Medusa, which turns everything around it to stone, are, it seems to me, self-evident—*luce meridiana clarius*. The lost overseas trade is excellently expressed by the waves which have been thrown into a corner. Cats are turning the globe without knowing what they are doing! Bishops' mitres become receptacles for comedy texts. Jewels made of leaves fill a maltster's hamper. This could be nothing else but assignats[1] for jewellery, and that tremendous wealth is threatened with destruction by a burning tallow candle. There is *sans-culotterie* everywhere here; even the one pair of trousers lies abandoned. A furious cat has its tail cut off; does that not mean Robespierre's tail? The threshing flail, symbolizing agriculture, lies in the corner. The empty trunks are as clear as can be. A sea-goddess from the West Indies presents a *sans-culotte* with her last remnant of rum, and both of them are crying. She herself is thrown up on dry land. The monkey who plays his tricks with the helmet, possibly of Pallas, cannot be misunderstood. Also the search for garments in the clouds has its meaning. So it goes on through the whole picture, and the assembly in which all this takes place is entitled:

Senatus populusque Romanus

and so on (see pp. 155-172).

---

[1] French paper money issued by the Revolutionary government.

IV

As is well known, Chemistry describes three stages of fermentation: wine fermentation, acetous fermentation and putrid fermentation. But these terms could also apply in quite other fields than Chemistry. One might find analogous processes wherever organic matter of any kind, combined with a volatile portion of *je ne sais quoi*, life-force or spirit or whatever it is, in varying proportions of quantity as well as intensity, takes part in the cycle of Nature, which is characterized by stability amid constant change. This is true of the life of individuals as well as of States, in the whole as well as in part. The first fermentation of life, O how it rejoices the heart of man! In what long draughts he imbibes enthusiasm and delight from everything! A little time goes by and it is no more, as happened in the last war, or whatever period the historian may choose. The pleasant taste has gone. The drinker puts down the half-drained cup with a grimace and a disgusted shake of the head. He no longer sees the sense of it; it is forbidden fruit; it is abominable—and up comes the sour face. But the process still goes on. Age makes for carefulness, carefulness for mistrust, and mistrust makes a man still older. Instead of with figures, he calculates with hyphens—upon the forehead, and many a time between supper and breakfast makes a costly midnight feast off his own fat. Thus one tooth after another falls out, one lock of hair after another goes, and one faculty after another fails, and so he goes on, without teeth, without hair, without faculties, or as Shakespeare says, 'sans everything', through the last stage of fermentation towards putrefaction. Oh! how he stinks! Away with him into the box with its wood-shavings; off to the Resurrection

A Harlot's Progress Plate IV

field with him, with the mighty Thing that will never be seen again! Such is the life of man. Is it otherwise with States and cities? All that remains from the glories of former times are tombstones above a mighty corpse, or miserable off-shoots on a decaying stump which drop off with every passing winter.

But life does not always pass so slowly and so regularly through all the stages. Some people get through all their fermentations in the time which for others is hardly sufficient for the first stage, and this is often the fault of the fermenting agents. Lord Rochester, a notorious witty old pig-skin, had grown old by his thirtieth year, was converted in his thirty-first, and died, utterly bored with life, in his thirty-third. All this is quite possible, even with a constitution intended for a hundred years of life. For that genius, as he himself used to boast, had once been drunk for five years on end. Every calendar year he used up, on an average, three years of his life, that is on a biometer whose scale is divided according to the durability of the human body. Have there also been States of this kind? Two years' wine fermentation, two years' acetous fermentation and two years' putrefaction! It might be possible with a proud and rash people who always acted first and thought afterwards.

All this is really meant for you, poor Molly. Your fermentation too is going forward very quickly. Barely twenty, and already nearing the end of the second stage, whose progress that brewery scullion in the apron beside you there will have difficulty in arresting.

Our heroine has, in fact, been brought to the penitentiary, of which this apartment appears to be the refectory or Activity-room, for the purpose of beating hemp during her leisure hours, and of such, alas, the day mostly consists here; or if she does not make a success of it, to let herself be beaten. In that event she will have leave to rest, like the fellow behind her, who a boy once thought, when he saw that engraving, was looking for sparrows' nests.

At a perfunctory inspection, it looks as if they were not too badly housed here. The company is fairly numerous, not entirely wicked, and, although in prison, they are at least not in imprisoned air; all is very airy and high, and that is something, especially on the border line of—putrefaction. She stands on the right wing of the file as file-leader, in a 'winged' cap, and altogether very much be-winged. Apparently she has been caught in the guise of a night-butterfly, and incorporated in that motley collection, or she has at least the colourful apparel in which she used to flutter at night around the lantern. But this item deserves a closer inspection. How is it, one might ask, that the girl has arrived here so decked out, since she has been fetched out of her bed and would hardly have been given time to dress up like that? For supposing she has tried on her head-gear four or five times, and every other article of clothing on an average about twice, and this surely is the least that can be assumed, she could easily have taken from two to three and a half hours. At that rate the butterfly-catchers would not earn their shoes. And then let us not forget the miserable mirror leaning against the punch bowl, which would reflect hardly a fiftieth part of that magnificent structure, and which would have to be shifted from zone to zone, each barely a few hands broad, all round the firmament, for her to see whether there was too much here or too little there. Do not some ladies require three hours to attire themselves for a Ball, and that when four hands are at work, and with a mirror in which, as they step in front of it, they can survey the whole sky? No, that would not do; so much patience cannot be asked of bailiffs, and could hardly be expected, if it were asked. For we cannot help observing in the hand of one of them in the third Plate the very instrument which the man here, whom we have just designated as the brewery-scullion, is also holding. Wherever that appears, it is never as an emblem of patience. I believe it is called a cowhide whip. Thus I can see only two ways of solving this puzzle. Either this is not the first arrest, one that ended perhaps merely with a private castigation, which however had no effect. I should be very sorry if that were so; and so we come to the second (and surely the fairest) interpretation: the girl was taken away covered only so much as the cool air and the gaze of curious nature-lovers in the street made necessary, and had her wardrobe sent after her. Now we know that in England nobody may be sentenced without a hearing, and that in the places where people are heard, they are also very much seen. It is an important moment for a poor sinner who relies to some extent upon her pretty face and figure. She knows for certain that her misdeeds will find an inexorable and incorruptible judge in the grave individual who sits opposite her under the sword of justice. But she knows, too, that among the non-professionals around her, her face, her figure, her hair, and her whole bearing will find many a judge who will not take the matter so seriously, people who have not sworn an oath to regard a pretty girl as immediately reprehensible or even distasteful, just because she had been caught while on duty. If therefore in England a woman is brought before the Judge, and if in addition to a pretty face she possesses of good manners at least the form, and of clothes either possesses, or knows how to procure, the substance, then one can be sure of something worth seeing. The name of a Mrs Rudd, who in the year 1775 brought the twin brothers Perreau to the gallows, from which she escaped herself only through that kind action of hers, is surely immortalized by all the magazines of that time—if the magazines themselves are still in existence. Everything she wore was described and painted ribbon for ribbon and bow for bow. Her head-gear, which decency itself seemed to have arranged, was analysed, and painted for the benefit of those who might perhaps have felt the desire to catch a few Perreaux themselves; greater honour could not have been accorded to a Madame Siddons[1] as Cordelia or Desdemona. That was going rather far. But who would reproach a girl like this if she rakes together her all (which is so little) against the day of reckoning? The jury are of course forbidden to let themselves be dazzled by it, but the poor sinner is not forbidden to believe in the possibility. Even if the blow itself could not be averted thereby, still it might awaken some Samaritan or other among the spectators who would afterwards pour oil into the wound; for in London there are some queer Samaritans, and among them, no doubt, somebody upon whom such a creature with its heavy mule-trappings would make just as great an impression as did the dancing Grace, Julie Potocki,[2] upon a certain man of the world, and one of the finest sentiment.

Molly was found guilty at the Bar and sentenced to be privately whipped, and also to serve a term of hard labour, beating hemp. And it is of course a slight intensification of the punishment to make her start in that attire. When she has run the gauntlet of her fellow-prisoners' tongues, she will make herself more comfortable. Already, over there on the wall, hang a crinoline and a braided hat which are no part of the prison livery. How dull her eyes have grown! The dark rings around them are very noticeable, even in an engraving. Her mouth, how helplessly agape,

[1] One of the greatest actresses of this century, equally worthy of reverence, and indeed revered, for her art as for her irreproachable character.

[2] See the exemplary description of that lady dancing in *Travels of a Lithuanian from Riga to Warsaw*, Part 2, p. 197.

and her whole face, how puffy! What a few false steps in the world can do, if they are the kind that lead to the medicine bottle! How heavy her poor heart must be! And how awkwardly she holds the hammer! With the left hand high up and the right a long way down. This is not the way to beat, at least not hemp—nor sugar either. Alas! it is a hopeless task for her, she cannot bear to look at it, she cannot and cannot beat. But 'thou shalt and must' is written on that face of bronze beside her, in letters which without punctuation can be read and understood the whole world over. It was quite unnecessary to stress the words by an *accent grave*! I mean the oblique cowhide is quite redundant—the face speaks for itself. Is he not a rogue of a warder, as if designed by Nature for such a herd? Just like Daphnis in Vergil,

Formosi pecoris custos, formosior ipse[1]

'Lovely little swine, the swineherd even lovelier.'

But do our readers know who it was that torturer resembles as one egg another? Mr Magister Thwackum, tutor to the two brothers Blifil and Tom Jones. Fielding says so expressly.[2] As is well known, that learned man provided the religious instruction in the boys' education. Did he too give his lessons in a white apron, I wonder? It has a sort of domestic-preparatory look about it, something exciting expectation, and at the same time suggesting to a bad conscience the idea of fleecing which, if used only as a deterrent, cannot possibly do any harm. That fellow's metal, though, is not altogether base; indeed, his upper half might even inspire respect if one were to put in his hand, in place of the cowhide, some instrument which had at least a different name. In order, however, not to prejudice our readers too much against the man, or to make them apprehensive for the poor prisoner in the charge of such a tyrant, we ought to mention that people of that sort have always at their command, apart from the faces for which they are paid by the municipal authorities, and those which they have to produce gratis, at least half a dozen others which can be bought against a small considera-tion. These are usually served up entirely without cowhide, and some of them, as I have been told, even with a genial cross-slash beneath the

[1] Eclogues, V. 44.
[2] *Tom Jones*, Book III, Chapter 6.

44

nose, from one ear to the other. What we see here is only ordinary fare, by way of entrée.

Immediately behind our heroine stands the wife of that Master of the Ceremonies, holding over the sufferer's head a whip of quite another sort which hurts only the soul—the lash of the most impudent derision. Should the Devil decide to animate one of his puppets in the world for some doubtful purpose, his fingers and expression as he grips the wires could hardly differ much from that woman's as she fingers the lace and ribbons or the handkerchief here. Could one easily imagine a more satanic physiognomy? And yet her expression is still of the kind which fits such faces best; namely, the ironic. Illuminated by rage and brandy it would gain tremendously in force, and still not be caricature. Oh till you have set eyes on such a creature, you have seen nothing of the world! If she is not actually removing the handkerchief from the pocket, as Ireland believes, she is surely drawing a witty comparison for the amusement of her husband and the gratification of her own heart, between the bridal adornment of the lady and the tomb in which she has been buried here. One of her eyes is not so much shut as non-existent, but the face loses nothing on that side in the way of light: all is richly compensated by the splendour of the ivories which that rattle-snake displays so inimitably that one hardly notices her eye is missing. If the greeting 'I'm absolutely delighted to see you here!' has ever been heard in that establishment, it could only have proceeded from such a slash of a mouth. So much for the torturer's—torturess.

Just let us run down the row of penitents—what a hammer-scale it is! What music! Curiously enough there are just seven of them—Doh, Re, Mi, Fa, Sol, La, Ti. The pair in the foreground do not count, since they are not performing for the time being. Whether something is in need of repair, or whether they have finished playing for today (since their hammers are at rest, and also there is no hemp lying on their block), I shall not venture to decide. Also there seems to be something like a small ditch between their place and that of the others. This may indicate that even here there are two classes, *prima* and *secunda*. Or is it that our Molly stands upon a platform as an example to the others, and that she works here in the pillory? That only half of the dog is visible really indicates such an elevation, and since rank is unthinkable without its insignia, just at that raised spot a ring is let into the ground, attached to a buttress-like stump of wood to obstruct or lessen movement. But let us return to our musical scale and to the hammer-mill.

Next to our keynote Doh there hammers Re, quite a dignified old man. I once saw an old copper-plate engraving of an ambassador being received in audience, who looked exactly like him, and who stood almost in the same attitude, only there was no hammering there, though maybe there was some talk about it. Really if we were to see that man in an honest workhouse in the guise of a Superintendent Police Inspector, or as a tutor in his study, we should think in the first case that he practised hemp-beating like the Chinese Emperor ploughing, and in the second like the dogs who eat grass when they have an upset stomach. How could he have landed here? The interpreters believe he is a card-sharper. They deduce this from the torn playing-card which lies on the floor in front of his work table. It is quite true, the man has something about him which usually characterizes people of that sort. Nature in her wisdom, while tolerating these poisonous snakes, usually puts into their appearance and apparel something which fills the office of a rattle, and gives warning to the bystanders without the snake itself being aware of it. There is always something not quite as it should be. Sometimes their clothing is out of season, sometimes even out of century. Full-dress uniform of the Peace of Ryswick period worn at the Coronation of Francis I, or magnificent furs on a cool evening in August. That is one of the idiosyncrasies of this class of human beings, and which class is without them? The card is an eight of spades, but there are no such eights with four spades in a row. Most likely it is an 'improved' nine. The two pieces say: three opposite five and one in reserve makes the *alterum tantum*. That certainly spells some fraud. Oh! if only the remark about prophesying from the coffee grounds had not already been made above, here would be an opportunity to sell ink without trouble and at a good price too!—like cinnamon oil.[1] But the point has its difficulties. We must not, then, pass it over too lightly. One might ask: how does the card come to be here? Has he pulled it out with his handkerchief, and why is it in two pieces? Was it perhaps so often bent over in play that ultimately it had to fall apart? The shallowness of the English commentators on this occasion is as strange as it is incompre-

---

[1] L. is here alluding to his writing for profit in the *Taschenkalender*. When coming across a cryptic remark like this, it is well to recall what Karl Kraus, the Viennese writer, once said: 'Lichtenberg speaks sometimes under the earth and one must dig deeply to hear him.' Ed.

hensible. Surely a point like that must have been easy enough to clear up at the time. After all, what is the point of writing if one adds nothing to the old capital? A foreigner can do nothing here but grope, and must be satisfied if he does not make a fool of himself before the native expert. So here goes.

To me the man seems not so much a gambler by profession as an old fortune-hunter who has tried his hand at everything, gambling included, and after being utterly ruined by it has taken to other paths which finally brought him here. With such a fate, a man might easily come to curse all playing cards, and on finding one still in his coat pocket might tear it up and throw it down before beginning—to beat hemp. I regard him as one of those notorious people who give the London Law Courts a lot of work every year, and who in English are called 'swindlers'. 'Swindler', incidentally, one of the words which the great Doctor Johnson has omitted in his equally great Dictionary, means in English a felon who through cunning subterfuges, and usually with the appearance of a man of rank and means, tries to defraud people of their property. For carrying out these stratagems, an interim wife, at least as decoy, is an indispensable article; she does the talking and he the job. I fear, I almost fear, our Doh and Re are such a couple. That their places are next one another, that they are both so magnificently overdressed and both in the same taste, adds weight to that assumption. Whether Re used Doh, or Doh used Re in the operation, we shall not decide; perhaps their parts stood in the relation of the three to the five on the torn card and thus differed from the relation of equality only by one-eighth of the total load. It may be that after long search they were finally arrested in their State carriage and brought here after a short trial, and the obvious distinction of our heroine would then appear to be a consequence of a second arrest, which is always connected with certain disagreeable attentions. Whoever finds this reason for Molly's presence here more plausible than the one given above, may adopt it; it is really only a matter of taste. That the braided hat on the wall belongs to our Re goes without saying.

After Re comes Mi, a mere child, the most wretched object in this Plate. Hardly in her 'teens, she is already under this roof, suffering for a crime of which she had no conception, and into whose mere form she had been forcibly initiated, like a poodle into its antics. Anyone coming from the seat of virtue, I mean from the small towns of Germany, to London, must feel his heart bleed if, of an evening, he comes across such little creatures of twelve or thirteen, dressed like ballet shepherdesses, being handled and intercepted with theatrically tender embraces. It really beggars description. They speak in a sweet childish voice and with a volubility obviously acquired through learning by rote, about things of which they certainly do not understand one word. One is therefore almost tempted to regard them as children about to be confirmed, if all this did not belong to a Catechism which only Charters or the Devil could have written. It cries to heaven.[1] The poor girl has something good-hearted in her physiognomy, and the zeal with which she is beating her hemp shows a willingness to follow any instruction. Good heavens! If this child deserves the penitentiary, what punishment would they not merit whose instructions have poisoned her innocence before she had time to reflect, and her youth before it had fully ripened?

We come now to the fourth note, Fa, the short, roundish thing who, propped on her hammer, is pausing a moment, a perfect little Satan. Her eyes, a charming pair of deadly-nightshade berries, seem to be directed upon a mosquito which is buzzing about in the air hardly three inches from her nose, but in reality they are aimed at the gaudy nightbird, No. 1 in the Cabinet, and its beautiful wings. She is taking a very sharp aim and is sure to make a hit when she lets fly. I should like to hear that girl talk. Near her Hogarth has added one of those touches which characterize him so perfectly; in these six Plates they are not very often to be found, but are increasingly apparent as his genius approaches maturity. It is a point which none of the English commentators has noticed. Behind the girl, there stands the well-known post with the iron collar, which can be seen in Germany, too. It bears the inscription, 'The Wages of Idleness'. Thus

[1] Since I have raised the subject, it is my duty to mention that in London they are trying to curb this abuse with all the energy which could possibly be exerted by a people proud of its liberty. Under the patronage and support of the Queen, the Magdalen Hospital has been established where girls of that profession who feel the misery of their position and repent are taken in and educated to become better human beings. In this way, a deep and pitiful corruption of human nature became an occasion for virtue to reveal itself in its greatest glory, to the honour of humanity. How little, however, some of these creatures are inclined to make use of it is shown by the following anecdote: One day a girl of that sort was being forcibly conveyed to the Hospital, evidently by well-meaning relations. She cried pitifully in the carriage. Passers-by who suspected an abduction stopped the vehicle, and asked what was going on. 'Oh!' cried the girl, 'they want to take me to the Hospital for Penitent Virgins, and I am neither the one nor the other.'

Fa is taking a rest immediately below the Tables of the Law which prohibit such respite, and not only that, since her Northern portion leans so far forward, her Southern parts are obviously turned against the Tables, which in every nation is recognized as a lack of respect. Here it is doubly indecent to direct that Pole upon a mere inscription, for although we know that this end sometimes accepts chastisement, we should not easily find an example of its ever having been used to receive a written warning.

Sol, the fifth from our heroine, is quite a goodlooking girl; anyone attracted by passive obedience could hardly take his eyes off her. I have come across just such a face once before, but whether in Nature or in a picture, on the cook of a Cathedral Chapter or on a Sphinx, I cannot now recall. A slightly mechanical aptitude for service and also a slightly Egyptian parallelism can hardly be missed in the face and in the whole way she is holding her head. Her hammer is very heavy; she seems scarcely able to lift it without supporting her elbow on her hip. By all the rules of perspective it is obviously bigger than those of her neighbours. Could there perhaps be lead in it? Mr Thwackum, perchance, has different hammers as he has different faces.

La is a negress, poor devil! And as I gather from her rotundity, a double one besides. What a nest of prisons for the embryo! Imprisoned in a mother who herself sits in the Penitentiary, in a world which again is a Penitentiary for her whole family. Oh let us be thankful that we were born with the colour of innocence and the livery of freedom. Thou blessed Sun, grant us only that and good health and our Ananas Troglodytes,[1] the rest we shall surely provide for ourselves.

Ti concludes the series. She is like Cordelia in *King Lear*—'although our last, not least'. She works more earnestly than all the rest, is also the only one who grasps the hammer with the right hand above. She sees little and we see little of her, and yet she does a good deal, or rather that is just why she does a good deal, just as in the great Workhouse of the World. After that little moral sermon from the coffee grounds, we now turn to the two *in secunda*.

The foremost is evidently the pug-nosed horror who poured out water for the tea on the third Plate. That she was brought here as well shows that she is something more than a mere servant. She looks rather pleased about the fate of her fosterchild, and appears to be giving the glad eye to

[1] Potatoes.

the cowhide which today, perhaps for the first time, is a good distance away from her. Hogarth had already provided her with an ample supply of bosom in the third Plate, evidently not without reason; here she seems to consist almost entirely of bosom and legs. The fancy stockings which she is pulling up here evidently do not belong to her sex, since they un-permittedly and quite indecently reach up too high, and have clearly not been woven for knees—of the weaker sex, which require more space. Hence the evident break-through in this region. Black with white clocks, or even silver ones! If we only knew the Court and town fashions of those days, we might perhaps hazard a guess as to who had lost them. But as it is, we must declare them, together with the embroidered shoes, as the acquired property of the woman who, in order to impress town and Court had, in the appearance of her legs at least, to try to imitate them. The whole figure is not a masterpiece of drawing, nor of light and shade. Where does the brightness under her skirt come from? Phosphorescence is out of the question, for whence should that emanate? And yet one can see so clearly. Most likely it is only a reflection of the light in the roguish eyes of the artist, which for one brief moment illuminated the character of that infamous creature so as to cause decency itself to look that way. To pull up the stocking she grips it, perhaps with a remnant of modesty, now at least, using her fist like a handle at the knee. The garter, to judge from the gentle undulations which it readily assumes, appears to have been cut from a piece of old oilcloth. Next to her sits another such creature. Mr Ireland says she is occupied with one of the Egyptian plagues; this is clear enough. Both appear to be versed in the beating of hemp; it is not the first time for them. Their finished task is in the basket above them. They thus have time before dinner to make their toilet, each in her own way.

At the very back on the right-hand side, on a window shutter or cup-board door, is a picture of the gallows drawn with chalk in guard-room style, with a man hanging from it, smoking his little pipe. The gallows are well drawn, they are familiar with it under that roof; moreover it often becomes the Estate of this aristocracy when they leave town. The man on it is a mere cipher. Above is the inscription S.J.G. (Sir John Gonson), the name of the honest man whom we mentioned in the third Plate. It is clearly the joke of a scoundrel carried out in chalk because he was too cowardly or too pious to do something like that with a stiletto. The pipe in the mouth has little significance. Every honest man engraved on a copper-plate has to put up with that sort of thing. I have often seen portraits of the most honest people, especially those who have been specially assiduous in the education of the young, decorated with that pipe by those very youths, and with a moustache as well which stuck out pitch-black beyond the powdered wig. It is a bad joke, but, of course, to allow a picture of oneself, beard and all, to be put in the front of a little school book so as to make oneself and the book venerated is not much better. To see such a figure, so very modern, and yet already engraved on copper, is a rarity; had it lain 1,500 years under volcanic ashes, we should not waste a word over it.

The fellow who appears to be bird-nesting is really standing in the prison Stocks, and so has first to work honestly before he can become a rogue of ordinary degree. On the board over the Stocks we read: 'Better to work than stand thus.' The scene needs no explanation except to mention that in all probability the delinquent (the squeezed-in one) has made a secret plea for his liberation to Mrs Gaoler by a correspondence which might quite easily be carried on here by way of their lower Poles.

Nothing else remains now but the dog, no easy item if one has to deal with such an unfathomable rogue as Hogarth. Is he meant to be here only as a volunteer, in evidence of un-human faithfulness towards a master whom he has followed into prison? This moral is somewhat too plain for our moralist; also we have already had an example of that with the Egyptian plague *in secunda*; and there it even had a moral tailpiece which is missing here, that is to say the reward which we are accustomed to expect in this world in return for extreme devotion. This does not fit. I think, therefore, it must be the sheep-dog of the lovely shepherd and his shepherdess who has to watch over and prevent certain movements of the herd while the loving couple is engaged on operations. What may not a dog learn? That he pricks his ears so much towards the wing commanded by his master is very understandable. Well does he know the voice which thunders against Molly. Evidently it is also the very formula with which he is sometimes received. He believes it is meant for him. For everything here is free and equal, so far as is possible under a cowhide.

V

HERE we have the transition to the last fermentation—she dies, and from the terrible consequences of pandemonial love. We should be grossly mistaking the intention of our great artist if we were to mince words here, provided we need use words at all. For it is hardly necessary. Everything speaks for itself. From the pale cheek and stiffened lips death has effaced the smallest trace of wanton charm, which art had erstwhile added from without or within. Closed for ever is the mouth from which, but a few months ago, flatteries or mild imprecations used to fly with double-tongued volubility at the passer-by, according to whether he fought weakly or strongly against its wiles; for ever extinguished is the eye that shot its glances around full of affected fire, less for the purpose of seeing than of being seen—and now it sees no longer, nor is seen. At this complete evaporation of all her cheap glitter in the sight of Death, she comes before him in the simple garment of her first naturally-good disposition, and implores his pity. She did not find it. Yet we would not wish to deny her ours—*Quiescat!*

She sinks back death-pale into the comforting arms of the woman who had hitherto the care of her soul, and was her faithful companion in the House of Correction, the abominable snub-nose who now suddenly loses all hope of leading her lovely ward, had she only lived and flourished longer to her own advantage, to the gallows. That is comfort indeed! She has been carefully wrapped up in a sheet. Perhaps the nightgown which is hanging on the line there to dry is her only one, and through the rapid change made necessary by nature and art, is still out of action! With her

A Harlot's Progress Plate V

right hand the creature enjoins peace and silence upon the two respectable gentlemen engaged in confidential discussion. Who these two men are we shall now explain. The matter is important, and the reader will there-fore grant us a little space for it.

In London there has appeared for many years now a weekly periodical which is turned out regularly, and always contains articles of more uni-form quality than any other weekly paper in the world. It has never lacked contributors or contributions. Everything it contains appears to have been dictated by Nature herself, although one knows that it was often profound human skill which guided the pen. This is not to be wondered at; it is even an observation apparent to anyone who under-stands human nature. For since a certain happening in Paradise, about which we may read in an old classical book that is not very much read nowadays, man has been so much thrown upon the left side of his nature that it has been a proper study to regain his right. Perfect order reigns on every page; everything has its appointed place here, so that the lover of such things may immediately find his way about. It is particularly strong in the touching, and the pathetic. Passages which cause the reader's tears to flow, and others where his whole being is shaken by shudders, are far from rare. These pages bear the heading: 'Weekly Bills of Mortality'. This little introduction was necessary before informing my reader that the two gentlemen he sees there are a pair of learned men who at that time were specially engaged in procuring for that journal the utmost completeness. They were, in every sense of the words, for this weekly paper what the famous Addison and Steele were for another, to wit the well known *Spectator*. Without them it could not have carried on with such completeness. So much is certain. But on account of the great number of collaborators, each of whom had his friends who wished to procure for him the distinction of being considered by Hogarth as de-serving eternal remembrance, the names of these honest men are not known for certain. This much is evident, that they are a pair of *Officiers de Santé* (Medical Officers) as doctors are now called in the Paradise of Europe (Paris of the Revolution), and, as we have reason to believe, have about the rank of prison warders. For apart from these persons, and occasionally some respectable experimentalist or elderly matron, no-body was allowed to supply contributions to that weekly journal. Now according to a reliable tradition, the rather corporeal gentleman with the convex belly is thought to be a German, the other more spiritual one with the concave belly a Frenchman named Misaubin. Of their manner of life, only a few trivial items are known, and are hardly worth mentioning. The first, so it is said, for some time played the clown with Fargatsch of Hamburg; from there he fled to London to evade prosecution for having prepared a tooth-powder from human skulls; for a while he practised there for dear life, and was ultimately hanged. People say it was for murder. If so, it was probably not a professional one, for it is well known that doctors in England enjoy the privileges *purgandi, saignandi et tuendi* as much as anywhere else. Thus there remain only two possibilitites: either he was hanged for his professional sins because he was not a proper member of the profession, thus not a doctor proper but a mere *lusus naturae*; or he killed the person by a contrivance which was not a legitimate one. Ten or eleven years ago a famous London doctor, Dr M'Gennis, almost ended on the gallows in that way (he was condemned to be hanged but was later reprieved). He had done no more than bring his landlord to the churchyard. They only came down on him so heavily because he had done it without the agency of a mixture or powder, but merely with a breadknife which he had sunk in the patient's body, and in this way had by-passed, as it were, the apothecary. The other figure, Dr Misaubin, was quite a good man, only he had rather too high an opinion of a certain powder and certain pills which he compounded in his own establishment; the latter being a sort of edible deer-shot. If death approached one of his customers, very well—he loaded the patient with the pills as if with grapeshot, and fired. In this way he skirmished and fought many a year with all possible diseases. Official reports of his victories are not available, but quite considerable loss of heavy and light cannon could regularly be traced in the weekly journal. I have heard that out of malice (when is that ever absent from merit?), they gave the honest man the nickname of Mice-Aubin. This was because in later years, when another would perhaps have rested lazily on his laurels, the good fellow tried his art on rats and mice. It is a bitter and bread-depriving name, and that means quite a lot to a poor devil who even without it had the *embonpoint* of a *rat d'église*. Highly unjust are such rat-like attacks upon the larders of one's fellow-men. And had he really behaved so badly? He could no longer visit patients but still had a good stock of his little powders; he therefore tried them out on whatever came to his surgery.

Oh! this is often the way of the world! How much good gunpowder and shot intended for partridge and snipe are used up on the way home upon sparrows and bats, whether out of boredom or to show one's skill, or because nothing better is available. And after all, is the pursuit of vermin so very far outside the scope of medicine? What then are lice, tape-worms and maw-worms and the Greek trichuriden?[1] Every occupation has its gradations. I am therefore convinced that the ingenious author of *Gil Blas*, in speaking of the *exécution de la haute médecine*, had a distinction of this sort in mind, something like game-shooting and rat-catching.

So much for the history of these famous men, and now for the use to which our artist has put it. The girl has fallen a victim to them, and how else could such a duel have ended? She fought against death and had none for Second but her own natural constitution, good in itself but often injured, weary, and neglected at every opportunity. And yet, perhaps, being a young woman of 23,[2] she might still have beaten her adversary. But He who knew this well had chosen for himself a pair of Seconds, each of whom could have taken up the fight alone against a dozen lives. That is why it went *veni, vidi, vici,* and suddenly there she lay. That this is the true explanation of the matter is all too evident. For if the toad and the salamander who are quarrelling here had not been Death's malicious Seconds, but had taken the side of Nature, they would even now be striving to resuscitate the girl, whereas they are leaving that to—the last Trump, and merely quarrel about who is to have the honour of the deed. This mixture of mine in this glass, says the toad, was the true oil on the fire; and my fire, shrieks the salamander, had no need of your mixture. What a *conflictus pronominum!* 'I' against 'I' and 'you' against 'you'. These are hard blows, especially those of the 'I's. And how beautifully they are demonstrated here, entirely in keeping with the laws of impact. The 'I' of the German has little velocity but all the more mass, and consequently has impulse even when it seems to be at rest; the 'I' of the Frenchman, on the other hand, has velocity but little mass, and therefore it felt the need of support from tables and chairs and whatever else came in handy. How gratifying for a German to observe how by the forceful thrust of his countryman, the French mass, which had only been pieced together, falls apart in all directions! Chair and table and plate and spoon and ink bottle—

[1] From Greek *trichina*, hair-like worm, parasitic in body of man, swine, rats, etc. Ed.
[2] The next Plate gives the necessary information about her age.

everything separates from the tiny kernel and collapses at the impact of the other's quiet remark: 'this is my little mixture', while *his* chair stands at rest, as it always has and always will.

But there is still more to this group. It is of inexhaustible significance. Would it be possible, one might ask, to depict a congress of diseases, or what comes to the same thing, of quacks, more eloquently than here with this dropsical individual and this hectic one? The one inflated, heavy, phlegmatic and stolid, the other concave-bellied, feverish, mobile and skinny? How Dropsy squats there! Medicine bottle and cane gripped as if they were the insignia of his blood-brother—hour-glass and scythe; Hectic, on the other hand, having surrendered scythe and hour-glass to his colleague, retains for himself the skeleton shape and the deadly powder in the pill box, which proclaims better than all the hour-glasses of his friend that the hour has struck—the rat powder. The eyebrows of each reach up towards the adjacent hair, the wigs, with a sort of longing which, they say, tends to signify inner conviction combined with a touch of righteous anger over a failure to impress. Here, however, especially with the dropsical subject, these hair curves come rather *too* near to one another, nearer than with his hectic companion, and this rather detracts from this interpretation. If I am not mistaken, such an elevation of the brow signifies rather a consciousness of uncertainty which tries to hide under the mask of caution. With Dropsy it seems to have been brought on by mental conflict due to undigested reading; in the more determined eye of Hectic we seem to read the effects of physical indigestion. 'Oh dear, dear sister,' protests the former, 'do believe my word!' 'No! rubbish, rubbish, absolute rubbish!' gasps the latter. 'Here in this pill-box. . .' and from this explosion in front the recoil is so strong, as with guns in general, that chair and table collapse. This, as the reader will observe, is a second hypothesis to explain the revolution in that room. We intentionally put it side by side with the other which sought to explain everything by a blow from the German, and it will find favour with those who believe that if only the German can maintain his phlegmatic attitude long enough, his opponent from the volcanic nation[1] would burst of his own accord, or disperse into his constituent parts. But by no means, dear reader, considering the limitations of our individual vocabulary, and our lack of knowledge of the world, would we attempt to express in words

[1] An expression of Dumouriez, who himself calls his nation *Une nation volcanique.*

alone the constant and quietly operating forces, as well as the erratic and turbulent ones, which were at work here, together with the vociferous interference by snub-nose with her wormwood face, or to try to represent completely in the form of an idyll what Hogarth has so inimitably delineated with his stylus.

[*A passage concerning the novels of Johann Gottwert Müller* (1743–1828), *occupying about half a page in the original, has been left out here, as being of no interest to the English reader, and indeed of very little interest to the German reader either, Müller's novels belonging today to the limbo of German literature.*]

The explosion has overturned the little table and with it a spoon, a plate, an ink-bottle and pen, and a bulletin. The spoon has come off quite well, it lies on its hollow side and touches the clean floor as little as possible, thus differing from bread and butter, which always falls on the buttered side. But the plate!

> Broken, broken is the lovely jar, there lie the fragments!
>
> (Gessner,[1] *Idylls*)

This is a sad thing for a whole plate, but not quite so serious for a damaged one. From the visible fragments, at least, it would not be possible to piece together a plate capable of containing anything which the neighbouring paper poster could not hold equally well. The ink-bottle breaks and the earth receives in a wholesale way the black gall with which it was filled, and which as an ingredient of prescriptions and love-letters may perhaps have led many a poor devil to that very consummation. It has finished its service. The collar round the neck of the pen, which has saved it from ruin, protects it at least from further destruction, and even if it were trodden upon in the turmoil, which however will not amount to much in this corner, there is still another department where it could find employment. Isn't it a splendid thing to have apart from one's writing end also a wiping end? If as a writer you are no longer able to give instruction, *stilum vertas!* and you can still sweep. A moral which every budding author who has invested his spiritual and physical fortune in disastrous South Sea shares of wealth and immortality through writing should let his dry pen teach him every morning, before he dips it into the

[1] S. Gessner (1730–88), German writer of idylls. Ed.

ink bottle to preach with it his revelations to the world. The poster advertises a practical scheme concerning a new method for curing all kinds of diseases by neckbands or necklaces. We can see an illustration there of the necklace in question. At the top is the word 'Anodyne' written from right to left, and below from left to right the word 'Necklaces', which even in the original is difficult to read. The lines are meant to curve rather in the form of a neckband, for they really make a circumscription, a sort of band around the neckband, and perform here in reality for the project the service which the project itself merely promises to the patient. Thus 'Anodyne Necklaces', necklaces which are to take away pain. A circle of words, half Greek and thus half mystical, drawn round an entirely mystical amulet, could not fail of its purpose with a certain class of person. It is really incredible, the success that device has achieved—I mean the outer band around the inner one.[1] For whether the inner one had benefited the patient himself has not, as far as we know, become public knowledge, if we except the wall mentioned below. However, that poster does not lie here simply as a satire upon the innumerable advertisements for medicines which in London are daily thrust unstamped into people's hands, and even into their pockets, by some kind of postman; its meaning lies much deeper.[2] This is one proof out of many which we shall come across that Hogarth in his works, just as Nature in hers, knew how to achieve, often with one and the same touch, more than one end, and knew also how to spread warmth where one might have thought he only wanted to shine. For these anodyne necklaces were originally intended by their inventor only for the use of children suffering from the so-called English disease (the Rickets), about which the unfounded prejudice prevailed in England and in many parts of Germany that it is usually the fruit of tainted love. This, therefore, refers to the poor little bastard who near the fireplace there half kneels and half sits beside the chair of his dying mother,

[1] Mr Ireland assures us that in the year 1790 a complete house wall in Longacre, a London street, was still covered with the names of diseases against which these necklaces could be used, and frequently had been used.

[2] These and similar little letters from philanthropists of all sorts are the only goods which, so far as we know, are put into our pockets gratis in London. In fact, however, this putting in is only a sort of superfine taking out. They are bills of exchange which cunning draws upon credulity, and by which they are often honoured in cash. In a similar way some journals appear to offer the medical lies at the end of the paper for nothing, although they often make one pay more dearly for them than for the political ones—I mean the political truths which appear in front.

and who, untouched by that dying and by the learned bellowing of the disputing gentlemen, and by the screaming intervention of the woman who presides over all this, quite peacefully roasts over the fire his pain-alleviating chop. Considering that he may be suffering from rickets, he could from his size be about six years old; deducting these six years from the mother's twenty-three, brings her age when she was infected to seventeen. This is what Hogarth tells us by means of a slip of paper which lies there between the fragments of a twice-broken plate and some pieces of furniture of rather equivocal form. If the stout gentleman on the upright chair there were to have been the inventor of these pain-alleviating necklaces, as he could well have been, the satire would acquire more branches still. For, as we remarked above, our learned doctor himself died through an anodyne necklace, the rope (*laqueus anodymus*), which the law prescribed for him, and which in London works wonders.[1]

Diagonally opposite, in excellent contrast with the death scene, is a little scene of acquisition. At least there is certainly a good deal of grasping going on there. An old woman, perhaps formerly a sort of chaperone to the girl, or else a relation of hers and of the smiling heir, or what is most likely, her present landlady to whom something is probably owing for rent and expenses, is now securing possession of the girl's little all, or at least she is reckoning it up, for the sake of her peace of mind. The death rattle, the snorting and snarling of the doctors' fight, even the hissing of the pot boiling over, do not distract her; she knows that people are mortal, and that doctors will quarrel, and even that for the refilling of a pot which has boiled itself dry, nothing in the world serves better than the appropriation of a full trunk. A face like that is very necessary if in such a den of murderers one is not to make mistakes in calculation; it is the very image of deafness on principle.

There is something about the contrast between what the woman is pulling out here and what corruption is appropriating over there in the armchair which, as every man of feeling will recognize, rises far higher than Hogarth's genius usually aspired, but which, notwithstanding, has been as adroitly executed as if it had been entirely within his natural

---

[1] Whole books have been filled with the stories of these miraculous cures: *The Lives of Celebrated Highwaymen, The Bloody Register*, etc., which are very widely read. There are also books containing advice on how to avoid the terrible diseases which call for such heroic medicine. But although people buy these, they do not read them.

reach. Here lies first the dark negro mask with which the friendly, sunny, Yorkshire face had darkened itself for a while at a Ball with artificial ugliness, so as to dazzle by contrast a chosen few in a tête-à-tête with all the charm of bought favours. The fan, since the fire of glances has ceased, sleeps quietly in the embrasures, and perhaps mysteriously leads many an imagination to attributes of the Tragic Muse, even through the mummery of love. Next to it stand quietly the dancing shoes, whose form and movement and gold and twinkling and glitter like so many will-o'-the-wisps, used once to throw caution itself, the pedometer, into confusion, and lead on to where retreat was no longer possible. Behind them lies the hat which we have seen before in the third Plate hanging under the bed canopy, below the comet. Ribbon and domino are unpacked too. Were we to cover the whole Plate except for that corner, should we not think that an old chaperone was employed in gathering together a costume for today's Masked Ball, for the little lamb in her charge? But now remove the cover and cast a glance at the picture of misery there in the armchair, the former owner of all that finery! Heavens above! Her present domino, how limp, how pallid and how still compared with the rustling silk which billows from the trunk. Her present mask alas! how pale, the make-up provided by the cold hand of death! And the dazzling light of her eyes, how deeply sunk into eternal night! They see not and are seen no longer! There is no mummery here. Those eyes in the wan face have really been pierced by the solemn arrow of death. With the black mask of luxury over there it was a dagger fully congenial with those eyes, a closed fan, not dissimilar in form as well as in use to the sword, I mean the rattle of—Harlequin. And where now are the little will-o'-the-wisp feet? Answer: the lithe, hopping red-breast needed them for her living on the thorny lust-hedges of Drury Lane; the heavily draped Bird of Paradise there upon the armchair no longer wants them.[1]

Just as we have drawn a line of comparison from the chair of the candidate for corruption to the travelling trunk, so we could draw another between the candidate for the gallows and another trunk that stands in the right foreground. Of course, the latter is more a chair than a coffer, or just as much (or rather more) a coffer to sit upon as a chair to shut something in. It is partly covered, partly surrounded by all sorts of

[1] The interpreter's belief in a winged horse gives him a right to believe also in Birds of Paradise without feet.

60

trivial articles of which alas! shovel and coal are by far the cleanest. Oh, we were always afraid of that corner in the fifth Plate! If, however, we succeed in bringing our readers safely out of it, there remains but one other, in the sixth Plate, before which we are already trembling. We confess this in advance, not only frankly but even not quite without a beneficial intention for ourselves, at least. For if someone has made up his mind to a rather disagreeable task, not entirely without persuasion and not altogether of his own free will, nothing exculpates a possible human *faux pas* so well as an open-hearted confession in advance: that one is in fact very apprehensive of not getting through without some unpleasantness.

Not to leave the subject too abruptly, which is sometimes dangerous, and would be specially so here, we must first send a few remarks in advance, for one of which the reader will be just as ready to let us off without proof as we shall be pleased to give it for the other. The first is that every freeborn human being, even one who is not censor-free, has a natural right to say what he likes about chairs of all sorts, as long as he leaves in peace the people who honour them with their behinds. And the second, that there simply does not exist in the world an utterly contemptible type of stool. The last sentence is especially important for us. In order to persuade people of it one need only bring the matter near enough to the ancestor- and family-sense with which nature has endowed everybody so conscientiously that almost as much enlightenment is needed not to honour an otherwise unimportant man of family as not to worship the sun. So here goes.

In the whole realm of furniture which, to the best of my knowledge, has not yet found its Linnaeus, the class of chairs (*classis sellarum*) is not only the most revered but also the most extensive; it is a class which not only flourishes at all points of the compass, but has discovered how to make itself indispensable. In a word, it is among furniture what the class of mammals is among everything that lives and feels. There are, of course, great differences between chair and chair, as regards form and weight, just as with mammals, for instance between the whale weighing more than many a house together with the inhabitants, and the Siberian shrew whose weight rarely comes to 30 grains. But as all these animals have as a common characteristic that they suckle their young, so all chairs have this in common, that when in service they are presented with quite a respectable part of the body to support. To them belong, apart from ordinary

61

stools and chairs with and without backs, and with and without arms, first all the thrones and all the cathedras from which, as is well known, the world is governed, and which, run into one by skilful carpenters, formerly represented what was called the Holy See. Next, all the Judges' chairs, the heavy chairs of sorrow to which some of the foremost thrones of the earth are said to belong, and the light bergères (armchairs) to which again belong many a throne and many a cathedra. After these comes the genus of benches, which are nothing but systems of chairs. Here belong the aristocratic and learned benches, all slaughter houses, the so-called lazy bench and the eternal long bench—the whale of the genus. These are followed by the Sedan chair and the Bath chair, the ivory *sella curulis* of ancient Rome, as well as the so-called chamber-chair between table and bed for those suffering from gout and rheumatism. In conjunction with this comes the cabriolet; the English storey-high phaeton whose name derives from 'turning over'; all flys, all carriages, all travelling and mail coaches from the German rib-shatterer to the English cradle on springs and the majestic State carriage for which, instead of making the gates wide and the doors high for it to pass through, they more modestly took first the measure of the doors and gates.[1] Immediately next to the benches and opposite the Bath chairs comes the species of sliding chairs or the so-called sledges in hundred-fold form; from the magnificent structure which to the silver sound of a thousand bells overtakes even the wings of a winter Zephyr, to the mourning-sledge which to the simple sound of the tolling bell moves to the place of execution. Then come the riding saddles (also a *genus sellarum*), the men's as well as the lesser known feminine side-saddle, which nowadays the fleetest and proudest of all horses, Pegasus itself, no longer disdain. From another side, and stretching far into the distance, we have the Inquisition chairs of Holy Justice and the torture seats for the accouchement of confessions, and the medical-surgical chairs for achieving more substantial extractions. Of the latter type an extremely rare example is to be found in a museum at Rome, though I have forgotten its name. After a considerable interval comes at last the Désobligeant[2] which is here under discussion, and which takes its name from the Goddess

[1] This is based on a folk legend that a Prince once in order to enter Frankfurt in procession on as large a scale as possible, first had the measurements taken of the gates of the town before having his carriage built. A precaution which shows much experience in the task of government, but which probably is not true.

[2] Called thus, like Yorick's carriage, because of its being a single-seater.

of the Night.[1] '*Ah! quel bruit pour une omelette!* Could you not have told us that at once?'—Impossible Madame. 'Why not? I would merely have said: with all due respect.' And so more or less without any respect—No! what can be said only 'with due respect' must also be said respectfully, and that requirement we believe we have now fulfilled.

After this if not diplomatic, at least diplomatically circumstantial exposition of that seat's genealogical tree, and consequently of the proof that it is in its right setting, we now expect from our gentle readers a free passport for its companions. These comprise a small tin vessel with a handle and, immediately behind, a rather equivocal bowl, and on the ground a no less equivocal earthenware pan covered with a tin lid. The little vessel is clearly a Dutch spittoon (*Quispedorje*) and in more than one respect fits rather well into the suite. It is standing on an advertisement of the immortal Dr Rock (see p. 280). Can those be pills which are lying on it? Pills which lie between the name of Dr Rock and a spittoon are mercury pills all right. But the pipe? Perhaps it lies there only to mask the spitting, just as brandy drinkers of some standing and principle are said to drink brandy out of tea-cups to spare the feelings of their weaker brethren. Or is there perhaps such a thing as mercury-tobacco? Or was the last favoured lover perhaps a sailor from the land of cleanliness?

We have called the bowl up above and the pan down below equivocal; this they are in a very high degree. How if the first turned out to be a butter or dripping bowl and the other a frying pan which has just been lifted off the fire with a wet rag? That would be some evidence of orderliness, and also of precaution, namely that these chaperones had made some provision for themselves on such a day. In any case, somebody's goose is being cooked here. Perhaps death appeared suddenly after a happy expectation of complete recovery and they began too soon to think of feasting, for which pots and pans and bottle are as indispensable in England as drum and trumpet with us. On such occasions one offers thanks to Heaven, without forgetting oneself in the process. Everybody according to his customs—that is as it should be. But there may be another interpretation, which almost seems to be the right one, and that is precisely what makes that corner so—dangerous. What, one might ask, if the object which stands there behind the *Quispedorje* were something of the same type, only bigger, for instance an *archi-quispedorje*? And the pan down

[1] A chamber-pot in German is called a night-pot. Ed.

there a mere satellite of the worthy stool The assumption is somewhat strong but, according to our feeling, so much in Hogarth's spirit that we cannot possibly withhold it from our readers, especially as we have made such a profound apology. Besides, it is only the suite which is under discussion.

We mentioned above a line of comparison which might be drawn from the gallows-bird Quack and his consort to the corner under suspicion. The reasons for the comparison are these. Everything has been done to save the patient, but in vain. But in the hour of death both doctors hit upon an idea which might have saved her, had they thought of it sooner, and that is the medicines which they hold in their hands. Of course, each counts the other's medicine among those which could never be given too late. Both bottle and box, with the new medicines, are still unopened, and therefore the patient died. But where are the old medicines with their consequences? They lie partly in the armchair beside the fireplace, and then—in the corner under suspicion. In a word, that corner contains in various forms, the products into which those medicines were transformed. One grasped what was nearest to hand and sought for help first here, then there, and as speed was necessary, the vessels had temporarily to be deprived of their function in the kitchen and were transferred to the department where the stool presides. Thus afterwards one knew at least *obiter* where one was. On the pan lies a plate on which we can distinctly read the word 'Cook'. Evidently it belonged to the neighbouring chop-house. We shall not disturb it.

To that corner also belongs the bladder of well-known form, which has found a nail to hang from above the mantlepiece between a couple of medicine bottles and a broken jar. This is the best position for display in the whole room. If I am not mistaken, Hogarth wanted to intimate through the intentional elevation of that instrument and by bringing into prominence the allied vessels that the doctors had specially adopted the vomit and lavage method. With this I would agree. If however his intention was to mock, he was very much in the wrong. Does he not know that this method is almost the only one whose efficiency, so to speak, could be demonstrated geometrically and even elegantly? That the girl has died of it, what difference does that make? Good Heavens! what could one not die of? Did not the postman Jablkowsky of Warsaw in January 1792 die from 300 oysters? Since that demonstration, which is really due

64

to Dr Swift,[1] a well-known physician for sick souls and sick governments, has not become general knowledge as far as we know, we shall give it here translated into our somewhat learned book language, whereas Swift expresses it so that a child could understand it, and that would not do. Since diseases, as everyone knows, are said to be nothing but reversions of the natural processes of some functions in the body, it is not even thinkable that they should be reversed again, that is brought back into the right direction, so long as the old disorderly habits of life continue which brought about the first reversal. This, it seems to us, is so clear that the proof requires nothing for completeness but a reference in brackets to a preceding paragraph, which however everybody will here find in his own head. But since, furthermore, all who fall ill have, up to the moment when this happens, eaten or ingested *in dubio* with their mouth, which we shall call A, and have effected the emission with the opposite end B, it is impossible that, *rebus sic manentibus*, the disorder should be halted and their health again restored. Again as clear as daylight. What then is to be done? The problem answers itself: one must start to eat with the end B, and transfer the emission to the end A, *id est*, to give lavage and to vomit. Nature hesitates, bethinks herself, turns round, and in this way everything ends as desired.

Now finally let us glance at the furniture in the room itself. The mirror seems to have been discarded since the truth which it told began to be somewhat troublesome, and to have been relegated to the corner next to the fireplace, which is not very accessible and by no means the spot in that rather composite room where one would choose to disrobe and admire oneself, at least it is no place for an *Os sublime*. It hangs, of course, next to the fireplace, if one starts from the chimney; if one starts elsewhere, it hangs differently, etc. On the mantelpiece, where the household gods usually find their place, there stand here, too, the present Penates of that happy family, together with some sacrificial bowls dedicated to the past ones. Those are merely symbolical, the three Parcae in the form of three medicine bottles with their necklaces, and then the Ibis with its famous beak in the shape of a bladder. Here should have stood the super domestic god, the mirror which never smiles more graciously on its priestesses than when the fire on his altar through their chaste cheeks and eyes full of devotion is sending up to him light and glow.

[1] *A Voyage to the Houyhnhnms*, Chapter VI.

Above the throne of these goddesses floats a canopy of damp, perhaps still dripping, washing which stretches over the seat of the dying and by its influence transforms that apparently warm place into a veritable *sub Dio*. The time and place of the drying, as well as the number of pieces which are to dry, testify to deep poverty. How wretched are the households where these three points are among the family secrets. Where the shirt on the washing line has to pretend to the chaste invisibility which it rightly preserved on the body. There luxury at least is out of the question. The whole change of service is then usually a change of one with one, or one with none. The last object on the line on the right hand side seems to be something padded, which is only hanging there for the purpose of being aired; one cannot tell quite what it is nor how it keeps its balance; but in the original it is drawn more as if it covered a similar piece as its counterweight. Probably it served itself for the purpose of padding, and would then be an impostor.

Opposite the chimney-piece, high up on a nail beside the door, hangs a round disc, perforated or indented, whose meaning Nichols, in his *Life of Hogarth*, has correctly interpreted. It is a Jewish Easter cake, Mazzos as they are sometimes called, which English Jews (as in some parts of Germany) send to their customers, more as a symbol of a substitute than as a real substitute, and which therefore they tolerantly treat not as victuals but as hardly more than an emblem of food. In England, the righteous of the fourth social class make fly-traps out of them, evidently by covering them with some sticky substance or, at least, with something which would for some time keep the dried mucilage in suspension. Nichols has repeatedly seen them used like that by people of that class. Whether it was Hogarth's intention to point merely at the class habits of the person occupying that room, whose whole Christianity had been reduced to that noble remnant of a cheap contempt for Jewry, or whether, as seems more likely to me, the cake at the same time represents a remnant of the past splendour of the second Plate, we gladly leave to the reader's judgment. In any case, the little moon was sure to reflect much light on to the sick-bed and, as Hesperus, would shine powerfully into the dying woman's conscience, which in the eventide of life is said to be very receptive to such reflections. At the Bell Inn she was betrayed, and that was a misfortune! In the Portuguese temple towards which that star is pointing, she betrayed and sinned on her own account, and that was a crime.

That in this room there must have been better and happier times than now, happier too than in the House of Correction, of that we find incontrovertible evidence on the ceiling. Almost over the bed we read the well-known 'M.H.' written with a brand, the initials which we saw upon the trunk outside the Inn in the first Plate. That trunk is seen here again, only somewhat aged. Such inscriptions, executed by some *bel esprit* who had to climb on table and chairs, are seldom made without a good amount of high spirits. But this is not all. Behind this 'M.H.' stands another word which Hogarth has almost blotted out again, and thereby contributed not a little to its lasting memory. We shall not, of course, restore it, but merely remark for the benefit of lovers of unreadable inscriptions that the Latin translation of it can be found in the third Satire of the first Book of Horace. How salubrious and airy this little room must be, especially for a somewhat be-quacked patient, strikes the eye immediately. On one side the whitewash has peeled off the wall, and on the other the wood-work is partly rotten. On the left side, under the two tallow candles, it looks almost as if the wall had been patched up with a foreign substance. The door, it appears, owes its rigidity not to the usual firm frame into which the panels are fitted, but to a single cross-beam upon which the boards are nailed. The doors of pigsties usually have three such beams, either parallel or in the shape of a Z. This structure is also the source of considerable loopholes for healthy air and comforting looks, and these have been patched and pasted over with much consideration for elegance. Considering, moreover, the tender childlike sympathy with which the boy follows the fate of his mother, the silent despair with which the old woman, seeing that all is lost, throws herself upon her knees, the dull, albeit gentle, look with which the female minister to souls is still seeking, but hardly expecting, help from the compassionate doctors—then Molly's fate becomes almost enviable, at least for some people; it seems to me as if I heard their:

Où peut-on être mieux qu'au sein de sa famille?

67

VI

HERE at last lies our heroine quiet and still in her coffin, safe from Sir John Gonson's minions, Magister Thwackum's blows, and Dr Misaubin's pills. What powerful protection a coffin lid can give! And how lucky she has been, for where the little nails for her coffin were made, the big nails for the gallows are often hammered, too. On the lid we read:

M. Hackabout, died Sept. 3d 1731, aged 23.[1]

[1] That Hogarth had a good reason for choosing of all the days in the calendar just the 3rd of September for the day of her decease, nobody will doubt who is only slightly familiar with his peculiar genius. Perhaps it is a cut which was noticed only by the family at whom it was aimed. In the *Gentleman's Magazine*, September 1731, p. 301, we read: 'On the 3rd of September died Miss Betty Fish of Enfield.' I mention this not as the key to Hogarth's satire but in explanation of my own thoughts. A roguery of that sort would be just in his manner. I could not find anything else, though possibly somebody else may come upon something. In the Julian Calendar that day is called 'Mansuetus'. Not even the most potent fortune teller from coffee grounds could make anything out of that. In the Gregorian Calendar it is of course called 'Euphemia'. That would be suitable for the death day of a virtuous maiden, but one could not very well make use of it here. The English Calendars which I have looked into have only a few names of that sort and Euphemia is not among them. The Great Fire of London (1666), the anniversary of which is usually cited as September 2nd, is given by Hume as the 3rd. But surely in this case Hogarth would have chosen the day on which the fire was extinguished. Since it is the 3rd of September we have to explain, we cannot pass over in silence that this is the day made so famous by Cromwell and extolled by him as the lucky day on which he won his two great victories—at Dunbar, 1650, and Worcester, 1651; furthermore the day on which his first remarkable Parliament assembled (1654) and on which he (very much in accordance with the nature of that fanatic who, when his health was failing, began to employ his imagination against himself) eventually died. The day, already remarkable enough, has become still more so through the storm which, as is well known, raged on it, and which Waller in his famous Ode has described so vividly, though in such a courtly manner. That Hogarth should have had that in mind is unlikely, for that a whore should die on the same day as a usurper is nothing remarkable.

A Harlot's Progress Plate VI

She was thus carried off before she had time to become pious. She was fortunate in that, for there are instances of pious dames of her cloth having been hanged. Oh! how much could we not say here—if we were allowed to say it! But we fear the prayers of the pious, respect the coffin-lid, and—are silent.

If we survey that gathering only cursorily or from a little distance, we are almost ready to believe we have seen something like that before somewhere in the world, and expect to find something sad but still genteel. A coffin over which they are murmuring a tender 'Sleep well!'; a lot of crêpe; a figure like a parson and another like a sexton; a funeral escutcheon on the wall; a child in deep mourning; rosemary, tears and white handkerchiefs; they are waiting for the hearse. Who in all the world would suspect anything reprehensible here? But just bring your eye a little nearer so that the parts become individually distinct, and you will find that you have never seen anything like that before anywhere. Everything changes and even partly vanishes. There is crêpe without mourning and howling without tears; not a trace of a parson nor of his sexton; the arms are a lampoon and the very coffin a counter—for brandy. It is abominable! Now what is going on here? This the reader will now partly hear and partly guess quite easily.

The room into which we are looking here is either a room on the ground floor of the house wherein our heroine died, or it belongs to the man who, against a certain fee, takes complete charge of the corpse.[1] This is the man here with the sexton face. The female part of the company consists entirely of sisters, prioresses and abbesses of the Order of strict observance to which the deceased belonged, undeniably one of the most numerous in the world. The Sisterhood of Drury Lane is said to comprise more nuns than London has hackney-coaches, whose number is estimated at a thousand; and though strict vigils and the martyr's death kill quite a few of them every year, and transportations to Jackson's Bay[2] have made considerable in-

---

[1] These useful people are called in England undertakers. They are in some respects for the exit from the world what the midwives are for the entry. But they proceed much more cautiously and undertake only the easiest part of the business, something that would correspond in a delivery to the washing, swaddling and bearing to the cradle. The main operation they leave entirely to nature or to the professions.

[2] To obtain that distinction a certain period of probation is necessary. Formerly it was arranged that, if one of the nuns was too ripe for this world and not yet ripe for the next, she was sent to a sort of intermediate world, the so-called New World. But since that New

roads, there is not the slightest noticeable diminution. They are waiting here for the removal of the coffin, which does not seem to happen quite on time. It is usually so with departures, except perhaps the departure from life, where everything happens much too soon; with the removal to the churchyard, on the other hand, the procedure is often as unpunctual as if one were hale and hearty. However, they know what to do here; they amuse themselves as best they can.

In that gathering there are thirteen living people, one dead, and then a sort of intermediate one, a picture in the mirror, thus fifteen altogether. Of these, three are standing by themselves, the other twelve are arranged in pairs. Two pairs of living ladies together with those separate subjects make seven; a living lady, paired with a dead one, makes nine; two highly alive Chapeaux with two ladies of the same quality, makes thirteen; and finally a lady with her reflection in the mirror—in the same capacity as the lady herself—gives fifteen. We shall have something to say about each, even if only a word. We begin with the left wing.

What strikes the eye immediately here is the big gun which has been posted at the flank. If compared but perfunctorily with the figure sitting beside it, it could easily be taken for a tear-bottle, but for this the shape has obviously far too much of the mortar and howitzer. It is really a drinking gun, a six-pounder at least, loaded with *Nants* (French liqueur). Very peaceful and merely serving the function of bonfire and fireworks for the column. The counterpart, a small mortar, is to be found near the right wing upon the coffin-lid, and for the same purpose. This fire from the wings, as we shall see, has an uncommon effect upon the centre. The moment has been excellently chosen by the artist. It is, in effect, the moment when age exalted by *Nants* approaches the feelings of youth, and when the gathering resembles the beautiful picture of the snake which with tail in mouth coils itself into a circle, to which everything perfect in the world must eventually more or less conform. It will stay like that—provided the hearse is not too long in coming and the coffin does not lose

---

World by and by began to grow aged itself and to start nunneries of its own, a second one was chosen in its place, and in that completely new one lies the above-mentioned Jackson's Bay. Now, since the Southern Pole Star appears quite high above the horizon there, the female Knightly Order has been named after it, and the noble Sisters are called Dames of the Southern Pole Star.

through the delay the respect due to it. But let us now examine a little closer how things stand.

The artillery is well served. The small mortar is taken charge of by the snub-nose whom we already know, and the howitzer by the fire-toad who in the corner there wrings both her fore legs and stretches out a hind leg. If someone does not know what *tragicus boatus*[1] is, he should look if he dares at that face. It does not bear illumination, and is in need of none; we only beg our readers to note that what shines so charmingly in the lovely mouth of that female gunner are not teeth (for of these she has only a few), but the most indispensable part of her swallowing-cursing-and-praying apparatus—her own unsmoked tongue. She seems as if born for her department, and the howitzer form of her waist cannot be mistaken, at least it would hardly be possible in a human being for the ends A and B to be nearer one another than here; a deft surgeon could attend to both with one hand. Moreover, it almost goes without saying that she only sits like that so long as she is not drinking or pouring out. Might it be the woman who was kneeling in front of the coffer in the last Plate? The faces, to be sure, are not quite alike, but Laocoon also looked quite different on the day before his misfortune from how he has looked these last few thousand years. And the figure? Well on such a day one puts on all the clothes one has.

Next to this Patagonia face, which is one of the unattached, we see the first of the couples, of European-London culture. Mr Undertaker, who is helping one of the nuns to don her mourning-glove, makes use of that favourable opportunity to submit to her a little request of easily understandable tenor, and he does so with such good manners and with so much modest fervour that it cannot possibly remain without response. In fact, there is already something like the reflex of a gracious permission in the very eye of the supplicant, although the sign by which it was granted is not disclosed. But his assistance in putting on the glove was probably given in the form of a question, and thereby gave opportunity for a reply which, however, had to remain invisible. The contrast in these two faces is capital: the undertaker has no other design but what eye and mouth betray, he is utterly concentrated and as one-sided as possible—for the moment, at least; the girl's eye on the other hand speaks of all-sidedness and design. However dim it may seem, it certainly is not only the Spiritus

[1] Howling in the tragic manner.

rector of this assembly which is dimming it; there is play-acting here which would betray itself by the obvious traces of a triumphant smile at the blindness of the poor trapped devil to anybody who does not happen to be that poor devil himself. Drury Laneites do not forget themselves. With them every movement, no matter how small, is meant not only for the hearts which they openly attack, but, at least secretly, for their handker-chiefs as well. No sooner does the harpy learn with the surface of her right arm that the heart is full, than she already begins stealing with her left. This is the so-called small souvenir from Mr Undertaker; the big one will follow suit.

Immediately after that first mixed couple come the four unmixed ones, one after the other, if we go from the left wing towards the right; the first of them represents an inspection. Both members are, as we see, of slightly more than middle age. In both can be observed a praiseworthy and most reasonable economy of bosom, with which the young, thoughtless vermin here are not yet willing to conform. One of them seems already of an age when spectacles can be mislaid. As we see, they are needed here. The second, a lean sufferer, has something between the fingers which seems to cause her pain and which is being examined by the first with surgical, serious, and really expert touch and subtlety. What could that be? Or is it perhaps nothing at all, and only signifies something? To be frank, we almost suspect here (Greek may do it) deep *esoteric* wantonness under a completely *exoteric* mask, about which, of course, one is free to say what one likes. Oh! how agreeable it is for a commentator if he can slink away from a difficult passage to which he has merely opened the door for the reader, without saying anything more than a few conjuring words in Greek. The sufferer has warts on her fingers and, as is well known, the dead know better how to remove warts than the living. The lady without spectacles seems to think only of ways and means of bringing a wart between the fingers in contact with the corpse. The problem is not easy. If the nose will not do it, nothing else will. This makes the poor creature cry. But only think what a rogue our artist is, even in his disguises. He conceals a wanton thought and the concealment itself is again an act of wantonness, deep too but more comprehensible than the first, though quite unconnected with it. I have heard of a type of politics, deep and unfathomable, being disguised as another, also deep but fathomable, and unconnected with the first (newspaper politics), but I never heard of this

72

sort of satire. The wart-remover, who is in charge of the operation here, has two of them herself, but on her brows like horns sprouting. Having brought the interpretation as far as this, the moral becomes easier and easier, which is evidently that of the beam and the mote and the brother's eye.[1]

Behind that pair stands the third; a pious sister in conversation with another, who shall have no name, in the mirror. Undoubtedly the happiest couple of them all. In every combination by pairing in this world, a certain compensation of defects and accomplishments in the subjects is necessary if the common happiness is to be lasting. What you lack, I have, and what I lack, you have, is the firmest foundation. But in the combination of which we are speaking here, that is quite unnecessary, and for complete satisfaction it is quite sufficient if only one of the members either has every possible accomplishment or, what amounts to the same thing, believes she has them. Thus in our case the girl who presents her back to us is young, and beautiful, or at least she thinks so herself; now if this is granted she need not care a jot about the characteristics of the other, and yet only see with what loving admiration they gaze at each other; like two angels who pass and do not know one another. Each sees in the other a higher creature, each admires and is admired, each bends the knee and the scene ends in mutual adoration.

We shall postpone for a little while our contemplation of the fourth couple, that is the union of the living and the dead women, because Hogarth has used them, and rightly, it seems to us, as the coping stone of the Ark; we shall turn now to the right wing, and thence proceed towards the zenith, as we did before with the left.

Of the pair who fill the right wing, we have a good deal to say, and even more to be silent about. Hogarth's honour demands the one of us, and the respect which we owe to our public the other. Yet the scene must and shall be understood, although we may have to take the liberty of not always writing expressly 'devil', but instead something like Mr Satan, or a mere d. . . .

This time, he as well as she are admittedly portraits. The girl was a notorious creature called Mary Adams who after innumerable acts of debauchery, committed while she was a young girl, was ultimately des-

---

[1] Mr Ireland still believes that a mourning ring is being slipped on here; we thought that too, long before Mr Ireland, but thought better of it later.

patched in her thirtieth year, not to the New, but because of very aggravating circumstances, to the Other World, for theft. She was hanged on September 30, 1737. Portraits have been made of her, and the present one is thought to have been modelled on one of them. Now since these Plates had already appeared in 1734, and thus three years before her death, we can infer from it, at least, that she owed her notoriety not to her last crime alone, or to the way in which she died. This might easily have been due to her personal charm, which the face does not lack even here, where English complexion and English teeth do not come into play, and where all the life which a beautiful face should express to the world seems bent in upon itself. The man beside her is not a clergyman. We beg our readers most earnestly not to entertain such a thought; anything like that would necessarily be prejudicial to the artist, and thereby the whole impression which this piece should make would be lost. There is merely a clergyman's frock. The thing inside it here is one of the few eminent scoundrels to whom Hogarth has justly accorded an infamous immortality; a Charters in his way. Would not the artist have done better, someone might ask, had he spared the cloth here as well? We regard that remark as very well founded; indeed, we are even convinced that it would have been better. But since that is how matters stand, we must hear the artist's defence as well. We undertake it with genuine pleasure and in the sure hope that he will be acquitted.

In his works Hogarth has made attacks on three occasions upon people in parsons' clothes, that is true;[1] but that he ever attacked the profession of clergyman as such, we cannot recall. Out of these three, two are portraits of well-known people, about whose despicable character the voice of the public had already decided long before Hogarth voiced his opinion. He has thus done nothing but what every honest man had done before him, except that he drew and painted where others spoke or wrote. Whether the picture of the third is also a portrait, we cannot say with certainty, but it would still show no disparagement of an honourable calling if it were not. The fellow is only a bit of a gourmand, and on an occasion which regularly occurs but every seventh year. Apart from this he does not hide his doings in a corner, but makes his feast, so to speak, right in the lap of his constituency, before the eyes of his flock, who feast

[1] Once, as we shall see, in the 'Midnight Entertainment'; a second time here, and again in his 'Election Dinner'.

together with him, and it does not cost his family a penny. Such conduct can hardly be called reprehensible. But here, here the situation defies description. Hogarth certainly felt this very keenly. He therefore did something which he had never done in any of his works, so far as we know; something which is hardly compatible with his manner of satire (though in order to exonerate oneself completely, even such extraordinary methods may be necessary). On the 1,200 copies for subscribers, he marked that vile creature with a capital 'A' which referred to a footnote under the Plate where it is clearly stated who he was, and where and how he managed to escape the law. Now just imagine what a lawless creature that abomination must have been, when an honest, well-known and well-esteemed man like Hogarth does not scruple to draw him thus for all the world to see, and, in addition, virtually invokes justice against him. In this way, or so it seems to us, he has not only proved that he did not intend to attack the clergy's estate, but on the contrary, he has shown how much he had its honour at heart. When hunting out subjects for satire, an occupation which he tirelessly pursued, many an object that knew how to evade the activity of the police and the law fell into his snare, and he acted rightly in delivering them up to the authorities, or, if the authorities let them escape again through carelessness, in giving them at the next opportunity the *coup de grâce* himself.

This scoundrel, evidently the Spadille[1] among the trumps in hearts, as the other black ace, the Undertaker, is the Basta,[2] was so well known under the name Couple-Beggar (because he copulated for a few pence) that Hogarth's interpreters have forgotten his proper name, a feature which in itself speaks for his great eminence in the profession. We have been assured that, apart from that other occupation, he united himself regulariter a couple of times a week—with the gutter. Not only symbolically, as the Doge of Venice marries the Adriatic. Instead of throwing a trifle into it, he threw in everything which he still had left in the evening —himself. A Divine he has never been called, he was merely an adept at holding Divine Services, and even there he just babbled through the Marriage and Funeral service—for a few pence. His spiritual hand, as it was called, never fished for more, but fished all the more often—while his worldly hand demanded stole-fees wherever they could be found,

[1] From the game of Ombre.
[2] ibid.

in pockets with and without bottom *ad infinitum.* This is well known. Whether Hogarth tried to hint at something of this sort here cannot well be decided. In his so-called spiritual hand, the left one, he holds the funeral brandy very badly and stains his handkerchief with it. Where the worldly one is, nobody, so far as we know, has yet been able to decide. People have looked for it under Couple-Beggar's hat, which the Manille[1] is holding very carefully in front of it, but it has not been found there either. We therefore willingly abandon this *locum difficillimum* and pass over with genuine pleasure, in the way of commentators, to an easier one—to Snub-nose. She stands at the foot of her friend's coffin with a mortar in her hand, like a female sutler before the inn counter. I call that feeling! And yet, to the honour of human nature, there is in her wild look a kind of unmistakable disapproval at the behaviour of the neighbouring couple. It absorbs, as one can see, her whole attention, and although her mouth speaks of much latitude in such matters, yet her eye seems to find place and time and hour somewhat unbecoming. It is a fine touch of Hogarth's to put even into that unfeeling tiger-face an expression of disapproval at such bestiality, and thus to make even the stones cry out about it. In passing we would beg our readers to recall for themselves what that creature has done and suffered so far, and what sort of a life that is, and yet even as we read this, it is still lived by countless women! But we do not wish to prejudice the views to which this might give occasion about the inheritors of the Kingdom of Heaven and their spiritual guides!

Right in the background near the door we see the fifth couple. If anyone does not know yet what it is to be befuddled, he ought to look at this. We should almost like to melt with them when we observe how these two hearts, which probably are not yet entirely depraved, fuse into one. What bliss! They have the sensation of floating towards a Heaven of love and friendship, and do not realize that the house of cards erected by the liquor will, in the ensuing quarter of an hour, collapse beneath them and will send them with acceleration into the depths where police, pillory, quack doctor and the hemp beating association are ever ready to receive them.

One of the members of the sixth and last couple, the living one engaged in contemplation of the dead, Hogarth has not put for nothing into the centre of the picture. He wants us to take special note of her. Just as she is at the apex of the semi-circle formed by the assembly, where the two

[1] From the game of Ombre.

wings converge, so also converge in her role the moral lines which the artist here wishes to draw. That is why the girl is also one of Hogarth's beauties. This is a point to remember, for it might pass unnoticed. Moreover, the girl is not altogether bad. Youth and freshness are there at least, and to these qualities is addressed the moral which can best be expressed by the words from the coffin:

What thou art and how thou art, I was too but a short while ago. Abandon the path thou art treading; if not, think of this: what I am now, thou too shalt be, and in a short while.

Whether the little goose has heeded these words, cannot be ascertained from her face; but that, if she has heard them, she will have forgotten them even before the hearse arrives, this I think can be predicted with certainty.

Almost beneath the coffin, just as formerly beside the death-chair, sits again the little heir, occupied with a pain-alleviating instrument. There it was a chop which he turned on the spit; here he winds a top which he is going to spin in the chamber of mourning. It looks as if the anodyne had worked well on the little chap. However, it may also be that what one takes for the cause here is really the effect. The boy does not grieve, but not because he is roasting his meat and winding his top, but he roasts and winds because he does not grieve. Why should he fret? Just as he has no father, since nobody knew who he was, so he had no mother either, because in the society where he lived nobody had time to be one. Oh, the words father and mother mean very much more than we usually find in their dictionary definitions, and more than people think when they read them! Just as many a child whose true parents are far beyond the grave finds, thank God!, a new father or a mother, so, alas! there are fatherless and motherless orphans whose parents are thoroughly enjoying themselves day after day. Evidently the poor fellow has often been pushed from one corner into another; but since the decease there will be one pusher less. Even supposing that snub-nose will sometimes throw him into the corner now, there is still nobody near at hand to throw him back again. From the boy's puny legs we might almost conclude that the anodyne necklaces have not been of much use. That Hogarth has dressed the boy up as chief mourner is a mockery in more than one respect; children are never used in that role; it must always be a man of some presence who would not disgrace an afflicted heart. But the expression could also imply 'the chief among the mourners', and in this way the situation becomes almost ludicrous. For if the most deeply afflicted is winding his top shortly before the cortège leaves, we can easily surmise how deeply afflicted the others must be. The dish with rosemary as well as the little table with the gloves and the glove-stretcher for the too-narrow fingers are plain enough, but the position of the pair of gloves is perhaps not without intention. They seem to have moved apart as if shocked, and so as to clasp each other again, and to shame by their example at least ten pairs of hands of flesh and blood among the thirteen which are assembled here and are occupied in a somewhat worldly manner.

About the mourning escutcheon on the wall, although we shall describe it in accordance with our duty, we shall take good care not to give an opinion, either as regards the aspirations which are to be immortalized through it, or the demesnes which it is meant to indicate, since we value peace, together with an ounce of family pride, more than all the honour which we might perhaps win on this occasion with our heraldic penetration. The instrument which we see here in triplicate on the blue field is called in English 'spigot and fosset', better written faucet. It is a sort of bung for barrels. This consists, as we see, of two parts, of which the smaller, the spigot, is stuck into the larger, the faucet, just as the latter is itself stuck into the barrel. In drawing wine, only the smaller one is drawn out and, when the bottle is full, is pushed in again. It is the simplest cock in the world. Despite our promise, we should be glad of permission to add a little remark about that escutcheon because, as the reader will see immediately, our promise will not really be broken thereby. We only gave our word as regards the interpretation of pretended claims to relationships and demesnes, but by no means of the wanton misuse which our rogue of an artist could make of a matter quite innocent in itself. He has drawn the three cocks, probably with intention, in such a way that, seen from a distance, they could be taken for the three French lilies. Fine praise for the girl in her coffin to hang above it the French escutcheon! I believe the rogue would have liked to hang the three lilies themselves there had he not feared that one of the English Kings-at-Arms would rap his knuckles for it. Were Hogarth's English commentators apprehensive of some similar reward for their interpretations? Not one of them says a word about it.

In the window sticks a body of such equivocal substance and form that one is not quite sure whether it has been pushed in from the inside to close the gap, or from the outside, and in that case, whether it was not the object itself which made the hole it now fills. This latter type of interference with the glazier's trade is something to which the virtuous young hooligans of London are very prone, when they suspect so much vice in a room, and especially a funeral with the French escutcheon. One might even be grateful if they calculate the hurling of the missile in such a way that, as here, it cures at the same time the damage which it has caused.[1]

Finally a remark about Roucquet's opinion of this Plate. He holds that Hogarth would have done better had he finished the story with the death scene, and he says of the present Plate, *c'est une farce dont la défunte est plutôt l'occasion que la cause.* We are accustomed to seeing Frenchmen often treat very serious matters as farces, and very trivial ones with gravity. This only means that with the French all things are possible. But Roucquet is really not entirely wrong. He has only missed the main viewpoint from which the picture must be apprehended, and has looked at it from another one, from which alas! it has also been conceived, and this in other words means so much as: Hogarth has really made a mistake. If Roucquet had hit immediately upon the first viewpoint, his whole criticism might not perhaps have materialized; Hogarth undeniably meant to say, as Gray in his superb Elegy has expressed it so beautifully, that even the most miserable and depraved, no matter how unsung they may die, find comfort in the respect of some they leave behind and long for it. It is not only insult after death (for who could remain insensitive to that?), but the mere thought of laughing heirs which embitters the last moments even of the most light-hearted. Do not the English regard it, for instance, as an aggravation of capital punishment if the additional sentence is pronounced that the body is afterwards to be taken to the dissecting room? And in other countries, is it not some mitigation if the headless body is to be buried not beneath the gallows, but in a corner of the churchyard? But what sort of funeral is it here? There are not many steps, to be sure, between this sort of honour after death and a burial beneath the gallows. This was undoubtedly Hogarth's idea, and the funeral scene fits very well

[1] What makes it the more probable that this is a stone which, in being thrown, stuck in the leaden lattice, is the fact that Hogarth in one of his later works has quite unmistakably made use of that feature. There it is a brick which remains stuck while others are flying through freely.

into the whole, but how has he executed it? Certainly not particularly well. With such ceremonial; with a chief mourner who is only a child, and even the deceased's own child; with an escutcheon, an inscription on the coffin lid, and altogether with such pomp, no whore is buried in London, unless she were one of some social standing. Nichols says a cortège of that nature would not have been able to proceed, especially in those days, when the police were so very bad. Satire of course is there, but unity is missing, and looked at from that point of view, this sixth Plate does in a way acquire the appearance of a Comedy after the Tragedy.

Marriage-à-la-Mode

Foecunda culpae saecula nuptias
Primum inquinavere, et genus et domos
    Hoc fonte derivata clades
      in patriam populumque fluxit.
          HORACE, *Carmina*, Bk. III, Ode VI, v. 17

Marriage–à–la–Mode

I

OUR great artist has often been reproached with having presented only the seamy side of human life. His genius, if he had any, is always at home, they say, in the lower regions of society, and is only at ease in the dirt of the streets. This piqued him eventually. He boldly ascended into the so–called higher regions, portrayed what he saw in Heaven, and presented it to us in the six Plates which follow. This *Voyage pittoresque* received quite unqualified applause. Even the higher world itself is said to have been not entirely displeased, perhaps out of self-esteem, at having to decide between the alternatives: either to admit that Hogarth really understood their 'high life', or that this famous high life was nothing but low life trimmed up, and no more than a sort of rabble world. That in a dilemma of this kind they would grasp the first horn goes without saying. Thus through their choice Hogarth's genius was vindicated; through their embarrassment in making it, he got his revenge.

He called his story 'Marriage-à-la-Mode'. The first of these words has been naturalized in England and is English proper; the last part of the phrase was at that time (the scene is the year 1745) French. So the title is half English and half French, just like the morals of that province of the higher world which he here delineates. In England the common man marries according to the custom of his forefathers, eats his steak and murmurs his 'Our Father' as they did; the gentleman, on the other hand, not infrequently has his marriage *à la mode*, just as he has his beef *à la mode* and his religion *à la mode*.

The moral tendency of these pictures is excellent, and the poetic justice the strictest imaginable. The evil-doers one and all die an unnatural death. What a pity that such justice should be only poetic! Will Nature never learn to appreciate poetic justice? For more than 6,500 years already, as *Batteux*[1] has so excellently demonstrated, poets have been imitating the beauties of Nature. I should certainly have thought that it would be only just if Nature were to come to her senses and start imitating, for once, the beauties of poetry.

How correct Hogarth's observation was, and how truthful his portrayal may be seen from the fact that, when these Plates appeared, Christian charity was somewhat at a loss to know at whom they were aimed. As histories, they fitted equally well, with some minor reservations, Lords X, Y or Z, and as prophecies they would have fitted half the alphabet. Hogarth who, so the rumour goes, had particularly in mind a certain Lord W . . . is in the same predicament as that fanatical preacher who, in the heat of his sermon, was about to hurl his hymn-book at an adulterer in his congregation when he noticed, to his astonishment, that as he raised his arm, half an alphabet of heads had ducked.

In the first Plate we see, in a richly and heavily furnished drawing-room, two portly gentlemen sitting opposite each other at a silver-plated table. The one somewhat old and palsied, the other still robust—in sound health, at least. One is His Grace the Earl of Squanderfield, a man of publicly attested blood and safely established honour; the other honourable merely in money and credit, an alderman and, to judge from his golden chain, a Sheriff at that time of the City of London, and so honourable at least *pro nunc*. They appear to be occupied either in concluding an agreement or in executing one they have already concluded; the occasion and the mutual relation of the parties are something like this. His Grace, though one would hardly believe it to look at him, is just as bankrupt as he is gouty, and his financial potency is, if anything, rather less than his physical. In contrast to him, the honourable gentleman is just as title-seeking as he is wealthy, and yet in the veins and arteries of his family all is as miserably middle-class as his coffers are princely. The former, therefore, is prospecting for the citizen's money to fill an empty, high-titled purse, and the latter for aristocratic blood with which to infuse his middle-class veins. Since the need on both sides is urgent, an agreement is speedily reached, and on the following terms. The Earl will transfer to the merchant's

[1] A French writer on the *Philosophy of Art* (1713–80).

Marriage-à-la-Mode Plate I

family a portion of his precious aristocratic blood in the person of his first-born, his Grace the Lord Viscount Squanderfield. In exchange, that family will open up its strong boxes to his Lordship, and hand over the daughter and sole heir to the immense fortune on condition that the above-mentioned Lord Viscount Squanderfield will perform, execute and complete in a legal way the inoculation of the aristocratic blood on the said girl of the merchant's family. All this is here given under seal. For the purpose of sealing it literally, a lighted candle burns on the table. Some imagine they notice a so-called 'thief' on the candle,[1] which would be an evil omen for the marriage lines. So much is certain, in any case, the candle is melting and omens of weakness are no good in matters like these.

The group at the little silver table is well worth a closer examination. The alderman as he sits there is tense, attentive and preoccupied. His legs do not even seem aware that he is sitting: the shins inclined somewhat beyond the vertical, as if ready for a jump, the feet parallel, the stout shoes with their coarse Stock Exchange soles planted as firmly as his credit. His Lordship's legs are also firm, if not in a fix—alas and alack!—just like his credit. The right, though not yet wholly in the grave, is deeply bowed in sackcloth and ashes, and the left peeps miserably through the lattice of its lazaret.[2] That the latter looks fairly presentable is merely through the contrast with its suffering brother.

The alderman peruses the heading of the marriage contract with a concentration which his Lordship is unlikely to have devoted to its contents. This type of attentive reading is not learned in books nor from books, but only through the enjoyment of great ideas—in bills of exchange. But perhaps there is in this attentiveness something more than mere caution. It may at least be possible. Think of the beautiful Gothic script of the English calligraphers, and of the golden words written in that beautiful hand: *The Right Honble Lord Viscount*, and foresee in this Viscount the future son-in-law, and in the son-in-law the future Earl, and in the Earl the inevitable Lord in the House of Lords with all his right and might until the end of the world. Indeed, if such a prospect could not bewitch the eye of a proud alderman, what in all the world could? He has, no doubt, pondered all that often enough, but he sees it here for the first time, written out in such heraldic magnificence and in morally ineradicable script.

[1] A projection on the wick of a candle, causing it to gutter. Ed.
[2] Hospital for the diseased poor, especially lepers. Ed.

Beside him stands, hat under arm, his old, devoted clerk, desiccated by sixty years of service in his counting-house. It is he who executes the contract, and hands over to the old Earl in the name of his master what is known in this house as 'the alderman's daughter'. It is he who, so to speak, performs the marriage ceremony. It would certainly require much philosophy to look upon the table where that marriage ceremony is proceeding without some secret agitation. Bank notes with highly significant rows of noughts, as if adorned with pearls, are lying there on heaps of guineas, and similar embroidery is to follow. And yet these are, as is generally the case with the visible charms on such occasions, only accessory items. Just in front of the old man lie yet more purses which deserve special attention, just because one cannot tell how much is in them. However, the most secret and therefore the most important item in the whole collection is obviously the document with the title 'Mortgage'. I come to this conclusion because even the accountant, with good-natured curiosity, seems anxious to observe the impression which such an unexpected blessing will make upon his Lordship. For in all probability it is an IOU which the alderman is returning, and through which a part of his Grace's patrimonial estate had till now been held in captivity. 'Here, my Lord, take back your estate,' says the old man. The gift is extensive, and from the manner in which it is offered, there is something about it which is not quite in the nature of a commercial transaction. This is also felt very clearly on the part of the aristocracy; the dowry is grasped immediately and without loss of time so as to send the pack of commoners quickly back behind their natural frontiers. 'All right!' says the Earl, 'that is what your girl brings to our house, and this which pulses under here [pointing to the fifth waistcoat button], my blood, and here [pointing to the family tree], this cedar of Lebanon, my 700-year-old title, these are what my first-born son is bringing into your plebeian establishment.' In order to feel fully the immense excess weight of these words over the deed, we must consider the oriental pomp which accompanied their pronouncement, and upon which we should like to comment here only so far as it immediately concerns this group.

The old Earl is seen sitting immediately beneath a state-and-audience canopy, with an Earl's coronet not actually upon his wig, to be sure, but on the canopy; garbed in lofty, golden, heraldic splendour, and as if he were himself a sort of magnificent coat-of-arms, with two crutches as his shield-bearers. Each crutch is stamped with the emblem of the coronet. At the present moment he does not need them. The responsibility for his support has been taken over at the other end by one of the finest private thrones which gout has ever ascended on a festival day. The sick credit leg is upheld by a stool which even the most delicate fragility would not disdain to accept as support for temple or brow, and this stool also bears for its services the golden coronet. Near it lies William the Conqueror with his coat-of-mail, shield and sword, admiring the noble fruits of his 700-year-old-tree, on each branch of which hangs the golden ornament of the coronet. Poor alderman! What is now the jingle of your temporal purse compared with that magnificence and the trumpet sound of an ancestral glory almost a thousand years old? That family tree is really no great comfort to the alderman. With his spectacles on, at least, he should not come too near it. For if I see aright, the noble Norman has with his sword hewn down a branch because that branch bore a coronet which had married a non-coronet. The little branch with its mildew could not remain on the tree of aristocratic knowledge which had struck its roots right down into the entrails of William the Conqueror. That the black zero which we see falling denotes an unaristocratic zero is almost certain, but whether a tradesman's daughter or a valet's or a footman's is not revealed.

Behind the alderman, in quite a charming nook, sit the two lovers themselves—*in natura*. It is not altogether easy to describe how they are sitting. That their hearts are not turned to one another is pretty certain, or else the hearts would have to be differently situated in them than in other people. To express it by way of a simile is not easy either, at least not in any of the usual comparisons used in marriage songs. One could not think here of turtle doves and their billing and cooing, for instance, for who in all the world would bill and coo in that position? Perhaps the most fitting simile would be to say that the bridegroom is sitting beside the bride like a sick angora rabbit beside a hot lady hedgehog. He with the light and fire of his eyes already dimmed, and with a *bon ton* plaster behind the ear that speaks volumes, takes a pinch of snuff with superfine elegance. His hardly perceptible smile is a smile of the most empty self-approbation accompanied by extreme indolence of body and soul. What keeps him going is perhaps a half-jealous attention to a small whisper, to which we shall ourselves listen anon. He sits—yes, he does—but no matter what with and whereupon, so much at least is certain—he sits miserably. His feet too, just as his father's, are eloquent about credit. Even while he sits they raise themselves upon the toes, probably to diminish as much as possible somewhere in a higher region the point of contact between seat and sit-upon. His face is turned towards the mirror, but only because the mirror hangs on the side where his bride is not. With the mirror itself he is not concerned. All he could see there would be, at the utmost, a little of the silver embroidery on his magnificent sleeve. For it is a catoptric impossibility that, as Mr Ireland thinks,[1] he could see himself in the mirror or could watch his bride in it. It gives one quite a queer feeling if one compares this fragile marzipan puppet with the iron Norman there whom it takes for its ancestor. And if the courageous, fiery, ambitious and anything but soft-hearted William with his sword had been here in person, the safest little nook in the room for his Grace, provided he had his jumping legs with him, would have been near the window.

Now for the bride! Gracious Hymen, what are you doing here? And how was it possible to contemplate such a match? Just look at them. If we deduct the trivial item (the only point on which the two good people are still in agreement) that they both, as one can see, hate each other like the devil, they most emphatically differ in every other particular. It is too bad! As for the commercial transaction which is proceeding at the silver table with purses and family trees, all that is acceptable but—as to the performance of the contract *in naturalibus* there on the settee, it is too bad for words. Just consider: he with the slender, weak, but refined remnant of flesh and blood, which he has precariously saved from the fire, posed in the most beautiful of Hogarth's lines of beauty; she still sound, but in an attitude *à dos d'âne*,[2] and bent over like a sawing-jack, which even her clothing cannot conceal. His arm, how gently propped up! And the hands how lightly poised! *Antinous* and *Adonis*, if they had ever wanted to take snuff, could not have done it more charmingly. Hers, bent in parallel angles, hang down like lame hooks on an old bag which have lost their eyelets. He dallies with the snuff-box and the snuff and, in this way, at least three-quarters of the purpose of these toys are fulfilled; she, on the other hand, dallies with the wedding-ring, through which she has drawn her

[1] And so does Hazlitt, loc. cit. Ed.

[2] Since descriptions of ladies' clothes are usually given in French, it would seem quite appropriate, when describing the ladies themselves, to do the same, especially since the difference between them, in the great majority of cases, is negligible.

fine, soft handkerchief, and which she twirls and flings and will probably—fling away.

The wedding ring is to her just a pinch of snuff which she has taken this morning for her honour's sake and which, since it was not to her taste, she will get rid of at the first opportunity. Some people want to find a deeper meaning in the toys of these two lovers. That may be, but there may also be nothing more to them. I, at least, do not wish to put deep meanings into toys. His mien, how sweet! Somewhat languid of course, but gentle; with some traces of debauchery but of good breeding, too. But hers! God save and protect everybody from such an ornament on their own shoulders, or on that of their future domestic honour. It would not do even as a figurehead on the family sledge. It would hardly be possible to draw a female creature looking less womanly. Uglier, perhaps, but in so few strokes, hardly more malicious, pig-headed, stubborn and yet sly. Indeed, the contrast in this couple goes very deep; it is not only concerned with head and heart, it extends even to parts which, especially when mankind goes on all fours (which no doubt will happen again in the not-too-distant future), are as distant as possible from head and heart. I mean the good people are not even sitting, or sitting down, the one like the other. The bridegroom, does he not float above his chair, light as the God of Spring over the silver gossamer of a mist of dew? The bride, on the other hand, is she not sitting there exactly in the attitude of a 'Boots' who is trying to close the lid of an over-filled trunk by means of a few rough, final hits with his behind? He sits, or seems to sit, as if he were afraid of needles on the seat; she just the opposite, as if she noticed in it an emptiness to be filled, and there are such seats in the world.

On her right sits the man to whom she is to give her right hand in marriage, and on her left stands another, a young, virile, matrimonial adviser who is in fact about to execute with her a similar proceeding for his own person, but in a left-handed way. The fox is aware that everything on the right appears to the bride as not quite right, and he begins an exposition forthwith on the left, not of that for which he sharpens his pen, but of that for which she pricks up her ears. The young man is not a clergyman, as many Germans would perhaps conclude from his black gown and his collar, but a lawyer, a sort of solicitor and attorney. In England, indeed, both higher faculties are constantly in mourning when on duty, whereas the faculty of medicine, for which that colour would, perhaps, be most appropriate, wears all the colours of the rainbow, just as in Germany. From the title of a speech of his which appeared in print, and of which we shall have something more to say below, we learn that his name is Silvertongue. And indeed he must be whispering something very silvery, since he succeeds in inducing such attentiveness in that owl as can be inferred from the tension throughout the length of her neck and back, and all while sharpening his pen. That she accompanies this attentiveness, which comes right from the depths of that spoilt creature, with the coarsest expression of vulgar indignation, is, it seems to me, an excellent touch of Hogarth's; for here he no longer characterizes the lady, and still less the mere creature of nature, but human vulgarity, be the fault whose it may. Has the father perhaps risen from fishmongering? As to the legal collar of our solicitor, I must draw attention to the fact that he does not wear that decoration throughout the story, but shortly before its end the Law presents him with another one, and with great solemnity.

This small scene on the settee contains the seed out of which our artist with the utmost subtlety develops the whole tale. Here glimmers the spark which by and by becomes the glow and finally the blaze through which the whole structure collapses. Hogarth, therefore, lays particular stress on it and explains what may still be obscure with a few excellent touches from the inexhaustible treasure-chest of his symbolic language. On the floor immediately in front of the young lord, the settee group is mirrored in the history of the two retainers belonging to the family's hunting establishment. They are a hound and a bitch. The hound, en-nobled to some extent by a coronet on its side, is already somewhat aged, somewhat broken down, and somewhat weary. The bitch, a simple commoner, but fast and lively, has no inclination to sleep, at least not when *he* sleeps with whom she is united by the coarse chain around their necks. The little beast looks round quite greedily for something, most likely for a solicitor. The black spot on the hound's ear is not a *bon ton* plaster. On the wall above the settee Hogarth has placed a candelabra. The arms holding the candles are twined round one another (also a betrothal), but the two candles themselves burn just as little as the two hearts beneath. Or do the candles point more to the left wing where the solicitor is in command? This seems to me more likely, because both are still fresh and unlit, and because the one arm of the candelabra really comes from the side and against all laws of symmetry entwines itself with the main arm.

Had Hogarth intended to point to the right wing, then it probably would have held a burnt down stump. They are not yet burning, but are quite ready to do so. To light them, only night is needed, which will come.

Before the open window stands yet another mourner of the second Faculty. He seems to be of somewhat higher rank than him of the left wing, first because he does less, and, secondly, because he really wears upon his head, the golden fleece of the English Themis. For nobody wears that fur who has not already stowed flesh and fowl safely in his larder. In his left hand he holds the plan of the old Earl's new palace, and compares the design with the execution. He works himself into such a state of admiring astonishment over this that his lower jaw and nose, which in his face are usually close neighbours, fall apart, and so do the five fingers of his right hand. If his admiration is not hypocritical, so much is certain, it is not that of an art connoisseur, but only that of a lawyer, for the building is abominable. The upper columns do not meet the lower ones; the column bases are round, fluted blocks; the basement windows are triangular; beside the main entrance lies a dark coach-house which admits some doubtful light through a round hole, and has an arched entrance cut so low that coachmen and carriages, when entering, could not possibly escape being cut off too. And so it goes on. But to reveal the old gentleman's lack of taste, his stupidity and mad squandering is not the sole reason why the artist has raised the window. There is no money there, he wants to tell us: a scaffolding and no workmen, the building has come to a standstill; nay, it almost seems as if here and there time had already started to break off parts of the scaffolding. Those swarms of people in the courtyard are not workmen, but either idlers from this establishment (superfluous servants) or the servants of other gentry who have come to look at the building and poke fun at it, and all this in honour of the descendant of William the Conqueror.

Just as the interpreter of these Plates was about to address himself to the collection of paintings in the room, he realized that with the guinea which lies there half covered with dust—the gratuity-box of the servants —the same had happened to him as to the three match-makers at the table with the chinking original itself. He had almost forgotten it over all the other treasures in that picture which are waiting to be discovered. The oversight was advantageous this time: it contains in itself the best object lesson, and therefore, at least to the gentle reader, the best excuse.

On the walls hang pictures which, apart from their diversity in other respects, are all terrifying portrayals of temporal misfortunes: war, murder, torture, inundation, pestilence, famine, cannon and comets everywhere, and all that in a betrothal chamber. Really! If Henry IV before his betrothal had consulted the coffee grounds, and the gipsy had shown him such a picture gallery in them, the famous massacre of St Bartholemew would certainly not have come to pass. Here, however, nobody seems to notice any bad omen, and so this Blood-marriage takes its course undisturbed. We need only look and see.

Just above the bridegroom's head, they are racking Saint Laurence on his wedding-bed, the grill. Oh! if only you would give this a thought, poor Lorenzo with your snuff-box down there! On the opposite side, Cain and Abel warn Mr Silvertongue of fratricide. Above the holy Laurence, the story of Herod, the September *briseur*[1] of Bethlehem, points to infanticide, and opposite it, Prometheus, the fire-thief, has his liver gnawed by the vulture of remorse. On the other wall there stretches a huge Goliath, his body on the Eastern and his right leg on the Western side of a hill, whence the boulder of his head is shortly to roll down. Underneath it, another head is rolling already, the head of Holofernes into the work basket of his faithful Judith; and beside that, poor Saint Sebastien receives the arrows in his breast. Thus, there is blood enough here. As to blood, it will in fact be forthcoming, also some similarities with the stories themselves may be found with some ingenuity of interpretation, everything in short—except the Saints.

We must ask the reader to give a little attention to the man whose portrait on the wall there occupies the space of four murder stories. It is a family hero, and whoever cares to see wind, storm and thunder without hearing them, should pause before this picture. The hero in a sort of wig which, despite the many recent advances in meteorology, would still, and rightly, be regarded as belonging among the thunder clouds, is in the midst of the turmoil of battle. That he stands at the head of his army is certain, but where that head is, whether in front or behind or on the side, has not been clearly indicated by the painter, following the manner of journalists. With a mien full of self-approval, he surveys the rich harvest of victory, and is just casting his eye to the side where the most successful

---

[1] This refers to the 'September massacres' in France (1791) when prisoners were massacred as the armies of the Holy Alliance were approaching Paris. Ed.

harvester stands. His right hand has, with mercy and compassion, transferred the lightning to his left, where it plays peacefully with the Brussels lace of his ruffle. The right rests without weapon on his iron hip. Forty to fifty yards of drapery flutter around him, and full against the gale which is blowing on to it from three pairs of inflated cherubs' cheeks. The hero has thus his own wind. However, part of the external gale seizes the main tail of our hero's wig, and lifts it fearfully. He stands there inspiring awe, and could even defy that comet's tail which is hovering above him, considering how nearly related such omens are. Below, a cannon goes off right under the hero's cloak, almost as if the explosion emanated from his trouser pocket. His pocket pistols are to the cannon, as his pigtail to the comet tail. How magnificent! The cannon-ball seems to have been copied by the artist *ad vivum* in a favourable moment. That it appears somewhat small must be forgiven him because of the speed with which such objects must usually be observed. Around the whole portrait is a magnificent frame of gilded woodwork, which is decorated above with a grotesque carving, something between a tiger and a monkey. The picture on the ceiling is a seascape: Pharaoh with his army depicted just at the moment when his chariot up there, above the solicitor, takes to the water. As a counterpart, the Ptolemaic system of the stars on the carpet seems quite appropriate; considering the topsy-turvy domestic arrangements. Thus, in a way, the whole betrothal is proceeding at the bottom of the Red Sea, and something of the sort could really have materialized here if all that blood represented on the walls had actually flowed, or if it had started the stream to which the comet's tail points so ominously.

Finally, a small calculation: the Earl's coat-of-arms appears here definitely nine times and probably eleven. Once upon the canopy, twice on the crutches, once on the stool, once on the alderman's chair, once above the family Medusa on the candelabra, once above the mirror, once under the mirror table and once upon the sleeping hound. The two probable ones are: one hidden by the old Earl's wig, and the other hidden by the hair-bag of the young Viscount, on the backs of their chairs. Our honour as commentator forbids us to complete the dozen with a third probable on the bitch, for we are determined to believe that this lively animal was only a commoner. On the family tree, the coat-of-arms may well appear a further fourteen times. Such a thing really looks like omnipresence.

For the benefit of the owners of the original engravings, we should like to mention that in our reproduction, through our having intentionally omitted to reverse right and left, everything is now restored to how it stood in the original painting. The solicitor again sharpens his pen with the right hand; the hero carries his sword once more on the left side, and the old Earl again puts his right hand upon his heart. I believe that this translation of the English engraving back into the primitive good manners of the painting is not entirely without merit. What man of breeding would, by way of assurance, put his left hand on his heart? If his intentions are not honest, then, of course, he cannot expect the world to say in the end that he had meant everything honestly; but this at least, it seems to me, a man of breeding may ask: that if he cheats, the world should say that he has cheated with dignity.

II

THE old Earl, it seems, is already disintegrated and gathered to the bosom of William the Conqueror! Neither the son nor the daughter-in-law whom we see sitting here appears to be specially moved by the fact that Death has won at last his eighty-year-old lawsuit against the old gentleman. They, too, are contending here, not with Death, but with his half-brother, Sleep, and as one sees, with rather unequal success. She, certainly, is fast losing her case, and he, since his own ill-humour is taking his part, will certainly win his. They have both slept little or not at all last night; she, in this house here, and he in another, perhaps a mile distant. The course of the story is as follows.

It is still early morning here, the clock on the wall may show what time it will; they are still yawning, still stretching themselves, and still break-fasting. Whether this is right or not is none of the plebeian sun's business. It is, of course, a somewhat topsy-turvy state of affairs, but then so are the fishes up there in the trees. It is the custom in this household and it cannot be helped. The young gentleman who, by the way, has aged over-night through rather heavy debauchery, seems to have just flung himself down in here after being unloaded from his carriage. Obviously, he has stumbled over the chair with the fine Cremona violins, has fallen and broken his sword. The figure is a masterpiece, and undoubtedly one of the best Hogarth has ever done. It is a true picture of impotence after the wildest debauchery of every kind. Nothing holds together in him through inner force. His position has been reached through force of gravity, through mechanical reaction, and, passively, through the shape of the chair. Waistcoat and stockings hang upon him just like his hat and his hair. The hair-bag is gone, the watch is gone and the money is gone. In place of money there are now only empty hands which search for it and find nothing but a melancholy support for themselves, and for the long heavy arms which have become limp as leather through sleeplessness and excesses. What has suffered least in the tumult is the black seal of the Faculty behind the ear. On what does his gaze rest? Outwards it certainly reaches no farther than half-way towards the overturned chair; inwards it must look uncommonly deep on this morn of domestic peace. Even through the mists of headache which hover round his brow it is still possible to recognize some traces of deeper heartache. This is what happens to little fishes once an over-frivolous jump has thrown them too far out of their element. Intoxication, which, at its onset and during its progress, raises the drinker above his usual state of mind and heart, lowers him again at its expiration below that state, so that in every kind of mood he can usually find some rung on this ladder from which he can, without much trouble, survey his whole being. He seems to calculate; but no, he only feels in a dull sort of way what would happen if he attempted to calculate. This is the ill-humour which, as we said, takes the young gentle-man's part against Sleep. However prostrate he may be though, he has not left the battlefield wholly without booty. From his coat-pocket there hangs an object of muslin and ribbon which only rarely, and never without some great unheaval, finds its way into male coat-pockets. It is some small perfumed head-gear which has been discovered by the lady's lap-dog with its Boulognaise sagacity, and at which it is sniffing with peace-loving cautiousness. Thus, what could hardly be regarded as an adequate security for a mere hair-bag has now become, apparently, the whole substitute for purse and watch! So much for the activities of the young gentleman last night, of which the little dog here has the scent—and now a word on the activities of the young lady, which the young gentleman himself is scenting out.

The whole night long she has entertained there in the magnificent Egyptian drawing-room, a company of card-players, young gentlemen and such-like, with a little tea, a little music, and a little dancing. They have gambled long and wildly; the candles are burning low; they burn up the daylight, as the saying goes, although it is a winter's day. One of the tables has its cards scattered on the ground; the Pandectae[1] of Whist,

[1] Complete compendium of Roman Civil Law made by Justinian. Ed.

Marriage-à-la-Mode Plate II

'Hoyle on Whist', have been trampled underfoot, and perhaps that chair with its costly woodwork—the violins—was also thrown over during some turmoil in this darkish corner. For apart from the glimmering light of the coal fire and the rather distant glow of the candelabra, there was no special illumination here, evidently with intention. At any rate, the two candles near the clock have not been lit. An excellent touch it seems to me! A few unlit candles on each candelabra would have provided sufficient evidence of how little the people here cared for enlightenment; that in addition we find the unburnt candles near the clock shows how little they cared for time either. Indeed, the proper time for the deeds of twilight as well as of darkness can be found without any clock; or if one needed to use a clock, it would be at a time when neither hands nor dial were visible.

The young lady is thus very, very tired; she shows it by certain gestures in which there is indeed very little breeding or, if there is any at all, it is very, very half-baked. She stretches a little, or, as they say in some parts, she threatens her spouse with the sign of the horns. She is certainly healthy, perhaps too healthy. Even the sleepy expression is not without force and indicates, like her whole attitude, a surplus of everything in which her poor husband is so sadly lacking. It appears she has slept a little, in the chair, and is soon going to sleep again if the conversation between her and her beloved is to continue with the same vivacity with which it began. What the little empty box or étui in her hand signifies is not easy to say. If there were a little mirror in the lid, then the matter—and greatly to her credit—would not be difficult to decide. It would obviously mean that on waking up she was fulfilling one of the primary obligations, I mean the duty of self-examination; that her face has passed that examination fairly well may then be clearly inferred from the placid stretching which immediately followed.

She has breakfast in front of her. It is, as one sees—and how could it be otherwise after such a matrimonial night?—laid and meant for one. If only the lady were too! With such a husband one might perhaps forgive her a night like the last. But with those folds in her gown which no longer lie as they did on her wedding day, and which, alas!, on account of the new shoot on William the Conqueror's family tree *can* no longer lie like that— to carry on with cards, violins, and Pandectae till the early hours of the morning, Madam, that was really not nice, no matter how fashionable.

The gentleman, too, has just had his breakfast. It must have tasted abominably, for the old steward who had brought it in is carrying it away again completely untouched. It consisted of a sheaf of bills which were due to be paid that morning, and of which only one is receipted, and that is dated June 4th,[1] whereas now it is obviously winter. The paid one is signed and hangs on the steward's file. It was, of course, a nasty bit to swallow, and yet these were but little pieces of bread and butter compared with the loaf which he carries under his arm—the ledger. That can hardly have been even sniffed at this morning. To try to comment on the steward's head and the meaning of his expression and the gesture of his hand in words would surely be the most unforgivable misuse of alphabetic writing that could possibly be perpetrated. This is not what printing type was meant for in the world. The most scrupulous preparation of footnotes, according to their two great divisions, would come to grief with a text like this: not only those which expound in order to help understanding, but also the much more learned ones whose aim is to hinder understanding. If I were to say, 'Look, that's how it stands with his Lordship's finances', and pointed at that household god there, would anybody still ask, 'but what is the real state of his Lordship's finances?' Not a soul, to be sure— at least, not between Cape St Vincent and Nova Zembla.[2] Conversely, that head is meant to help us in our interpretation of the rest, and we therefore count confidently in advance upon our readers' indulgence if, perhaps, in some of the following passages, nothing more is said by way of explanation but: *videatur* the Steward!

But although the meaning of that face needs no words, the man's history requires a few. The face is said to be the portrait of a certain Edward Swallow, an old honest wine-steward of the then Archbishop of Canterbury. Hogarth, who was at that time in search of a model for the steward's head, had long been minded to fix on that one, on account of its honest simplicity. At last a friend of the Archbishop took Hogarth to Lambeth. There the painter sketched him unobserved and as he re-entered his carriage he whispered to his companion, 'Now I have him!' The square-toed shoes, the old-fashioned coat, the uncurled hair, all indicate that the man does not belong to this world, and least of all the world to which nine-tenths of the English servants of such homes now belong. He appears to be a Methodist, at least that is what Hogarth has made of him, perhaps

[1] Not the 4th of January as Mr Ireland read it.
[2] Novaja Zemlija. Ed.

out of mischievousness, for out of his pocket peeps a book *On Regeneration*, and, as is well known, the word regeneration is the permanent pass-word of that spiritual Corps. Moreover, discussions on the subject form a pious occupation in many of their gatherings, a sort of spiritual whist, and in this way Hoyle and Whitfield[1] come very well into the picture here together—*Pagina iungit amicos*. But the sly rogue, which Mr Ireland sees in that figure, I am quite unable to discover. It would have been easy enough for Hogarth to find the appropriate physiognomy for such a character, and it is my firm conviction that the old and therefore tried domestics of an Archbishop of Canterbury will be surely the last class of humanity, not only in England but perhaps in the world, where a painter would think of finding rogue physiognomies.

Behind there, in the temple of the aristocratic Bacchante, among the candles which, as we remarked, are burning the daylight, there seems to be one which has run its course and is in the act of setting fire to the chair-back. It is really already alight. The matter could become serious. But fortunately another chair-back, against which a servant has dozed off while standing, becomes aware of the catastrophe, threatens to throw off its rider, and in this way will probably be the saving of its brother. The young fellow rubs and scratches head and breast to rouse himself, and does everything a low-grade domestic can do. For that is all he is; the properly uniformed ministry is still asleep.

The pictures in the drawing-room are not fearful and sanguinary as those in the betrothal room; on the contrary, they aim at pure, cold-blooded edification. Most of them represent saints with their haloes. Although it is not possible to see the halo of the fourth on account of the lights in front, we can assume its presence from the rest of the company and the uniform frames. Mr Ireland takes them to be the Four Evangelists. Now this is just what they are not. The central figure of the three is evidently Saint Andrew with the cross of his name, while the figure hanging on his right is a she-saint, perhaps a Madonna with a chalice, and the fourth holds a sword in his hand. What use would a sword be to an Evangelist? One does not write gospels with a sword in one's fist; one only interprets them with it, and that is a more recent innovation. The most sacred figure among them all appears to be the one of which the curtain permits us to see only the little naked foot. What a pity! Had we come earlier, when the young

[1] A notorious Methodist preacher.

99

gentlemen were still here, we could have seen everything. Oh! Madam, Madam!

Just as our artist has indicated, through the lascivious contrast in the pictures of the drawing-room, the moral principles of our young couple, so he shows us now their aesthetic principles in the decoration of the ante-room. This is a point which ought not to be overlooked, especially in these Plates. For Hogarth has, with great delicacy and wherever he could, tried to expose the complete lack of feeling for beauty and art in these two families, especially in the aristocratic one. It must have been his intention to show how much better it would have been for this house had the taste of its owner been a little better formed in his youth. It cannot be denied that at least the blunders on a grand scale which are a source of misfortune within the family and, according to the perpetrator's calibre, for whole countries, proceed as a rule from people who combine with great fortune or great power a complete lack of feeling for beauty, except perhaps in women.

The whole mantelpiece here is covered with the most abominable works of art from north-east Asia: Chinese gods, apparently in an advanced state of pregnancy, sit there naked so that the folds of their garments should not come out of crease. Others have their hands outstretched from their shoulders, wanting to make the sign of the horns but unable to. Vases stiff as railings and little bottles dumpy as corks alternate with curious objects of nature and with artefacts such as chance will sometimes produce. Most ludicrous of all is an antique bust. It is a pity that its head is new and the nose still newer than the head. It must have been bought for a Faustina.[1] On the whole there reigns among this junk an admirable symmetry and the most meticulous order. Every little bottle has its counter-bottle, and every freak its freak to match. This seems to be the most orderly spot in the house. As one sees, they are quite capable of keeping order under that roof when it suits them, and when it does not suit the object. The picture on the overmantle represents a Cupid who has had a miserable fate, or at least has it now. His temple has collapsed, his bow has no string and his quiver no arrows; nothing remains for him but the bagpipes and the pipe upon which he now fingers his monotonous lament.

No matter how ridiculous the clock looks up there, with its fishes in the

[1] The wife of Marcus Aurelius, suspected of unfaithfulness by ancient writers. Ed.

trees and its cat among the fishes, it is possibly not only the greatest work of art in the room, but even the greatest masterpiece of the clockmaker's art. I believe, in fact, that we may conclude from the solemn position of the cat, which seems to do nothing but just sit there idly, that the clock is a cat-clock which mee-ows the hours just as there are cuckoo-clocks which cuckoo them. A clock upon which a very finely carved dog barks the hours has, as a friend of mine writes, been offered for sale by an Englishman not long ago, and at a very high price. This gives not a little support to my assumption. But Lord Squanderfield's clock exceeds that one by far, especially if one considers that the quarters might perhaps be mee-owed in a different tone, or even by kittens. From what I hear, a pupil of Le Droz[1] is said to be even now employed in constructing a clock on which a wild boar grunts the hours in short snorts. Probably he had the idea from the celebrated Pig Concert of the conductor Pepusch[2] in Berlin, in which the voices of the pigs were blown on bassoons as *porco primo, porco secundo*, and which earned such resounding applause.

The eighteenth century has thus given us, among many other novel inventions, a menagerie of clocks under which we shall surely sleep more merrily in future than with the eternal *memento mori* stroke of our tolling bells, which properly belong on steeples. The two fishes look to me as if they too were stuck in a wave which is connected with the clock. Who knows whether they may not make their hourly carp-jump as well? It would be a delightful idea, and all the more remarkable in that it takes place in the tree-tops—an event only rarely indeed encountered in Nature.

[1] Either the clockmaker and ingenious inventor Pierre Jacquet Droz (1721–90) who worked on an astronomical clock, or his son Henri Louis Jacquet Droz (1752–91), who also constructed clocks and curious mechanical toys, and had set up an establishment in London. Ed.

[2] J. Chr. Pepusch (1667–1752), German composer. Ed.

III

LORD ORFORD,[1] in Part VI of his *Anecdotes of Painting in England,* where he speaks about our artist, affirms that the main idea in his work was always comprehensible. True as this is for by far the greater part of his engravings, it does not quite apply to the present one. There are, if I am not mistaken, no less than five different interpretations of this scene. This circumstance alone would be sufficient evidence of its obscurity, but an anecdote which Mr Ireland quotes to the same end is too remarkable to be omitted here. On some occasion when the well-known poet Churchill[2] was asked about the meaning of this engraving, he confessed that it had always seemed to him so ambiguous that one day he had asked the artist himself for an explanation, but he, like many another commentator, had left it as obscure as it had been before. 'And I am therefore,' proceeded the poet, 'quite convinced that he based his tale upon an idea of Hoadley, Garrick, Townley, or some other friend, and never rightly understood himself what it meant.' In this remark one can sense the cynic's bitterness. Mr Ireland further comments, in connection with the story, that this opinion of Churchill's was given at a time when the unfortunate quarrel between him and Hogarth had already broken out.[3] It may happen, though, to

[1] The title to which Horace Walpole succeeded. His *Anecdotes* were published in 1771.

[2] Charles Churchill (1731–64), a satirical poet, as famous in his day as Pope, known especially for his long poem 'The Rosciad' criticizing the actors and actresses of that time, and for his feud with Hogarth (see *Epistle to Hogarth,* July 1763). Ed.

[3] Unfortunate that quarrel certainly was, for it accelerated Hogarth's death. The notorious Wilkes, his bosom friend Churchill, and Hogarth were good friends until Hogarth had the idea of dabbling in politics and of attacking his friends' party with his stylus. Had it been done with

Marriage-à-la-Mode Plate III

the most honest man that in a fit of philosophical penetration or poetical inspiration, especially just before Mass, he will write something which he himself no longer understands when Mass is over. These are the lightning flashes of genius, and lightning does not take aim; nor do flashes of genius, any more than natural storms—especially thunder without lightning—leave any trace, either in the element from which they come, or in that into which they go. But a work of art like this one is not just flashed on to the canvas by a single *coup de main*. Each separate line of the attack must be planned and visualized before it is executed, and afterwards it must undergo still more aiming and planning, for days, even weeks, and it would be a queer thing indeed if the besieger were not to see what he wanted to take by storm. Hogarth certainly saw it, and saw it clearly. We shall now see whether we cannot indicate, by a few slowly convergent straight lines, the proper direction of his manifold ordnance, and thus the position of the main targets. We shall not prolong these lines as far as their meeting points; our paper is too small for that. We therefore beg the indulgent reader to transfer them from here on to a somewhat larger canvas and then apply his own ruler to them, and everything else will come by itself. And, after thus reducing the solution of the problem to a mere linear plan, we can, I think, afford to be brief.

It has already been hinted several times, and fairly distinctly, that the young Viscount was neither quite healthy nor otherwise quite *comme-il-faut*. But all this was mere rumour. There was mention of a plaster behind the left ear and of some muslin and ribbon in his pocket and so on. But here we obtain reliable official confirmation that all is really so and, so to speak, straight from the Viscount's own mouth.

We see him here in the consulting room of a certain Monsieur de la Pillule, a French doctor who specializes in that type of disease which the linguistic usage of all nations has made a co-national of Monsieur le

the wit and esprit which pervades his other work, it could have proved a very dangerous weapon. But his engraving 'The Times' is a very mediocre allegory. Wilkes then attacked him in a Number of his *North Britain* (No. 17), and when Hogarth produced a caricature of his adversary, he brought on himself Churchill's famous *Epistle to Hogarth*. Hogarth in turn portrayed his friend in copper in the guise of a bear with a jar of porter and a joint, but all this did not heal the wounds he had received. His adversaries were superior to him and his satire this time had public opinion against it, although Churchill's poem is not among his best works. Lord Orford correctly judged the controversy when he said, 'Never did two angry men of their abilities throw mud with less dexterity.'

Docteur, and which is probably treated by him, on account of that relation-ship, with profitable care and leniency. His name we learn from a copy of the impressive tome which lies open there on his right, and the success of his practice can be inferred from the whole appearance of the elegant room with its vaulted window overlooking the street, and from what is loudly proclaimed not by architecture alone but by all the realms of art and nature on the walls.

Presumably this is also the establishment where our hero was stamped behind the ear. Together with the poor immature creature who stands on his left, he has just arrived at Monsieur de la Pillule's, to whom he has also invited, or brought along, the more than mature witch on his right. Now the quarrel develops, the cause of which is as follows: his Lordship has hired the little creature from the old woman's educational institute, to serve as companion in his extra-domestic household, for an indefinite time and at a high price. For this, the Mother Superior of that Nunnery guarantees in her novices immature youthfulness, innocence, complete ignorance of gallicism of any kind, and therefore complete security. The last item was very necessary on account of his domestic household, and the immaturity was really made an explicit condition, mainly because of fashion, but partly also because of the increased security. And in this, alas! his Lordship found himself miserably and quite irreparably damaged. He is surely within his rights, for the old hag, instead of remonstrance, immediately draws her pocket knife against the defamer of her institute. But he, for his part, is about to produce an argument against which the mere tongue-wagging of the procuress will be powerless. The young and candid creature has, in fact, confessed to him herself that she has used the doctor's pills before, and is still using them. They have therefore brought the whole supply with them to lay here before the tribunal. His Lordship holds a little box open in his hand, and shows it to the quack, who is perhaps one of the girl's underwriters, probably with some such words as these: 'Look here, Monsieur, are not these the self-same pills which I've already taken myself more than a hundred times?' He may be presenting them also to the Mother Superior: 'Aren't these the cough lozenges which you provide for your nuns?'

I believe this is the simplest solution of the puzzle, because it also ex-plains the expression on the face of the poor victim, in which predominates an eloquent fear of the old dragon, and of the castigation awaiting her in the nunnery for telling tales. The supply of pills was not negligible, since the child has another little box in her hand, if it is not the lid of the open one, and yet another lies on the chair in front of his Lordship, from which it would certainly fall were it not that the angle formed by his Lordship's thighs had made a suitable resting place for it. That his Lordship has sat down for the poor creature's sake, as if to put himself on a level with her, and even takes her between his legs, is a very subtle and striking touch of our artist's. It shows how small, childish, and in need of help the little creature appears, even in the eyes of a good-for-nothing. Had he been a sincere defender or avenger of innocence, surely that position in itself would have secured him the spectator's affection. As it is, it only increases our horror of the disgusting, brutish voluptuary. It seems unlikely that he raises his Spanish cane to administer a real thrashing— he only brandishes it a little so as to give the ironic amiability of his face and the light mockery of his words the proper cudgel-like solidity, by which alone it is possible to make oneself understood in such society. The Mother Superior's defence with the knife cannot be of any special consequence. Nothing more comes of it. Probably Monsieur de la Pillule interposed with the volubility that belongs to his nation as well as his profession. This would be quite in his line; a main ingredient of pills like his was always the gilt of oratory: it would thus not be difficult for him who had concluded so many more difficult peace treaties between ego and non-ego, in which this gilt was a main ingredient, to conclude one so easy as that between cane and pocket-knife, through the gilt alone.

Be that as it may, the pious dame now grasps her pocket-knife, just as her adversary the half-raised stick, as a stress accent for those who might still find anything equivocal in the expression of their faces. On her bosom can be seen the letters F.C., probably etched with gunpowder. If the English police had found it advisable to subdivide into companies the Light Regiment in which that piece of hussar had served forty years ago, then the letters might denote First Company; also Free Corps, or Filia Carissima—in the nunnery, that is; or if the kerchief covered the name of the founder, owner, or landlord, then they might also stand for the well-known Fieri Curavit or Faciendum curavit N.N. According to Dr Nichols, the letters stand for Fanny Cock, the daughter of an auctioneer named Cock with whom Hogarth had a quarrel. Whether he also had some quarrel with the daughter is not known; probably she herself had one with the public. But whatever the letters may mean, they are characteristic enough in this context, for among all London's pious dames, Mothers Superior and Prioresses, those with burnt or etched mottoes are the most infamous.

Now for a glance at Monsieur de la Pillule himself. It is to be hoped that the reader will be fully indemnified thereby for the nausea which the rest of the company may have caused him. It is impossible to look at this man, who either gilds everything he touches or turns it into money, without feeling a few years younger. Only look at his gold mouth! What a source of comfort, especially when he spouts broken English! And beneath it a nose which surely represents the most perfect saddle ever ridden by spectacles. Do our readers recollect perhaps a description which *Fabre d'Eglantine* has given of the blessed Marat?[1] *Oh, c'est Marat tout craché!* Even if a touch were missing here and there, no one could easily miss 'the eye, naturally gentle, even charming, and yet penetrating, the short thighs and the bow legs' of Marat. If the wig was only perched a little more to one side, I should believe it was Marat himself drawn immediately after the box on the ear which led to his theory of light.[2] He wipes his spectacles for the inspection of the *corpus delicti*, which he can hardly avoid doing. Upon his table lies a book which has the appearance of being clasped by a somewhat curious skull that had evidently in life been gnawed by the compatriot disease. It is permissible to draw conclusions from such a padlock about the contents of the jewel box; there must be something of the *momento mori* in it. In that case, it could either contain the mysteries of the doctor's poison-brewing art, or it might be the book of life in which he enters the names and the debts of the blessed cured.

Opposite that closed book, at the other side of the consulting room, lies an open one. An arrangement like that is almost reminiscent of the

---

[1] The description is in Herrn von Archenholz' *Minerva*, April 1794, p. 12 f. The words below in inverted commas are taken from that description.

[2] Marat who, as is well known, bungled in medicine and physics before he took to politics, one day read a paper on physics before a learned society, which was criticised by one of those present. Marat took this in so bad part that after leaving the lecture-room he attacked his unarmed opponent in the street with his sword (here one already sees the future statesman). The man, however, who must have been just as brave in a fight as he was learned in discussion, grasped Marat's sword with one hand and with the other gave him such a stout blow on the head that he staggered away; and this, it is said, led him to invent his theory of light.

German promotion ceremony for the Doctor's Degree at which, as is well-known, the candidate is recommended in a fatherly but serious manner to apply himself not only to the opening of books but to their shutting as well, at the proper time. In France, however, to the best of my knowledge, that custom is not in fashion; at least, there is nothing about it printed in the protocol of Doctor Molière. Moreover, the open book of our Doctor is his own work, and in any learned establishment such books surely open by themselves. The full title of the work, which consists of two moderately sized volumes, is as follows: *Explication de deux machines superbes, l'une pour remettre les épaules, l'autre pour servir de tire-bouchon, inventées par Monsr de la Pillule. Vues et approuvées par l'Académie Royale des Sciences à Paris.* Thus it is a description of two machines, one of which serves to set dislocated shoulders, the other to pull corks out of bottles, both examined by the Royal Academy of Sciences at Paris, and approved forthwith. That means something. Such an honour is only shown by the Academy of Sciences to people whose value is already established. If he is a poor unknown devil, they will either examine his work stringently, or, if there is no time for this, they will only glance at it and reject it. From the appearance of both machines which Hogarth shows us here, the verdict of the Academy appears completely justified. One need only look at them to approve of that. In the first volume, as we just read in an old review, the author shows the use of the machine for dislocated shoulders: he explains how the patient is to be properly strapped on, made rigid, and screwed down. By one of the springs which we see here, the end of a napkin gathered into a ball is pressed into his mouth, and as the tension and therefore the pain increases, more and more of the napkin is intruded, so that the patient is completely prevented from crying out. Upon the great jagged pole at the back is fixed a very finely adjusted measuring scale which he calls *points de démembrement*. If now the machine is set at the proper point, depending upon the age and strength of the patient, one may boldly wind like an organ-grinder without fear that the patient will be torn apart, since before this could happen the great hook (a sort of lock) will fall into the third wheel, and stop the machine, and the patient remains whole. One more revolution and the patient is torn apart (*démembrement*); hence the name of the measuring scale.

In the second volume, the author shows how the machine could easily be used for uprooting old stumps of oak trees, and even raises the hope that it might serve for restoring leaning steeples to their proper elevation. Very modestly, almost like Archimedes, he requires for this only a little spot of earth on which to stand. But vigorously and strongly though it performs one of its functions, so gently and tenderly, one might almost say kindly, does it perform another. For he claims to have extracted with it the teeth of personages of high rank, even the corks of the bottles on their dinner tables. The part which serves for drawing corks he has worked on specially, so that it can be separated from the rest and used by itself, and this is the marvellous idea which we see materialized there on the floor.

Although it is evident that Hogarth has displayed all this here *in majoram gloriam* of the noble simplicity of the medical art in general, and of French surgery in particular, which, as he intimates, is capable of dispelling diseases of all kinds without much ado, whether rooted like oak trees or sitting lightly like corks, the downy bird still cannot suppress his mockery of the venerable de la Pillule. He has carried this so far that with the best will in the world to think the opposite, we are inclined to believe that Hogarth's sole intention with all that machinery was to indicate that Monsieur de la Pillule was a charlatan and a shark who made preparations for cutting nails as if for amputating a thigh, and afterwards, in the Book of Life, entered his charges accordingly. One need only look at the cupboard with the glass doors over there; that sort of thing could not possibly be meant as a recommendation. On top of it we see a rather curious tripod. It is hardly the tripod of *Pythia*, although the whole shelf looks like an antique shop. It seems rather to be a tripod of another sort, from which, instead of the unknown being foretold as at Delphi, something well known is proclaimed. Yes, it is quite certainly the sort of tripod whose sight has comforted many a poor traveller in Germany whom some landlord has despoiled of half his purse; he sees that on the highway, at least, he need not worry about the other half. It is the well-known legal tripod—the gallows. It hovers here like a halo or a coronet above three figures which represent man, and more especially the laboratory of his thought, like the three layers of an onion—the skeleton, the skin, and the wig. Unfortunately, the noblest layer, the wig, is none other than our doctor's. That it sits here upon a somewhat more beautiful carving makes no difference. From the outside he might really have looked like that in earlier years, and from the inside they still probably resemble each other.

The group would bear more than one explanation to be sure, but none would be able to explain our doctor away from beneath the gallows. The naked figure, it is believed, might be a patient, and the other two, doctors in consultation, one of whom is our doctor here, and the other the famous *medicinae practicus* of whose humane behaviour Horace sings as truly as beautifully,

Aequo pulsat pede pauperum tabernas
Regumque turres.

The latter, though, does as if he were angry with the former, but only because the patient is listening; fundamentally, both are making common cause. Or, one might be already in bliss, and has come to succour the other who is not yet quite so far gone: 'Are you going to "cure" him to a skeleton as you did me, you scoundrel?' Or both might have been hanged, one dried honestly in chains, the other dishonestly dissected, for which he is making the bitterest reproaches to the Faculty. 'It's still a question,' he says, 'which of us two is the more [de]pendable, you or I.'[1] Or they may represent a *Concilium medicum* in general. In a word, one sees that the three-leaved clover in the cupboard is a gallows-pendant, and our doctor the 'pendant' (in the metaphorical sense of the word) to the skeleton.

The laboratory at the back seems to be a mere show-piece—a chemical kitchen in which no cooking is ever done.[2] The glass apparatus in it apparently serves the same purpose for the doctor's pills as the oak tree extractor does for his corks. He himself does not draw his corks in this way, nor does he make his pills in that. Everything here has been chosen, not for its necessity and usefulness, but to impress with its splendour and pomp, together with a dash of terror. Quacks are good at that. They know that without window-dressing the masses cannot be served with physical or spiritual food, nor with the foods of the chemist's shop either, which are something between the two.

[1] What the situation in London is like with these graduate claimants to the gallows may be seen from recent newspapers. In a number of the *Hamburg Correspondent* in April of this year (1797) there is a report from London, whether meant as satire or in earnest is not clear, that one of the two English Universities had set a Prize Problem, whether in England as many people die through the Quacks (in the same time, of course) as in France some years ago by the Guillotine.

[2] In the decoration of model kitchens they have even gone so far in a famous German town as to have the firewood consist of beautifully planed and colourfully dyed logs, which were even mounted with brass at either end, always carefully polished for Festivals.

On the wall above the cupboard hangs a whole encyclopaedia of show-pieces of every kind, evidently intended to inspire his patients with feelings of awe or perhaps to afford them some preliminary entertainment until the doctor had made up his mind on the appropriate final jibber-jabber. It is a well-established fact that many people can talk, if not very well, at least tolerably, on matters of which they understand nothing, provided they are allowed, for the fortification of their inner confidence as well as the increased energy of their jaws, a little time to dwell on things which are familiar to them, and of which the listener understands nothing. As such a running start to the main objective, the collection up there is not at all badly designed. For there will hardly be a soul except the owner who would understand all the little object lessons hanging up there. Beauty is hardly represented, but rather the great and the sublime. The collection begins on the left with a huge narwhal's tooth which, if seen as a horn growing out of the procuress's head, adds not a little to the fury in her face. But this is not the meaning of it, at least not the only one. That is still to come. Then there follow a few bricks, probably baked more than 2,000 years ago, a barber's basin, shaped like *Mambrin's* helmet, a urine bottle evidently for the reception of some *aqua regia* of pre-history; giant bones, giant children's heads with small pipes or tubes to emit smoke and fire, gigantic combs against gigantic pests, and between these colossal magnifications of the small stands the colossal diminution of one of the most uplifting objects in the civilized world. Next to it hangs—once antiquated but now again the dernier cri—the high-crowned hat; more properly the felt knock-and-shock absorber. That is why it is left partly empty. That emptiness extends, when even the best heads are stuck into it, to at least half the height, with others to two-thirds and over, and, occasionally, according to the kind of heads, to the whole. Then follow the insignia of nobility, the spur, the shield and the lance of youth and the slippers of old age; two crocodiles, one with amputated legs and an ostrich egg, since no better was available, and the other with a chain on its lower jaw; finally, a monster and an insect almost too big and too many-legged for the giant comb.

Whether Hogarth had a purpose in displaying just these relics is difficult to decide; but it is quite possible, even if we regard the whole cabinet as a perfect general satire upon certain collectors of all the rubbish of Nature and Art. For nobody understood better than he the art of adding, with inimitable roguery, to what is of general appeal in his art some other ingredients which would only act with full force upon such individuals as would be specially sensitive to it, by reason of some hidden defect. A touch of this sort is to be found here, one which hits at the learned descent of our Monsieur de la Pillule. He has had the unfortunate idea of putting up his narwhal's tooth at a slant, thus transforming it into the generally recognized shop-sign of the barber (the barber's pole),[1] and then, an untoward fate caused him to place *Mambrin's* helmet, the barber's basin, and the urine bottle so close to the pole that through that hieroglyph the well-stocked room of Monsieur de la Pillule becomes a barber's shop and he himself a urine-wise barber, who could only jabber about medicine.

Thus the doctor's collection may perhaps be interpreted partly historically, partly prophetically, indicating his life-history as follows: he began as a barber, then became a urine diviner, surreptitiously gained the doctor's hat soon afterwards through his cures, though just missing the gallows by a hair's breadth, and now even reckons upon a knighthood, if he has not won it already.

The two pictures hanging on the left wall of the room represent two monsters, one of which has both arms growing out of its head. It is perhaps, as Mr Ireland believes, one of Sir John Mandeville's cannibals:

> Whose heads
> Do grow beneath their shoulders.

Its arms hang down in the painting like the ornamental wings of the noblest type of wig. The other monster has, without a trace of further reduplication, simply two heads. If these creatures really existed, which I do not doubt, we can only regard them as some well-meant attempts on the part of Nature to give the writer's profession a better foundation at last. The two ways in which this purpose could be quickly achieved are obvious: either each writer should be given two heads, one for the daily domesticities, for smoking, taking snuff, compilation and mystification, and another for solemn thought, for the uninterrupted acquisition of knowledge and for writing proper; or if, as hitherto, everything has to be accomplished by a single head, then such an important instrument for the

---

[1] In England, barbers in general advertise their shops by such poles or lances. On the fourth Plate of 'The Times of the Day' (Night) a barber's shop is shown with just such a pole. German barbers attract their customers with a barber's dish; English ones with a lancet.

writing of books as the arm with its hand should not be suspended from the shoulder, but rather from the head itself. Why this beautiful project has not materialized I do not know. Perhaps the booksellers were against it.

On the right, over the door leading to the kitchen, hangs another picture; also a monster. It is not clearly visible; however, from the brazenness with which it presents itself, that is, from the extended legs and out-stretched arms, we may conclude that it must have something curious to show. Having taken a great deal of trouble with this creature, I believe I have found that it represents a new variety of *Janus bifrons*, that is, one in whom the positive and negative front, I mean the face and the seat, lie on one and the same side, and who thus, wherever he turns, be it to the past or the future, not only looks at people, but shows them something too. For it is clear that with this creature, the navel does not appear on the same side as the face, from which it naturally follows that whatever as a rule is not on the side of the face must here appear on it. That the Janus of ancient Rome, before he shut himself in at the conclusion of peace, never showed himself to the people like that, is pretty certain. But what he did or ought to have done in modern Rome before he recently shut the temple door there cannot be determined.

If somebody wanted to draw the life-line of Monsieur de la Pillule through this fifth point also, I would suggest his considering whether the picture cannot be interpreted as the dog-like fawning and flattery of that class of human beings; for my readers are aware that some little dogs do not know how to make their masters a greater compliment than to approach them wriggling like snakes and showing them, just like that picture at the conclusion of peace, both fronts simultaneously.

Above the quite sizeable medicine chest on the left, a terrible hyena head, or whatever it is, threatens with destruction anyone who comes near it. Certainly a very telling symbol for the poison chest above which it hangs; a proper *noli me tangere*, keep away from me! Or it portends cannibalism. From this viewpoint, the head would fit in very well with Sir John Mandeville's cannibals. Of course, Monsieur le Docteur will interpret it quite differently by pointing to the diseases which have found their inevitable end in his jars and boxes.

Next to the poison chest Hogarth has excellently, it seems to me, placed two mummies. Out of their infinite security and after their thousand years' truce with the healing faculty, they look down, evidently with proud contemptuous looks, on all the quack turmoil and the drug trash of this world; which one can do if one is—a mummy.

The doctor's overcoat and hat, thrown upon the floor, are evidence of his activity, his haste to save life, and his great practice.

IV

IT is well known that in some ladies' calendars the longest days in the year are just those which are followed by a night of dancing. Oh! those hours! So long, so long! It is as if a stroke had paralysed the hands of the clock and time itself. There is no dealing with the sun; night will not come! It is just such a day in this picture; indeed the hours are even longer here, for there is to be not only a ball, but—a Masked Ball! If therefore some remedy could not be devised, time would not move at all. Lady Squanderfield has accordingly summoned everything to her aid, so as to make time feel the spur and compel it, if not to a fast trot, at least to the regulation police walk which she herself adopts on days when the following night is to be for sleep. One therefore rose this morning *numero rotundo* at ten, breakfasted till about eleven, rushed afterwards in a light, fetching dress to a saleroom to 'fetch' the dandies (here, the rumour goes, time actually moved apace), wounded a few gentlemen, acquired a few modern antiques which are strewn here on the floor, and so returned home. This brought the hour hand quite considerably beyond its zenith through the descending numerals.[1] But there are still three or four hours until dinner, and for a healthy idler those are the most stubborn and heavy-footed of the whole morning because, for someone with a good digestion, dinner is said to have just such a prolonging effect upon time as have ball nights

[1] This expression can, of course, only be used of clocks hanging on the wall or standing or in a tower. For with watches it can suddenly happen, even if they are properly kept in the pocket, that at least some of the ascending numbers are changed into descending ones and vice versa, very much to the disadvantage of the man who carries them, a sad example of which we shall see in the next Plate.

Marriage-à-la-Mode Plate IV

upon the time of somebody who loves dancing. Lady Squanderfield has a remedy for this, too. And what is it? It forms the content of the fourth picture.

She is holding her levee here, and in a style wherein are tastefully combined the dignity of the Earl's wife and the familiarity and condescension of the commoner. She accepts confidential morning visits in her bedroom; like a lady she has her hair dressed, and like a duchess gives a concert, small to be sure if one only counts the number of performers, but were they to be weighed on the scales of art or those of the goldsmith, very great and very costly. For to remark in passing, the singer is the famous eunuch, Carestini, and the flautist the renowned Weidermann, a German and a genuine man. It is a *Privatissimum*. That is going to cost a pretty penny! I refer here to the housekeeping book and the pious expression of the righteous steward in the second Plate.

The lady herself sits by the unveiled mirror, under the hands of her hairdresser, robed in a powder-mantle for the chaste draping of—the chair-back. Of the inner strife which we noticed on her brow in the first picture there is no longer any trace. In addition, all the rust of the city seems to have been polished off, and all the awkwardness which stuck to her from boarding-school has been cultivated away. We notice rather, and not without pleasure, a certain ease in her person, evidently a consequence of pleasing visions from the past or of the future. Oh! if only domestic happiness, and especially the event of which we see a very telling symbol hanging from the chair-back, had a greater part in it! It is a silver rattle with a teething coral which is hanging there; the lady is a mother! But alas! alas! not a trace of motherly feelings; all capacity for that has long been—cultivated away! If we try to imagine the source of the contentedness in that little sugar-face, we could hardly avoid pulling a long face—like the steward. Of the duet which is proceeding over there from Weidermann's flute and Carestini's little golden mouth, she hears nothing, or almost nothing. She listens simply and solely to the enchanting solo of her beloved lawyer, Silvertongue, who there in her own bedroom is lolling on the sofa opposite her, with oriental, effeminate indolence, as if in a harem. In his right hand he holds a ticket for today's Masked Ball, which he offers or actually hands to the lady.[1]

[1] This, at least, is the interpretation of all who went into the question, and I am not sufficiently familiar with the form of such tickets to contradict them outright; but it does not

What Mr Silvertongue is discussing here is a proposal that they should meet that evening, if possible, at the masquerade. This is sufficiently apparent from the lawyer's pointing to the Spanish screen where a fancy dress ball is depicted; but it acquires certainty from the fifth picture where we shall find that they have in fact met at a Masked Ball. It looks as if he were pointing particularly at a nun who in the foreground there is confessing to a monk, and as if he were recommending that disguise to the lady for their common devotions that evening. They were to be monk and nun. This is a very natural conjecture which should not be entirely disregarded, but it does not seem to me justified. The main indication would have to be by mouth; with the hand it could only be imperfectly made, especially considering the direction in which the Countess is looking. The pointing gesture is rather vague.[1] In the picture which follows we shall see some of the ball costumes. And there the lady's costume bears as little resemblance to a nun's as she herself to a saint. Trivial though this pointing gesture may appear here, it will prove important enough for poor Silvertongue; it implicates, in fact, nothing less than a nail for his—gallows.

By his feet lies a book with the title *Sofa*. I do not know of a single

seem to me very probable. In the first place, the paper is not the right size for a ticket—those for concerts, at least, look quite different; and, secondly, it is evidently torn. Who in the world would present his lady, even if she were no countess, with such a rag of a ticket? Could it not have been plastered up on some street corner from which Mr Silvertongue has somewhat rudely removed it in order to refer to it for the date? Thus it would seem to be more of an advertisement than a ticket. Lawyers love documents and bits of paper, and orators have always been distinguished by the scroll in their hand. The words, '1 door', '2 door', '3 door', seem to refer to the buffets and the various prices of admission to them. What, however, the scribbles on the paper are supposed to mean, I absolutely cannot understand, nor can my English friends whom I have asked. If they were perhaps the marks of dried mud, it would have meant that the poster while on the wall had experienced the just ill-will of the honest, often very rightly feeling and properly thinking John Bull who, as is well known, was opposed to the introduction of these frolics. But why has Hogarth put no other writing on the whole paper but '1 door', and so on? This can only be decided by people familiar with the customs of those days. To discover the true meaning of the paper with its dirt and fantastic scribble would certainly be of advantage to the satire embodied in this scene.

[1] It seems much more as if the paper has just been passed by the countess to the lawyer, with her left hand, as a sort of token of affection or intimacy, and that it is nothing else but one of those curl-papers which her hairdresser is just using. That would explain the look of sly surprise on the latter's face. The lawyer then, to whom evidently nothing is sacred, points to the holy couple as being the antithesis to themselves in that respect, since if there is one token of affection which one cannot imagine passing between a monk and a nun it is a curl-paper. Ed.

interpreter who mentions this detail with one word, and yet we may readily suppose that such a subtle and cunning man as Hogarth would never have taken the trouble to draw even a plain book, let alone one with that title, without some meaning and purpose. Now, the meaning is not hard to find; it has even a double one. The book is in fact the infamous, hot-blooded product of the pen of the younger Crébillon,[1] entitled *Le Sopha*; *conte morale*, and is just as suitable for a lady's library as gilded oak-apples or candied night-shade berries for a Christmas tree. The touch is thus highly characteristic and surpasses even the finest touches which our artist has brought into this picture for the same purpose. The Countess is an abandoned creature. This seems to be the chief meaning and one which the whole character of the Plate unmistakably confirms. But, apart from all this, there is a secondary, a more comic meaning, which lies somewhat deeper, and which Hogarth, who must have known the book, undoubtedly intends to indicate. It is as much justified by the character of our artist's genius, as the first meaning by the character of the whole picture. Crébillon's fairy story is based upon the following plot: Almazéi, a sort of courtier at the Court of the Shah Baham, who was once as a punishment transformed into a sofa, related afterwards what he saw and heard in this guise, and a sofa, as we know, may well see and hear a thing or two in this world. There were certain conditions for his transformation and restoration—he was free to choose any shape, any material, any colour, any border, any embroidery, that he fancied; he might serve whomsoever he pleased, but he must remain a sofa until he happened to be present at an event which, of course, in the higher regions of society may be as frequent as the great conjunction of all the planets in the region of the sky—namely, innocence to innocence mutually lost. It is upon this Almazéi that the lawyer here reclines, and upon which the Countess has this morning placed her Crébillon. Oh! shuffle away, poor Almazéi, on your four legs; in this house there is no redemption for you!

Behind the lady whose silken lap, as we forgot to mention, appears to serve here as an ornamental case for her watch, especially if viewed from the sofa, stands the hairdresser. He is evidently of that country from which the English, at least the higher strata, have long drawn their servants, in order to have their hair dressed and their stomachs spoilt—

[1] Claude-Prosper-Jolyot de Crébillon (1707–77), author of a number of somewhat licentious novels, among them *Le Sopha*, 1745. Ed.

coiffeurs and cooks, that is. They provide decoration and indigestion—
of the stomach, I must expressly state, for to summon them or their
recipes, to induce an indigestion of the head, is a new custom. In fine, the
creature is a Frenchman. Hogarth's engravings, as our readers will have
discovered by now, have their own symbols for Frenchmen, just as the
calendar for the quarters of the moon. For every landmark in their
path, which they travel or dance or crawl over the British horizon, they
have their special symbol. This fellow here is still one of the hollow,
hungry ones; he is still developing. He is seen here occupied with a pyro-
metric experiment; he breathes upon the curling tongs and listens to the
voice of the advocate and in addition gapes at the—chairback. To do only
one thing at a time is impossible for such a fellow. Despite his expression
—*un mouton qui rêve*—one can wager that he already knows more about
the Masked Ball and its implications than all the rest of the company.
Something might come of that observation, provided he makes use of it in
the proper quarters. This leads in a most natural way to a little remark
about barbers and hairdressers. It is incredible for what great purposes
Nature employs these otherwise unimportant creatures. Just as some
insects carry fertilizing pollen to flower cups, which without that service
would have remained sterile, so these people carry little family anecdotes
from ear to ear, to induce a love of humanity which without these inter-
mediaries would never have arisen. Or perhaps more appropriate: just
as certain birds carry undigested seed-grains to inaccessible heights for
the promotion of physical vegetation, so do these people, for the promotion of a certain kind of moral purpose, carry many a little anecdote-
grain from the lowest quarters of the town into its higher regions. There
really is a resemblance, and the whole difference lies in the trivial dis-
similarity between the organs with which each deposits the undigested
matter with the authority.

On the extreme left, richly decked and adorned with British gold,
British diamonds and British fat, negligently draping an arm over the
neighbouring chair, sits the eunuch, Carestini, said to be one of the loveliest little pipes which the knife of song has ever cut out of Italian cane.
But just look at him now! Merciful Heavens! What an abominable bagpipe does the masterpiece of creation become when Art presumes to carve
a flute out of him. The tallowy lower jaw has neither beard nor force. The
stiff cravat with its glittering diamond cross, the holy cross of the most

unholy,[1] are only a miserable substitute for that defect. The little mouth obtains thereby a certain pappy, sloppy insignificance, and if it rouses any feeling whatsoever in a grown-up person, it can only be the desire to hit it. How the fat has driven all form and elasticity out of those thick knees, and the whole leg-piece! Looking at those weak, wobbling lumps of legs, we might take them for the wind bag of a bagpipe, which has just devoted a good deal of its content to a trill of the first water. Oh! if congenital neutrality in sex, though still in possession of its weapons, is said, as I have heard, to plane away the most important characteristics of the human face and human behaviour, in the eyes of knowledgeable men and women, what in the world can a creature unarmed, or even deprived of its arms, produce but such an abomination of bag growling. An unlovely work of art, to be sure, but valuable all the same. The sleeves and hem of his garment are heavily encrusted with gold thread, while diamonds glitter on each finger joint, on knee- and shoe-buckles and on his ear. Merely to achieve a setting for his voice, he has done everything possible.

Behind him stands our countryman, Weidermann, the famous virtuoso on the German flute. If I am not much mistaken, there lurks in the corner of his right eye, as well as at the corner of his mouth, a sort of good-natured roguery which, taken together with his hawk nose, speaks in favour of his honesty. He seems to smile in the very act of playing. In a company where every face and every gesture is so rich in the ridiculous, it is difficult to say what he is smiling at, if we assume that he has in fact looked beyond the music. But Herr Weidermann's honour as a virtuoso compels us here to assume that he has never taken his eyes off it. In that case, however, nothing would remain to explain the smile except a private estimate of the costs of their respective instruments. 'How much money did I give for my flute, and what did the eunuch pay in cash value for his pipe?' There is no neutrality in Weidermann's expression.

Next to the fattened Italian capon sits the English domestic cock, desiccated in service; in their extremes of physique, one worth as little as the other. There have been many interpretations of that figure. Someone has even made a Prussian Ambassador Michel[2] out of it. Of course, many

---

[1] Pope, in his *Rape of the Lock*, says of Belinda's necklace:
  On her white neck a diamond cross she wore,
  Which Jews might kiss and infidels adore.
[2] L. alludes here to the 'Deutscher Michel' as a synonym for simpleton. Ed.

a Michel in this world may have looked like that, and may look like it in the future, but, according to all the rules of interpretation, this is certainly our hero, the Earl Squanderfield. If Hogarth himself were to reject this interpretation, he would have only himself to blame for being misunderstood. Of course, his Lordship appears thinner here than before, and what is still queerer, thinner than later that evening. But what does it matter? The dandy may have risen this morning but he is certainly not yet roused. He is still only a caterpillar. His head is already in the chrysalis state—the rest will follow, and before the dinner bell sounds the butterfly will appear in all its glory. These are only trivialities; after all, hips are neither here nor there. Since clothes have come to make the man, Nature has lost much of its custom. It is certainly a little malicious of our artist to serve up this half-transparent kipper together with the fattened Italian carp,[1] as if on one dish. For really the legs of his Lordship are by no means the straws which they seem to a superficial observer. One need only cover over the two bamboo posts of the Italian, whose propinquity is obviously harmful to his Lordship's, to see that the latter are still a pair of legs upon which a man of some standing, who neither stands nor walks very much, may still stand and walk quite passably. But what has Hogarth done? With unpardonable malice, he has intentionally covered over more than half of his Lordship's left leg with the left leg of the Italian. Is that right? Indeed, if to cover over shortcomings in this way is not worse than to discover them, then I do not know the meaning of cover and discover. By this method, of course, one could in a moment turn the stoutest walking-stick of the most up-to-date Parisian dandy, or even of Hercules himself, into a mere matchstick. Thus the whole argument against identifying the former and future Squanderfield with this creature here, which is based upon the feeble legs of the subject, itself stands upon very weak legs. Besides, for an artist of Hogarth's vitality and wit, it would be harder than for others not to exaggerate the contrast once he had hit upon the idea. Oh! the best-trained wit, ridden by Reason itself, may run away with its rider once such artistic jumps are made. Then one usually tells only half the truth, or else six quarters of it, which, *mutatis mutandis*, comes to very much the same thing. But now let us listen to the other side of the argument: it must be Earl Squanderfield, for, in the first place, he sits there *en papillotes*, just as his love, or rather his semi-wife, sits over there, not with her

[1] As is well known, carp, too, are castrated, but not to improve their voice.

120

husband but merely with her lover. He is waiting for the curling tongs of the Frenchman whom they both employ. Nobody but a husband has the right to have himself nipped in that way at a lady's levee. Thus they belong together, *serviliter* at least; they are married *à la mode*. Secondly, just look at the head: is not that a horned animal *tout entier*? And who in the wide world could fail to see it? Even the little black boy there in the right-hand corner notices it and points with his finger at the *papillotes* of a miniature Acteon which has just arrived from the auction. Yes, indeed! brother Acteon with his ten-branched antlers even seems to point with his stump of an arm at the member of his Order, Squanderfield, who has seven branches: 'Just look, isn't that one of ours too?' And the poor devil of a Lord really seems to have just recognized his little brother. Oh, he already feels a pinch in some part of his being! For who would sip chocolate, even the hottest, like that, if he were not burning somewhere else as well? At present, his eye probably sees as little as his ear hears or his tongue tastes; it is spiritual food which he consumes or tries to digest, perhaps a few paper sandwiches from his steward, and something of the amorous collation to which Almazéi is listening over there. He surely is the husband—*à la mode*.

Thirdly, what speaks very strongly in favour of this interpretation is the expression, and even the attire, especially if one compares it with the Squanderfield of the second Plate. He loves fancy coats.[1] Even at the scene of the catastrophe in the fifth Plate, he wears one of these, whose cut is however different from that in the second Plate. But, one might object, the *bon-ton* plaster behind the ear is missing. Answer: that is what happens to plasters in the night, and behind the ear there really is something discernible which might well have deserved a one inch *bon-ton* plaster. It is also the first time that our hero has favoured us with his right ear; it was always the left that we saw. That an evil which is usually symmetrical should have thus broken the rule for once would, in this household at least (with the exception perhaps of the mantelpiece ornaments in the second Plate), be precisely in order. A stronger objection is one which I have raised myself: this gentleman has, if else I see aright, a hat with a cockade under his arm, which, according to English custom, would be an officer's

[1] The broad ribbons, especially those with little pom-poms, were called Brandenburgs in England, if I am right. Perhaps they had been introduced by some Prussian Ambassador, and from this arises the conjecture that this figure was, in fact, a Prussian Ambassador.

hat. His Lordship is not an officer, to be sure, but how if last night his Lordship has perhaps acted the officer, and has only just returned home, as the other day, or that in the confusion he has made an acquisition just as he did before? My readers may take their choice here, if they find it worth their while. Perhaps their choice will be made easier by the consideration that our hero might also have been brought into such close contact with the Italian to demonstrate that if in this world a man wished to acquire a sort of eunuch-credit for all kinds of courage and bravery, he need not always use precisely the knife.

The lady in the bonnet, already somewhat beyond the equinox of life, in the direction of winter, is a certain Mrs Lane, and the slumbering fox-hunter in the background, with the black wig and the black cravat, is Mr Lane, her husband. He was such a passionate adherent of that kind of hunting that he was nicknamed 'Fox-Lane'. After his decease, the simple Mrs Lane became the complex Lady Bingley. Thus, my dearest lady readers, you who are beyond the equinox of life in the direction of winter, and still walk without a companion, for God's sake, don't despair too soon! In our clime, at least, the sun of your luck behaves sometimes, even if not always, like the Queen of Days which bears its name (Sunday). It presents the Spring of life, and even its Summer, with tit-bits rather than solid, lasting nourishment. Only in Autumn ripens the drink of the gods which delights the heart of man. This is the season of the kingly Berga-mote, the refreshing St Germain, of the greasy *Poire de Beurrée blanche*, and our pickled cabbage, and all that keeps until the depths of winter.

Madame's glance is directed not only at the warbling half-man in the physiological sense, but also at the half-man in the military sense, pro-bably more to evade the melodious stream issuing from that contemptible orifice than perhaps to seek the source itself. She is delighted; she is en-raptured. The way she throws out her arms conveys to the eye what the ear necessarily misses—the cadenza to which Carestini's song is approach-ing, if he has not reached it already; just as the attitude of the whole Madame in corpore illustrates its ravishing beauty. If the cadenza does not come to an end soon, then indeed the cadence of the scale may become for Madame a cadence from the chair. How very differently her husband behaves behind there, if sleeping can be called behaving. Not a trace of resemblance, apart from the trivial circumstance that he, too, is as if carried away, and is not quite secure against a cadence from the chair.

But was it perhaps our artist's intention to insinuate something here to our eye which escapes our ear—that this concert is in fact a trio in which Mr Lane plays the third instrument, I mean an accompaniment on nasal reedstops? He seems at least to have the instrument tuned and set in position, and to judge from his strong and healthy chest, the requisite bellows will be in pretty good condition. How peacefully he sleeps! But oh! how he would start up if the Tally-ho! suddenly sounded, or if some English bass eunuch tuned up his 'the echoing horn calls the sportsmen abroad', etc., or even if instead of Carestini and Weidermann, Malampus gave tongue accompanied by Lalaps, Okydromus, Pamphagus and Hy-laktor.[1] Then, maybe, Madame would go to sleep. Is this, too, a marriage *à la mode*?

Immediately beside the unfeeling fox-hunter we notice, alas! as the eternal contrast to all wild hunting and shooting, the most sugary senti-mentality of behaviour, and the extreme expression in masculine shape of affected delight. What a little balsam box it is compared with the tar-pot behind there! What a pity that the little plaster on the lower lip, greatly though it heightens the charm of that dainty face, somewhat disturbs the effect of the appreciative smirk. Without it we might have learnt much better from his very lips what is, of course, demonstrated more or less by the fop's whole behaviour; that is, how to give expression to the ineffable. In order to indulge his ear in the highest degree, he de-nies his palate the chocolate and, probably, since he turns his back so care-fully on the man with the riding crop, deprives his nose also of part of the stable perfume which may emanate thence. Although the loud exclamation of wonder is necessarily missing, the five exclamation marks which he em-bodies with the fingers of his left hand unmistakably denote its silent presence. From the same hand, opened like a fan, hangs the folded fan of the lady herself. He has apparently taken it into custody in order to have it redeemed in the end by a kiss. That is how everything hangs together in this little man. Just add the age in the sixties, a parrot-green coat with rose-coloured lining, and a pair of shoes with red heels, and the future natural historian of the affections in the male of the species will have just about the complete characteristics of an old coxcomb.

[1] These are the names of five of the eighty-two immortal hounds which Acteon once kept in his stable, and whose names have been preserved for us partly by Ovid in his 'Meta-morphoses', but more completely by Hyginus in his Fables.

Behind the enraptured lady (I mean the one sentimentally enraptured of Carestini, and not the more realistic adorer of Silvertongue) we see a head, or rather a head stares out at us, which, of course, is not exactly the most beautiful, but certainly one of the most characteristic in the whole gathering. It is the head of the negro who is serving the chocolate into the blue. Truly with the three diamonds in his face, of which the one upon his nose is not genuine, but merely borrowed from the window, he puts in the shade, completely and absolutely, all the diamonds worn by the eunuch in ear and solitaire. Isn't that expressive language? And wasn't it clever to give more prominence to the symbol of the new moon which the African there carries on his shoulders than to the Italian full moon? If one tried to draw a little night piece like that one would soon find out. There is no affectation in it; it is pure, solid, human-animal instinct which draws the axis of his eyes so firmly towards the Italian. Probably it is not so much the voice of the singer which fascinates him, but the gestures which accompany it and the orifice from which it oozes out. He laughs about the little pap-and-rag mouth which once washed itself in the soft and feminine Tiber,[1] and himself reveals a mouth that has been rinsed in the Niger or the Senegal, and one of such dimensions that neither the Senegal nor the Niger nor any other famous river god would need to fear complaints about shortage, if he were to let his store, which had poured hitherto from his urn, spout in future from such a head.

We have already heard that the Countess was at an auction this morning. Here we see from the auction catalogue which lies on the floor to the right that some collection was put up for sale and the name of the owner; it follows from the kind of articles bought there, and which we see standing around here, that it was a collection of *objets d'art*. The English title of the inventory is: 'A catalogue of the entire collection of the late Sir Timothy Babyhouse, to be sold by auction.'

All the junk which her Ladyship bought there belongs, we observe, to the class of antiques which we saw on the mantelpiece in the second Plate. The articles are so arranged that the whole resembles a procession in which the members become more important the farther back they are. It is reminiscent of a triumphal procession. In front there trots on its four feet an unknown little animal which seems to have precedence only because of its unimportance; behind it crawl a couple without feet, next to

[1] *Uxorius amnis.* Horace.

it a little bowl, then an atrocious cat's head, a few enchanted princesses together with the magician, then a horrible pottery monster in the form of a candle-holder; now, more important, a butter dish, and still more important, a mystic pot with a mystic seven upon it, and, finally, most important of all, the Imperator Acteon himself with the crown of victory upon his head. He leans against a wash-basin of majolica ware hand-painted by Giulio Romano, a great rarity. Raphael-like rubbish of this sort is to be found everywhere; the picture itself represents a nude woman being bitten by a wicked goose.[1] The rear is brought up by a magnificent vase of the pot-pourri type.

Still more mystical perhaps than the seven on the little pot may be the round figure of 100 upon Acteon's belly, but this we shall leave an open question. In the counting-house of her Ladyship's father, such round numbers could have been seen on more important slips of paper. One of the figures is marked with the number four. Her Ladyship has thus attended the auction from the beginning, and held out till Lot 100—a very long time if it all took place the same morning. But there was a little statue to be bought for her lord and master, to hang his hat on in the evening. Thus the series of little nonsensical objects there on the floor becomes in the end very significant for our story. It is irrefutable evidence of crude lack of taste, coarse sensuality, and what is ultimately not much better (*videatur* the steward) of thriftlessness in buying, for want of a better occupation. What may she have paid for that doll with the horns? To form an opinion we should have to imagine another such creature being present at the same auction, or several more of them, each just as extravagant, wise, and well brought up as Madame. We must imagine, too, the noble contempt of money and the elevated feelings which so easily overpower ladies' souls in that sort of sales excitement, especially if their absent husbands are perhaps engaged with equal ardour in some similar glory-, rank-, or title-auction. Then one should only hear how those ladies, as if in vocal contest, now with alternating voices, now with simultaneous duet and trio, drive one another higher and higher and, like jealous nightingales, continue to warble till first one, then the other, worn out at last, falls down from the branch. Then what? Oh, the doll was not worth three

---

[1] This description of the picture is taken literally from the local paper of a neighbouring town, in which, on the occasion of the theft of a box with that picture on its lid, the famous story of antiquity was reported in just those words.

farthings, but the joke of buying a man with horns in the presence of so many gentlemen and ladies, and the pleasure of seeing the nightingales fall, one after another. . . For a satisfaction like that, as many golden sovereigns would be but a trifle.

Our artist has perhaps exaggerated a little here. Who in the world, many a lady might ask, would buy such jokes, and moreover such moral filth? *Fi donc!* Quite right. But how if we were to translate the numbers here into book titles, and in this way transform the whole collection into a modern lady's library? How's that to de done? Even supposing the little dishes and bowls *might* signify a cookery book or a recipe for making candles or boiling soap, this does not imply that they *must* have that meaning. Could they not just as well be instructions for face-tanning, for the improvement of the hair roots, and for painting a pink and white complexion? And if even the enchanted princesses, the dwarf, the gander on the dish, and, finally, the horned creature with the one and two noughts on his belly, were transformed into books, would the library look a jot more respectable than the floor does here? Hardly, hardly. . . .

The little procession becomes almost comic if we consider that it is making straight for Carestini, and if we then recall Orpheus—and why not recall him here? If Orpheus with his harp made oak trees and granite boulders approach him in a waltz, why should not Carestini with his pipe entice that Nürnberg ware? Either the one is not a true story, or the other is at least possible. To return to the idea of translation into book titles, the small, dainty animal which is trotting on its little feet at the head of the procession, just because it trots on little feet and is so dainty, would have to be a poetry almanack and, by the same token, its two legless, prosaic companions could be nothing else but a couple of prose almanacks (*Taschenkalenders*).

Close to Carestini's chair lie visiting and invitation cards, trump upon trump. Some turn upwards their acquired inscribed aspect, others their congenital printed one; still others show nothing, just as they happen to have fallen. We shall briefly review them.

Lady Squander (so she is called on all these cards, instead of Squander-field, perhaps because most of the fields are already squandered) is invited: (1) to Lady Townley's Drum (this is a sort of party where they gamble and talk nineteen to the dozen), and that is for next Monday. On the card stands Munday instead of Monday, a telling indication of her Ladyship's learning. (2) To Lady Heathen's Drum-major, where everything is more spacious and magnificent, gambling as well as tongue-wagging, and that is for Sunday next. Pious John Bull does not forgive a soul for playing and making music on Sundays, that is why the Sabbath breaker is called here Lady Heathen. But so far as I know, the Jew's harp of tongue-wagging, which is played at all parties, is as little forbidden on Sundays in England as it is with us. (3) To Miss Hairbrain's Rout (also a sort of party which, if it is what its name says, must be like a small riot). Finally, there lies with them No. (4), the card upon which a foreign Count Basset inquires after the health of her Ladyship. He has apparently gone to England to learn English, and here gives a proof of his proficiency, for which reason we quote it in full: 'Count Basset begs to no how Lade Squander sleapt last nite.'

By the pictures on the walls, our artist continues to throw more and more into relief his conception of the ladies' master-passion. He started with the Primer for Young Women over there on the sofa; below in the basket he continued his tale, and on the walls we now see the sequel. There are four pictures. We must be brief. On the right hangs the 'Consequences of Intoxication', a few rungs above the middle stage, in the story of Noah and his daughters. The explanation of the dish picture (p. 125) was taken from a daily paper which like a falling leaf (*fliegendes Blatt*) has long since flown away. The explanation of the present picture (the biblical), however, we should have to copy from leaves which are anything but flying, and which it is hoped may therefore never fly away this side of the Rhine,[1] wherefore we refer the reader to them. Next to this picture hangs the 'Consequences of Masquerades', in the story of the beautiful princess Io, where she, too, is bitten by the enraged Jupiter clad in his usual Thundercloud-domino. This is a copy of a very well-known presentation of that biting by Michelangelo Buonarroti, bought of course by her Ladyship for the original itself, and perhaps even paid for as such.

To the left hangs Jupiter for the third time, again *en masque*, for we must confess that the gander on the dish over there was this same Jupiter. Pictures like that might induce anybody to try his luck for once at a Masked Ball, especially if he is a friend of Lady Heathen's. Jupiter appears this time in the guise of an eagle carrying his Ganymede to Olympus.

[1] L. refers here to the French Revolution having done away with the Bible. Ed.

What is queer is that the King of the Gods is about to bite again here. It almost makes us afraid to look. Oh, if only Ganymede would do the riding this time; I mean if only he would be, as the French so excellently put it, *un cheval sur un aigle*! As he is now hanging from the eagle, this will not come to a good end. I tremble, I tremble! Jupiter who hovers there just above Carestini's head is listening to the divine voice of that mortal; 'I must have such a singer, too,' he thinks, and no sooner thought than done, proceeds immediately with his own noble beak to the operation.[1]

Above that picture, in Olympus itself and among the Immortals, there hangs, somewhat ominously, a portrait of Mr Silvertongue, quite undisguised, in all the exterior dignity appropriate to a Head of the House. At his feet there the horned animal felled by him gnaws at its chain. Good! We shall leave it at that. In the next two Plates we shall see both the hanging and the felling in more solid form.

Silvertongue's picture was hung just opposite the sofa for the sole purpose of promoting devotion. As soon as that ceases, he receives, as we shall hear, a different place, or rather, as soon as that idol obtains another place, the devotion ceases.

A trifle to finish with, for surely every puzzle is a trifle. On the canopy of the lady's bed the artist has put a French lily. Now how in the world do the French arms come to be on an English bed?[2]

[1] If this is, as I believe, the true meaning of this item, then it belongs indisputably among the most excellent touches in Hogarth's works. And how rich must a man's genius be who flicks a thing like that, which many a poet would have spun out to the length of a whole ballad, into a mere corner of his work; that is, into a little picture on the wall of a picture which itself is hung on the wall, without caring who will find it, or whether it will be found at all. At the same time, this is the most magnificent *réparation d'honneur* for the poor eunuch, if he had felt offended by the rest. Carestini could easily be made ridiculous, but hardly praised with more delicacy.

[2] Lichtenberg asks that question evidently with his tongue in his cheek, for he cannot have missed the point that the English believe the French to be constitutionally frivolous. The French arms on the lady's bed may well have evoked the same moral apprehension in the English spectator of those days as a yellow-backed French novel in the book-case. Ed.

V

How clear and how terrible is everything in this picture!—blood, murder, death-struggle and despair, in the depth of night! How gruesome if we add in imagination the tumult of the Watch as it rushes in, the terrified whine of awakened conscience and infamy unmasked, mingled with the drawn-out, monotonous moans of the dying. Is this marriage *à la mode*? Merciful Heavens! There he sways, the modish husband, stabbed by the lover of his faithless wife. His knees are giving way beneath him. The only support left him, his arm, grows more and more powerless with each precarious beat of his pierced heart. He may stand for a few moments longer and then—never again. His breaking eye no longer sees the light, that light which illumines for us here the signs of approaching death in his sunken cheek and fallen jaw. In vain does the whine of despairing depravity rise up to him from the lips of that abandoned woman; in vain her supplication for mercy for crime discovered. His ears no longer hear them, and his mouth no longer responds. Between the two of them, accusation and defence have come to an end; the case is closed this side of the grave. The remainder of the hearing and the judge's sentence await her in another world.

There she kneels now, the modish wife, barefoot, in her shift only, before the Beadle and the Watch, craving forgiveness for her crime, and suffering for it. If she were to hold in her hand the light which stands beside her, I would say she is actually repenting and praying for forgiveness, as did formerly the French king's murderers, as long as there were only a select few. How closely and convulsively she clasps her hands!

129

Hands so folded must surely be trembling, and the arms, too. This is no *mode*, it is pure nature. Her eye stares at the sinking features of that picture of despair, where the years of expected life are now dwindling to seconds. Each dull sound from the moaning man becomes a peal of thunder to her sleeping conscience, and even her numbed sense of honour seems re-awakened through the disgrace which in so manifold form has overtaken her. But enough of that terrible duo-drama.

The reader will, we hope, forgive the interpreter of these pictures his perhaps over-solemn introduction to this Chapter. He was just expressing his own feelings. The main content of the piece, I feel, is solemn enough, and would be still more so if the gentleman who makes his exit through the window there were less visible, or at least better covered than he is. Hogarth's intention was evidently to arouse terror, hatred, and revulsion with the first glance at this scene, and this he has certainly achieved. Of course, he could not entirely refrain from indulging his impish mood even here. But these features (with the possible exception of the large features in the window there) are all so much concealed that they really have to be looked for, and have therefore often been overlooked as well. They disturb the main impression so little that, on the contrary, it is they which, through the force of that main impression, are hardly noticed. But even if these touches were less recondite, what sort of human feelings would they be that would remain unmoved by such a scene, simply because the story was enacted in a ridiculously furnished room, or because at the same time there appear in it a few persons in queer attitudes? I am so little apprehensive of this reaction from my readers that I shall not hesitate to bring all these touches to their notice, and I am convinced that once they have considered them, they will themselves return them where they belong.

The occasion for this event was as follows: Lady Squanderfield and her advocate, Silvertongue, had, as will be recalled, a date for the Masked Ball, and they did in fact meet there. Excited by dancing and probably also by Lot's cup, they remember the miracles of the masked Jupiter, pointed out to them by Giulio Romano and Michelangelo, and, as true pupils of Crébillon, they leave the Olympus of the ballroom, glittering with countless lights, and settle themselves in the dirtiest corner of a so-called Bagnio, a sort of house which is open at all hours of the night to any miracle worker, and especially to those who descend from such a

Marriage-à-la-Mode Plate V

height.[1] Lord Squanderfield, who has got scent of the exploit, sneaks along behind them with sword drawn, bursts open the locked and bolted door (key and cross-bar are lying on the floor) and finds what he was looking for, completely unmasked, without domino and even without clothes, except for one quilt to cover both, which didn't amount to much. He rushes at the advocate. That much experienced, legally cautious fox also carries, at this delicate appointment, a sword, *in subsidium iuris*, and before the attack can materialize he flings himself out of the quilt and confronts his furious adversary in the open. A fight begins, and one, alas! in which horns are no help whatever. For rage, resolute and nimble though it may be as a murderer, is notoriously the poorest fencer in the world. To be brief, Lord Squanderfield rushes on to the sword of the advocate and falls. After this victory, the lighter part of the garrison emerges from under the quilt to celebrate it as victories are usually celebrated in civil wars. This is the celebration. In that sortie she entangles herself in the sheet, drags it after her and apparently falls. Here again, her character is in the balance. Did she sink on to her knee intentionally, or has she merely forgotten to rise?

In the uproar, the night-watch awakes, rouses the landlord, finally even the police. There they stand, the whole bunch, in the doorway, partly visible, partly indicated, and arranged in the most natural order in the world, namely according to the interest of the parties. First of all, the landlord, with the five exclamation marks on his left hand and a face which, if times do not soon improve, might well be worth storing among the printing blocks. The honour of his house is at stake. Behind him stands the constable, the representative of the police, with his staff. A lovely figure, and one that can be seen by the hundred in England; a genuine tough composition of beef and pudding, tawny red, shining, stocky and stout with enough behind for two; slightly in advance of him a digestive apparatus of the most comfortable curvature, the true symbol of national debt and taxation pressure. His right hand rests admonishingly on the landlord's shoulder; he seems to recommend cool blood and caution. It is no use having too much heart in cases like this, especially when naked swords are flashing about; if it were wine-glasses, or fragments of them, one

[1] In order to bring the necessary symmetry into the analogy of this adventure with Jupiter's, the indulgent reader is asked to perform a slight transposition among the actors, by which Lord Squanderfield obtains the role of Juno.

might perhaps do something more. The night-watchman, still more cautious than the police, heads the detachment, from behind; he dare not do anything nor does he want to; he does not even issue orders, he merely holds the light. We see nothing of him but the right hand holding the lantern, whose ventilation holes are projected on to the ceiling of the room according to the rules of perspective and there become a sort of canopy over a throne, which we shall mention in its proper place. Mr Silvertongue, though sure of his victory, yet takes to flight on account of that small detachment. As an advocate he would know better than anyone that the welfare belly there in the door belonged to the lesser troops of an invincible corps, namely the English Criminal Law Administration, and that this corps is rarely far away when such advance troops appear on the scene. But he seems especially apprehensive about a certain person employed only occasionally in that service, quite an unimportant person, by the way, whose acquaintance, however, cannot always be avoided, and who then becomes something of a nuisance—the hangman. That accounts for the great haste and the retreat by an outlet to the street from the second storey, with a rather abbreviated flight of steps which begins on the window-ledge and ends on the street itself. Moreover, it is a flight in winter, for the main illumination in this picture comes from the fireplace, and it is a windy night since the flame of the light indicates a sneezing draught between window and door. It is hard at such a time to be despatched like that, especially in one's summer coat. No victor surely has ever taken flight more scantily clothed. We can almost see Mr Silvertongue in his entirety up to his silver mouth, which is concealed here by his shoulder. What a ridiculous figure is cut by guilt when forced to expose itself in the so-called robe of innocence, from an angle which even innocence would regard as double nakedness. His position is awkward: he is about to leap out of the window from the second floor (for we do not see any window-sill), and straight down, silver mouth first, without climbing. It will be a dangerous jump. But then, what will a man not do to avoid acquaintance with the lower officials of the administration of Criminal Justice? It almost seems as if he wanted to throw something down in advance, perhaps a pillow, or something in the nature of an overcoat, or some underwear especially. For if Hogarth had intended to expose him on the street to the passers-by, or since they would be asleep, to some night-watchman, without pants, then he would probably have shown us

132

somewhere the pants without the man. But of these there is no trace, although parts of the battlefield are strewn with armaments which might properly be termed their counterparts, such as whale-bone harness of all sorts for hand-to-hand and distant fighting, corsets and crinolines,[1] hoods, masks, embroidered dancing slippers, swords and scabbards, and so on. In its sudden sortie from the bastion the young garrison came by mistake, it seems, upon the field medicine chest, knocked it over, and broke open some little boxes, releasing a hail of grape-shot (which pharmacy has taught us to cast from a well-known cold liquid metal), or whatever diabolic concoction that may be which is rolling about there under the address of that fine establishment and its landlord, as if under the protection of a patent.

Next to the corset lies something else for unlacing, to wit, a bundle of faggots; not unlike the former in appearance and very similar in stiffness. We may be sure that our artist has not thrown these two fascines so closely together for nothing; nor, in all probability, the two sticks which in the form of a sword point murderously at the nearer bundle. That almost looks like suicide. Oh, there are certainly prophetic voices in this room! And the sword there in the lower fascine presages very little comfort for the upper one.[2]

The faggots are lying in front of the fireplace, as we infer from the

[1] A very wide crinoline like this one hardly belongs to a nun's attire, for that would almost make her a sheep in wolf's clothing. Here I would like to add a remark. I said above that the lady was kneeling in her shift. Although this is not strictly true, the other clothes she wears do not contribute in the least either to her honesty or modesty; that is why, in the interests of forceful expression, I spoke simply of a shift. English ladies sleep with a light bed-gown over their night shirt, and this is also customary in other countries. Should they have to do without it on some occasion or other, they would not only feel embarrassed but, not being accustomed to it, very uncomfortable too. Since our lady is sleeping away from home, and in a Street Bagnio at that, where comfort of that kind is not to be had, she has put over her shift the loose sack which she formerly wore over her crinoline. The silken folds and the great length of the garment support this interpretation, and distinguish it clearly from the shift which, however, as we see, it does not quite cover. That incidentally a high degree of sensitivity to fashion and comfort goes quite well with a complete lack of honesty is well known outside England too.

[2] Our readers who are familiar by now with the artist's queer moods may find this comparison of a bundle of faggots with a corset, and of the faggot cross with a sword, and all its relations, not entirely improbable, or even in bad taste. If the artist himself, of which there can be no doubt, really used devices like that occasionally in his style, the just reader will forgive his commentator if he for once commits something of this kind on his own account in a rather obscure locum.

shadow of the tongs which stretches along the floor beyond the murderer's sword. It is thrown by the same light which illuminates the main group. But the fact that they burn half-rotten faggots here instead of coal, throws, by the rules of another perspective, yet another light upon this room. In a great city at least, and especially in public establishments, this, to the best of my knowledge, would always be evidence of disreputable stinginess, and in this case it shows what a cosy little corner the good people have chosen. Whether fire-tongs standing near a considerable fire could throw so sharp a shadow need not be more closely investigated here. The shadow is merely a half-artificial device to indicate the fire in the fireplace: it does not seem to be an entirely natural one. It is not the first time that Hogarth has used shadows in his pictures and, just as unnaturally, merely to indicate the presence of objects which he could not actually bring before our eyes. Also, it is difficult to see how these tongs would have to be placed in front of such a fire in order to throw such a shadow, since they seem to be neither leaning nor hanging. They would, apparently, have to be stuck in some crevice of the fireplace, or to be a pair of falling tongs, just like the falling rapier over there which also throws a somewhat unnatural shadow.

At this point, a few words about the falling sword. As a telling detail in the delineation of the story itself it hardly calls for explanation. A moment ago the dying man still held it in his hand, that is what the artist wants to say, and the very next moment, that is, the one which has here been seized and fixed by art, it is already too heavy for him; it falls, or rather it stands there—like its master. That is all. Now a little about this presentation, partly as a work of art, partly about the present reproduction of the picture; not through literary importunity, but because of certain criticisms which have been raised by friends of mine, and which might easily be made by some of my readers. I start with the last point. In the original engraving, which must be clearly distinguished from the original picture, the dying man supports himself with his left arm, and the sword thus seems to have fallen from his right hand. What is more natural than that, one would say, for surely he held the sword in his right? But this apparently justified objection can immediately be countered by the fact that in the original engraving his Lordship wears that part of the sword belt on which the sword had been hanging, on his right, whereas in our reproduction it hangs properly on the left. His Lordship, while he was still standing unsupported, apparently flung the sword away and sank against the table which stood on his right. In our reproduction we also see the right hand of the scribe, or whoever he is up there over the doorway, restored to its eternal and unalienable right which in the original engraving it had apparently ceded to the left. Thus here, too, Mr Riepenhausen's reproduction is in agreement with the original painting. Now to the first point. It has pleased me not a little that almost everyone to whom I have shown these engravings has found the position of the sword unnatural. And why did it please me? Answer: because I am confident that I could easily elicit from anybody who felt like that after some slight subjection to Socrates' torture, some theorems of higher mathematics. He feels, without expressly knowing it, that the painter of the living and moving— just because his painted representation is still and without life—ought to present only an infinitely small moment of time, and he also feels that the infinitely small moments of time must preserve their relations with one another, for otherwise the falling of a sword inclined towards the horizon, with its heavy sword hilt on top, could not be found unnatural if compared with the falling of its master. Now the sinking master could still hold, or have held, himself up; not so the sword. There lies the difference. On the coat-of-arms of a knight on the point of falling we might still read the device, but we could hardly do so with the name of the sword-smith or the factory of a sword falling in that way. The position of his Lordship approaches that of rest, that of the falling sword more the motion of the cannon ball which in the first picture flew out of the hero's trouser pocket.

On the wall facing us is presented upon wallpaper (whether *haute-lisse* or *basse-lisse*[1] cannot quite be discerned) the Judgment of Solomon. Solomon on the throne, though except perhaps for the crown, not in his usual splendour, but rather in the holiday attire of a Dutch sailor. Anyone not aware that this man was once at the helm of a powerful State, which he guided with great wisdom, would be inclined to believe that here, at least, he was guiding some coal barge or herring smack under the powerful influence of greed, rum and schnapps which clearly glow out of his eye and nose. Nor are the inanimate ornaments of the throne much more attractive than the animate ones. Not so much a terrible as a terribly-drawn lion's head, and a throne canopy with ten magnificent suns embroidered by the sombre rays of a stable lamp, that is all! Before him stands the

[1] Painted or embossed. Ed.

mother of the child that is about to be divided according to the principles of equality. Were she not grasping it so anxiously to prevent that division of the apple of her eye, one would almost be inclined, judging from her face, to regard her as the father. For head and headgear are entirely masculine, and nautical to boot, and for the sake of touches like these one could overlook a few small items such as, for instance, that she wears a skirt and is apparently again in an unmistakably interesting condition. That the beadle is about to chop up the child with his left hand is again no argument against Mr Riepenhausen's omission to reverse the original painting. Solomon here holds the sceptre in his right hand, as we feel sure he always held it. His wisdom required this of him, and this way of representing him must therefore be the rule for every artist who undertakes to portray him in all his glory. What does a single left-handed rogue of an inferior official matter? Oh, if we were immediately to reverse the whole picture because some inferior official performs something with his left hand that a wise governor has ordained with his right—there would be no end to reversals in this world.

Apart from this Old Testament story, Hogarth has hung two other pictures from the Newest Testament, which offer a peculiar contrast, if not with the wall paper, at least with one another. The one, we are assured, is the portrait of a certain Moll Flanders, a notorious Drury Lane trollop (Mr Ireland calls her, in his somewhat peculiar language, 'notified'). At the first glance, her appearance has something repulsive in it, which however more or less disappears once one has discovered the happy union of cowherd and affected fine lady, and it vanishes completely as soon as the intention of the whimsical artist is revealed, for he has really put her here in the pillory. She has a squirrel perched on her hand, a little dandy too, and behind is a parrot in its ring, also a chatterbox, evidently a cut at other affected damsels, not those of the cowshed but of the *bel-étage* of the house itself. But joking apart, such companions really have something to contribute. These little animals lend to lady owners of a certain age something of their own daintiness and, what is hardly less valuable, divert somewhat the lover's attention where too much of it might become embarrassing. In a word, as soon as two lovers, desiring to entertain one another, begin to forget their mother-tongue, which sometimes happens in the third quarter of life, or if they find themselves at a loss for something to talk about, or hesitate and wait for the prompter in their head, then a parrot and a squirrel may work wonders. The object which hangs down there from her right hand I have always regarded as the head of a riding crop. Mr Ireland, however, states dogmatically it is a butcher's steel. Possibly it is, but what in all the world could that woman have to steel or to sharpen? Now for the pillory. With genuine roguishness and with truly appropriate malice, our artist has hung the picture of this piece so that the legs of one of the fellows in Solomon's Swiss Guard on the wallpaper appear to be hers, and it looks as if her skirt had been cut off above the knee without her even having noticed it. This last circumstance makes the matter really interesting. That lucky cut, to be sure, transforms the creature into a Highlander, without the Highlander's famous second sight having given her the slightest inkling of it, although it happened in such close proximity that there was not even any need for a special gift of vision to discover it.

The second picture hanging on the wallpaper is—the mirror. And why? Oh! it was certainly not without intention that Hogarth hung the mirror there, so that its frame becomes at the same time a frame for the head of the dying man. 'If,' he seems to adjure foolish vanity, 'If you do not feel cured of your madness by a glance in that first mirror with the Highlander and the squirrel, very well, then look into the second! How's that? Do you recognize the make-up which covers those cheeks? What do you say? Oh! whoever in the world you may be, sooner or later the time will surely come when your mirror will look back at you like this one, little though you may then be capable of realizing that the features which it reflects with its wonted truthfulness are your own.'

Over the door hangs a third picture, which deserves attention. This time the subject is taken from the New Testament and, as can be seen from the halo of the man with the bull, evidently represents the apostle Luke, known to be the patron of artists, as Mr Ireland has correctly observed. He thus portrays here the remarkable story, and, as one sees, with the utmost zeal and close attention. Even the horned animal appears to be curious about what is going on down there. Perhaps it has the scent of the one who has just been butchered, at whose *papillotes* yesterday morning brother Acteon so mysteriously pointed. But I believe this is by no means all there is to it, and venture therefore an additional explanation, the more readily since it has obtained the full approval of a discerning Englishman and an expert on Hogarth's inexhaustible fund of allegory. London has, in common with all large towns, apart from a number of private lunatic asylums, two great public institutions for that purpose, which are pretty well known everywhere, Bedlam and St Luke's. The latter is particularly for incurables. That name and the hospital which bears it are so well known and their association so familiar to everyone that out of a hundred who hear the name pronounced, ninety-nine will think of the lunatic asylum rather than the apostle. Now our Saint Luke here, although the patron of painters,[1] but just as surely also the patron of the hospital, evidently holds a pen, not a pencil, in his hand, as we can see very clearly in the original engraving. Thus he is writing. Might he not therefore be entering in his register the names of those three candidates as very deserving inmates for his institution? They have lived madly enough at least, all three of them, and incurable they are too in another sense. It is possible to draw with a pen, to be sure, but this does not invalidate the last suggestion; on the contrary, the satire gains, through just that re-inforcement, its two-edgedness.

A slight emendation to end with. It is possible that Lord Squanderfield, after learning that his bed-fellow had been seen together with her lover in a house of ill-fame, proceeded more cautiously and more in accordance with English law than I have indicated above. He may have obtained a warrant, and thus arrived, together with the constable, at the house which without that measure he could not have ventured to enter by force. They burst the door open together, under the protection of the police. His Lordship drew his sword, the civil war between Squanderfield & Co.[2] broke out and was concluded; all in five minutes. Had it not even come to a fight, such witnesses would always have been welcome for the sake of the divorce. If this was his secondary purpose, then he achieved it too. The marriage is divorced. There, under the shadow of the fire-tongs, lies what cut the marriage bond.

[1] The Académie de Sainte Luc at Rome therefore takes its name from the Evangelist, and we were even shown pictures by Santo Luca at Rome, until the origin of the error was discovered by Domen. Manni (Del vero pittore Luca Santo in Firenze, 1764).

[2] A true sleeping partner, Lichtenberg would surely have called him, had the German language known that term. Ed.

VI

We have seen the crimes with some of their non-judicial consequences. The nobleman in his blood, the murderer in his shift escaping into the winter night, and his aider and abetter similarly attired, in the grip of her conscience. The punishment so far was light. Here in this picture it grows to a terrific intensity for both of them, to the highest pitch it can attain, judicially and non-judicially, this side of the grave.

Immediately upon the physical death of her beloved lord and master, and her own moral death which was bound up with it, the Countess leaves the fashionable world of the West End and exiles, or rather buries herself, together with her child and its noble blood, in the East End from whence she came, in her father's vaults, not far from London Bridge, which with its buildings is seen here from the window.

Here now, removed for ever from the magic of the heavenly music of the Court and the tumult of Lady Townley's and Lady Heathen's Drums and Lady Hairbrain's Rout, she had had the opportunity of making an acquaintance which might have been of infinite advantage to her had it come in better times—that is, with her own self. But it was much too late! Announced by a peal of thunder from her conscience, she appears to herself now for the first time. What a sight! Rejected in the West End by everybody for whose sake she had rejected many another in the motherly East End, and now herself rejected by these same rejected ones, without visits and even without visiting cards, without rank and, finally, without honour she is now the mockery and the derision, the talk and the news, of the first city in the world. Ever more clearly, she recognizes herself at last as the murderess of her husband; though not legally hangable, yet extra-judicially condemned to hang herself, towards which end one might, in solitude and ineradicable shame, make very rapid progress. 'Struth! Thus to await the *coup de grâce* from one's own hand is infinitely more painful than the rope which the law, by God's grace, ordains inevitably for the criminal.

Meanwhile, a feeble ray of hope still shone into her prison. Silvertongue, though arrested and imprisoned, was still alive then, and knew the wrong as well as the right side of the law; what more does such a bird need in order to escape from any cage, by the power of the beak, or the gab? Thus, there was still the possibility that these two gallows-birds,[1] even if not in the East or West End of the city, at least in some corner of the earth, east or west, might build their little nest once more. Soon after, however, Silvertongue is brought to trial, is found guilty and condemned to death by hanging. It was a very great step to take all at once on the path lawful; suddenly one had reached the final stage. The unadorned wooden portal with its entrapping noose through which the way led was close at hand. She still comforted herself: 'It's impossible—he cannot be hanged—he was too dear to me! Surely my departed husband was more to blame. Always drunk, always with his plasters and his pills! He should have looked after me better. Not to steal when some lovely object lies about in the street is not in human nature, any more than it is in human nature to let oneself be stabbed to death for nothing, if one carries a sword. And these, after all, were the only crimes of my Silvertongue. Oh! yes, there is justice in England, but there is mercy too. This, this is what I seek; this is my comfort; justice, but mercy too. Oh! certainly mercy. My Silvertongue lives and will live.' With dreams like these she was still deceiving herself this very morning when suddenly an event occurred with the most terrible effect upon the dreamer. It was nothing less than the thunder-clap: 'No, your Silvertongue will not live, and does not live any longer. This morning, at the stroke of ten, he was left hanging in the portal's noose; you can see him swinging there still, if you like.' That event we shall now report to our readers in simple prose.

This morning, as the lady might have known very well from the news-paper even if she had not heard it elsewhere, was the day appointed for the execution of her lover. Not being familiar with the fine points of the law, she thought she could easily remember similar, or at least apparently

[1] In some parts of Germany, ravens are very appropriately called 'Hangman's Doves'.

Marriage-à-la-Mode Plate VI

similar, cases, where a comparable crime had been punished merely by imprisonment or transportation. Upon this she based her not altogether impossible hopes, which love and wishful thinking raised now, as if by magic power, to certainty. Thus, to make that certainty doubly sure and with the utmost despatch, she sends a sort of Boots (the thing over there by the table that has concealed itself in a man's coat) to the place of execution. That poor devil now brings, perhaps without knowing just what he has brought, not only the news that Silvertongue has just exchanged the temporal for the eternal, and the legal collar of cambric for the hempen one, but in addition a forget-me-not leaflet which we see there on the floor, lying beside an empty medicine bottle. This document, whose seal nobody would easily mistake if he has some human feelings, contains nothing less than Silvertongue's swan-song from beneath the gallows, his gallows sermon.[1] This was too much for a tender heart. Her husband— that could have been endured, but her lover! Quick as lightning she grasps a two-ounce bottle of laudanum,[2] which she had evidently prescribed for herself in the first wild moments of her newly-gained self-knowledge, but found somewhat too powerful when it arrived—and drains it to the last drop. At lunch, the action of the poison becomes apparent; she falls backwards with her chair; they pick her up, carry her to the armchair, call the doctor, call the apothecary, and a good proportion of his drugs; all arrive, but it was too late; had Silvertongue himself been alive and, in a flash, appeared with a ball ticket, he could not have restored her. That it is too late may also be seen from the fact that the doctor is warily withdrawing to pay his respects to the departing soul before the front door. This is a brief sketch of the scene which we shall now describe in more detail.

She dies in an armchair with the insignia of the disaster which has befallen her, poison bottle and gallows, at her feet—and thus Squander-

[1] This is the *opusculum* to which we alluded above, and from which we learn that the deceased's name was in fact Silvertongue. Apart from that, in classical England, it was the same story with these speeches as with the speeches of the heroes in classical authors: the heroes themselves knew nothing about them.

[2] For the benefit of those among our readers who do not know what laudanum is, we mention that it is really a sort of Bohemian liqueur which used in drops externally or internally under the direction of an experienced doctor may be beneficial; but swallowed just anyhow, and even by the ounce, it acts like lead in pill form shot out of a pistol. More can be found about it in pharmacopaeia and in novels, especially the silly-sweet ones, where betrothels are made in the grave.

141

field is at length avenged. An old housekeeper, whom Nature had painted greyer than grey probably twenty years ago already, holds towards the doomed woman the child whose rattle we have seen before, hanging from a chair of a different type. This picture of despair puts its small rickety arms round her neck, and kisses the pallid cheek of the human form that was called mother, but who has never been much more of a mother than she is now, when feeling has left her for ever. On its cheek the poor creature already carries the seal of Squanderfield's blood, and delicate and light though the little body is, she already needs, as we can clearly see, laced boots with steel supports, to prevent the emaciated little legs from bending under their paper-light load. Throughout this scene, which could hardly be more movingly conceived, the old father remains as calm as if the whole daughter had been insured, apart from her rings, which latter, therefore, he takes care to salvage personally. The philosophical composure of that man is really incredible. If our readers will take the trouble to cover the left side of this stoic with a piece of paper so that its edge passes down his right cheek and the extreme tip of the thumb of his right hand, then in describing his movement they will find themselves at a loss to say immediately whether he is filling a fresh pipe, or cleaning out an old one in order to fill it. He receives this secondary punishment from Heaven as he probably received the primary also—with as much composure as if it were merely a bill of lading. What a granite-like imperturbability in that figure there, from the broad, cautious brow, which seems strong enough to resist a hatchet, to the two Stock Exchange flagstone-rammers which, in their sturdiness, seem to put in the shade even the timbered double footgear of the chair in which his daughter dies! And all that close to the corpse of his only child, and having taken her cold hand in his, not in order to press it once more, but to prevent her perhaps from bestowing unawares a ring on the woman who is to lay her out. Surely not even an elephant or a poodle would do such a thing; it could only be the work of all-embracing avarice. The interpreter of this Plate has often found confirmed in real life what Hogarth is trying to teach here: namely, that a certain collector mentality, better a sort of hamster instinct, intent upon saving every year certain 'little round sums' as these people modestly like to call them, by and by overcasts the heart of man with a good, strong callus, which protects it as surely from all moral warmth as soft swansdown protects the chest from physical cold; nay,

finally invests its owner with the enviable faculty of bearing every misfortune of his fellow-men, as Swift puts it, with Christian composure.
Incidentally, one notices, especially if one has a cold, how carefully that
sort of person, or whatever it is, knows how to combine his Horatian *aes
triplex circa pectus* with the homespun *pannus triplicus circa stomachum*. He
wears three coats; for in those happy days a coat and a waistcoat still stood
al pari, just like stocks and shares. One can see the man gives nothing away,
neither money, nor affection for his fellow-beings, nor animal warmth;
of all this he saves as much as possible. The chain under the girl's cold
hand is not one of his daughter's bracelets, but the golden chain of office
which the old man wears in the house, evidently so as not to leave it with
the coat in the counting-house quite by itself, for obvious reasons.

Behind the old gentleman, and apparently garbed in mourning-black,
stands a man upon so sturdy a pedestal of calves that it almost seems as
if Nature had ordained him for a butcher, and while shaping him had taken
into consideration the quarters of oxen which he would have to carry.
Nature has, however, made a mistake this time. The man merely became
an apothecary, who visited patients, prescribed and dispensed as well, and
in the end had the four quarters carried away by others.[1] That he is somebody of this sort can be recognized from the pharmaceutical extinguishing
apparatus which sticks out of his pocket, a small squirt and a bottle of
julep; the obliging man arrived here, however, only when the building was
already burnt to ashes. With his left hand he grips—and with just such a
grip as in former times the terrorist Gassner[2] used to grasp the foul fiend—
a rather loosely hanging State-livery by the collar, evidently in order to
drive out of it the poor devil by whom it is possessed *ad interim*. It really
looks as if the conjuring had had some effect, for if I read the face of the
exorcised aright, it seems to express, apart from great anguish of heart,
some indecision whether to jump out of the top of the coat or to dive down
and slip out below; just as the devil did with Gassner. The story is as follows:
the poor soul there, as we have already heard, is some kind of servant in

---

[1] In London, one frequently finds practising apothecaries, or doctors who also dispense.

[2] Jean-Joseph Gassner, born at Bratz in 1727, died 1779. A pastor who claimed to cure
diseases by exorcism. He enjoyed a tremendous vogue, patients coming to him from Switzerland, Germany and France. His theory was that illnesses were of two sorts: natural, which
could be cured by medicine, and diabolic, produced by obsessions, which could only be cast
out by a priest. He wrote a treatise in German, *Instructions for combating the Devil*, published
in 1774, which Lichtenberg may possibly have seen. Ed.

this household, a miserable creature who evidently serves for half-wages, but who also has nothing more important to do than to run as quickly as State-livery permits as soon as anybody calls *apporte*. This innocent domestic animal has, unfortunately, also fetched-and-carried the poisons which lie on the floor here, side by side, the dying speech and the laudanum. 'See what you have done there, you gallows' bird,' thunders the apothecary, pointing with his right hand at the poisons. 'Who asked you to do that? You deserve to be strung up yourself this very moment, you scoundrel.' With that, he shakes him furiously with his left hand and bestows on him a look which hardly leaves him in any doubt as to what the right hand is going to do the next moment. And the poor sinner who outside on the bridge would not have felt the slightest guilt, now in the claws of terrorism begins to believe, from intimidation, that he really deserves the gallows. Therefore the despair, and the mouth which seems to attempt something like a last dying speech. Is there anything one cannot make the Lord of the Earth and the Inheritor of the Kingdom of Heaven believe if only one can get him properly by the collar and shake apart his store of ideas to suit one's purpose? Then he will do and think and even feel just what is required of him. What a wise provision of Nature! How, otherwise, would it be possible to lead whole millions of such inheritors and guide them where they ought to go? But by this method their mind in the end feels the fist on the collar and its steady force just as little as their body the pressure of the air. Thus, with a sort of rapture, man perceives his name right at the top of Linnaeus's 'Who's Who', and even the monkeys tremendously far below him, without considering that by far the greater part of his species stands, according to a different, but perhaps more rational, system, below the dogs and the millers' donkeys.

The contrast between the two individuals is marvellous. The apothecary's expression, pure, genuine metal, full of bull-like force and resolution; the servant's like a miserable milksop's; his whole head, though not badly equipped, exactly like that of a sheep with St Vitus's dance; trembling, actively determined on nothing, passively open to anything. Oh, whatever becomes of the poor devil, he will certainly not make an *Orateur du Genre Humain*! The coat of the one almost like a waistcoat, and even buttoned up, so as not to obstruct the play of his knees as he walks the streets on his salutary visits; that of the other much—oh, much

—too long! A proper locking device for the fetch-and-carry, especially if the magazine pouches on both sides are well loaded; a true Spanish mantle. Moreover, the garment of the first sits firmly, not a cubic inch left vacant; everything is stuffed full; only one more pound of pudding and the seam will burst or the buttons fly. But the other's coat, oh gracious goodness—barely half-inhabited, with space enough and to spare to accommodate the whole pound of pudding together with the apothecary. There are certainly no buttons flying off there; they would even slip out of their buttonholes had they been fastened symmetrically; but they are buttoned up askew, and the tenth button is really poking out of the ninth buttonhole, and the eleventh out of the tenth, and so on. The device is not a new one, but if the poor devil has hit upon it himself, he has really displayed some talent for mechanics. For now the button side of the coat does not quite match the buttonhole side, but the former hangs on the latter; it is carried by it. If we now assume that the pocket on the button side will always be specially well loaded as a man's usually is, then if, for instance, when fetching bread the excess weight were only six pounds, the button can as little slip out of its hole as a nail on the wall out of the loop by which a coat hangs on it, no matter how wide the loop may be. The apothecary's stout leg pedestals we have already passed under review. The legs of the servant with the permanent curtsy of impotence which they are in the act of making, hardly deserve the name of legs and are altogether not worth mentioning. Thus only a few words more about the coat. This State- and everyday-livery is really an ancient servants' fief in that family, which at every change of personnel, at every sloughing, always reverts to the feudal lord. Now since under this procedure some saving will obviously be made in the course of time, they have been generous at the start with the material, and everything is rather strong and in full measure, so that it could be partly worn and partly dragged along by any man from 4 ft. 6 in. upwards to a height where he could perhaps let himself be seen for money. That one man will not be as well fitted as another is of course true, but this also applies to a certain extent, not only to their garments, but also to their—services.

Before we turn to a closer examination of the room and its appointments we cannot let the doctor in the doorway there get away without a few more farewell lines, little though they may benefit him. There is something comic about this figure which can be more easily felt than described.

Few have looked upon the retreat of the doctor without a smile, but wherein the ridiculous part really consisted, they could not explain to themselves. It is true that the broad knot-wig, the sword hilt in the coat slit, and the Spanish cane with its golden knob, held somewhat below its centre of gravity and gently raised in meditation towards his mouth, have a solemn but incongruous air. But is that all? Not quite. It seems to me that the man's appearance obviously suggests the idea of belated arrival, or the so-called race against time, a situation which in any case is extremely uncomfortable, but is absolutely deadly to an intended impression of solemnity. To be late, even when one is not to blame for it, does not specially become anybody, and can make one ridiculous if it is made with an air of punctuality. Moreover, the best of doctors does not cut a particularly good figure *vis-à-vis* a dead person whom he had hoped to save; for although, on the one hand, one knows very well and readily admits that the art of medicine is nothing less, and could and should be nothing less, than the art of making man immortal, yet one could not, on the other hand, take it in ill part if some people in such a situation should think that not to be able to help is an art which others could also practise. To evade such a comparison, or at least to cut it short, his Magnificence the Doctor now sneaks quietly away and leaves it to the less sensitive ear of the apothecary to listen to the mourners' complaints about our lack of knowledge and the fruitless expenses.

Hogarth has covered and hung the old merchant's whole room with very telling traits of the most abominable miserliness and that vulgar lack of taste which always closely attends on greed. The first thing that strikes the eye is the table laid for the mid-day meal. The Frenchman who once translated that term by *mal de midi* would not have been far out here. There is only one hot dish for the hysterical lady, namely a boiled egg balanced on salt. The rest consists of a dead joint (for there is also a living one here) which was to be picked over today for the last time, and half a pig's head, an animal which in life must have had its food worries and which, after death, through being frequently borne to and fro between larder and table, must obviously have suffered still more through desiccation. Although the palate is, as we see, but moderately provided for, eye and imagination are the more richly feasted. They are catered for by some heavy and ostentatiously magnificent silver plate, and particularly by a view of the Thames. With the latter, the generous man has really been somewhat extravagant today; he has opened both window casements: one would have been enough. There is hardly any evidence of plates for guests except a small one, apparently a family meridometer[1] for soup and vegetables.

What the huge ornamental silver vessel with the handles might contain is difficult to say; that is, of course, as far as one cannot see inside it; for as far as one can see, it is obviously empty. If, as is probable, the sly landlord has made good by the vessel what was lacking in drink, then it might at any rate contain stale beer—and still be an expensive-looking drink. The content of the silver jug on the floor is apparently honest-to-goodness, pure Middlesex 1745 from the Thames. This then is the meal at which death has overtaken the fair guest. Of course the poison was to blame. But indeed, for an appetite and digestive powers such as the policeman on the fifth Plate must have possessed, such a dinner, if repeated for only a few days, would surely have been followed by similar sad consequences. We need only look at the living joint there, the dog! Poor devil! Luckily for him, they are mourning the death of the daughter of the house, for otherwise they would surely have been mourning his today. He helps himself without recourse to the meridometer. Well done! There is certainly no one among our readers who would not wish the good animal a happy retreat with his booty. But it is difficult to see how such a retreat is possible, and to devour the booty before the enemy's very eyes is out of the question. To outflank the right wing is entirely impossible; the old man is in command there in person, and with the keen, constant wakefulness of a watch-dog, knows equally well how to guard diamond rings and old joints. It would thus seem more expedient either to outflank the left wing, where there is at any rate some mutiny, or to break through the legs of the apothecary so as to get in front of the old doctor and the departing soul, on whose discretion he can rely, and thus get ahead of her. Let us hope for the best.

In the magnificent bow window with its stained glass, the domestic dragon with her dust-and-spider broom has evidently gashed in a few ugly ventilation holes which gave the old man an excuse for dispensing with cleaning altogether, lest the whole window be turned into a ventilator. A cross-spider has taken advantage of this peacefulness to spread out her

---

[1] From μέρος portio, and μέτρον mensura, a portion-measure.

net in safety.[1] In this connection one can hardly fail to remember Churchill's verse in which he describes Scotland, though, of course, with southern, anti-Scottish malice, as the promised land 'where half-starv'd spiders feed on half-starv'd flies'.[2] For in very truth if the alderman does not feed his flies better than his dogs, then the above-mentioned crusader might indeed find itself in the position of its Scottish fellow-knights, since in this household even the skeleton of a dog falls upon the dried specimen of a pig. In the matter of repairing the transient, this man has his own methods. He has not attempted to patch up the window panes, not even with sugar paper, which does not look too bad as a rule, but, instead, he has worked on the backs of the ornamental chairs, and that in a way which does not look particularly well. Our readers will notice that the fallen chair must have had a similar fall before, in which both back supports were broken. These have not, perhaps, been glued on but, at least on one side, been reinforced by a stout splinter, which is really much more solid. As far as the appearance goes, it is certain that the mend will be quite invisible to anyone sitting in the chair, and hardly noticeable to others either. The only questionable point is the lack of symmetry in the patching. Indeed, it seems almost as if the splinter on the right is intended at the same time to cover the fracture on the left, since there the parts seem somewhat out of alignment; it may also be that the fracture is new, and once the chair was on its feet again, that little matter would soon correct itself. Little tobacco pipes are to be seen in various parts of the room, one on the window and even three in the small cupboard which contains the business papers. With such care does this parsimonious creature preserve something which every day-labourer in England throws away after he has used it, since he will get another for nothing together with the smallest drink he orders. But since, if I am right, the water-drinkers get nothing, he might be excused on that account.

The private library consists entirely of MSS: The *Day Book*, the *Ledger*,

---

[1] That the coat-of-arms, which is not only divided by a cross but contains a small cross as well, hangs there in the arch like a spider which also bears a cross in its coat-of-arms, has surely some meaning, which, however, I do not quite dare to decipher. But perhaps it is enough in the way of explanation that the landlord should carry the same device as that insect whose loving kindness and disinterestedness and inoffensive behaviour towards his weaker fellow-creatures who have business with him have become proverbial.

[2] A quotation from Churchill's poem 'The Prophesy of Famine: a Scots Pastoral', January 1763. Ed.

the *Receipt Book*, and, finally, the thickest of them all[1] next to the cupboard door, entitled *Compound Interest*. The little volume in quarto appears to contain the correspondence from the last postal delivery.

In the lower part of the bookcase, next to the pipes, stands a home-made tobacco pouch made out of a twisted quarto sheet, and, probably, a bottle of ink. Perhaps, however, the bottle contains an *ipse fecit* for the stomach to take of a Sunday morning in well water. The absolutely taste-less insipidity of this cupboard is relieved, at least from the gable end downwards, by an old inverted punch bowl. Since time, aided by careless-ness, has already, as one sees, cut a second spoon groove in its rim, it seems to rest up there in honourable retirement.

The adornments of the walls are, of course, less showy than those of the Squanderfields under the last two governments, but they are at least English workmanship through and through. The alderman's hat and gown hang on the pegs; next to them an English clock, probably with works of English wood. To judge by the calibre of the bell, its stroke and alarum regulate the business of the house on all floors. The hands point to five minutes past eleven. Dinner at this hour is not the worst institution in this household. Even from a miser it is possible to learn something. Eleven o'clock in the morning is even late for a man who at four is already poring over his rent book. In the West End of the City they sit down to dinner when here in the East End it is already five o'clock. This gives the City of London a moral[2] extension in length of six hours' time, corresponding to 90° longitude. Should it increase still more, which seems very probable, and should the King of Spain start boasting again that the sun never sets on his realm, then every Cockney could confidently reply that his home town alone is already so great that the sun, wherever it may be, always finds some family at dinner.

The remaining decoration consists of three paintings, apart from an almanack stuck on the wall. The originals were not, as one sees, of the Italian school; they were never turned out like that in Southern

---

[1] This feature is lost in our copy through a very pardonable oversight. In the original that curious MS. is almost one-and-a-half times as fat as the others. I take this occasion to point out other such errata on this Plate. In the original the table-cloth had a few quite noticeable stains, and the ceiling had been repaired by the decorator just about as well as the chair-back by the carpenter. Evidently both were done by the same artist, or were even maybe a small *ipse fecit*.

[2] In the sense of being more industrious. Ed.

Europe under a clear sky and on volcanic earth, but in some North-Western corner of our continent on alluvial peat soil and in a somewhat heavy, misty atmosphere. The largest of them contains the portraits—one could not call them speaking likenesses but rather tantalizing likenesses—of a leg of mutton, roasted on the spit, heads of cabbage, potatoes, carrots, onions, etc., all executed so appetizingly that the naked appearance of the pig's head on the table could not compete with them. This is what art can do. In addition, we see here stable lights which lack nothing but oily stickiness, little herring barrels complete apart from the smell, swill rags charming to put in one's pocket, if only they would not seem to drip like real ones.

Almost a quarter of this still-lifeless nature the owner has covered with a live Teniers, and thereby has given that kitchen paradise, so to speak, an inmate. A real masterpiece, this, by that Raphael of the Netherlands. It hangs there above the almanack, apparently in place of a morning devotion for the strengthening of the moral feelings, which, after all, is the purpose of all painting and was especially the whole endeavour of Raphael, the Teniers of Urbino. Even if that purpose should be somewhat out of place here, it is at least possible to test by this item of the morning routine whether one still has some moral feeling. It represents a great empty drinking vessel and another still more roomy, somewhat overfull, which have evidently exchanged their contents. The piece is not a complete Teniers, for in his works one sees at least a great number of faces everywhere. Is it perhaps cut out from a whole canvas, or did it alone survive from some destruction of the rest? This seems to me highly probable, since merely to represent that simple process of filtration of Dutch drinks, even a Dutchman would hardly undertake for the sake of its moral implications. But if it is a salvaged cutting, then it is again queer and contrary to an established procedure that in a wholesale destruction only that figure should survive who at the wall—looks. Above the door hangs the third painting, also of the Bog school. This marvellous picture can bear more than one interpretation. Either one of the figures is burning a nose-wart off the other with his pipe—such a thing might be possible; or Hogarth was thinking of Shakespeare and Bardolph's nose[1] which glowed

---

[1] Lichtenberg evidently refers here to the passage in Shakespeare's *King Henry IV*, Pt. 1, where Falstaff says to Bardolph: 'Though bearest the lantern in the poop—but 'tis in the nose of thee; thou art the Knight of the Burning Lamp . . .' (Act III, Scene 3). Ed.

in the dark like a coal, and the man is now merely re-lighting his pipe at it.

Without my drawing attention to it, the reader will have noticed that Hogarth in his pictures, by means of the wall decorations, pokes fun partly at Biblical murder stories and the subtle obscenities of the Italians, partly at the more peaceful cochonneries of the Dutch. As is usually the case with every man of value, he thinks himself better than anyone else. Bravo! Without such a faith not even a grain of sand can be moved, let alone mountains; so, in Heaven's name let us carry on like that; this procedure is most advantageous to the savings-box of Time and of Humanity.

I return once more to the most prominent exhibit of the lunch-time scene, the view of the Thames. The row of houses which we see are the famous, and ultimately infamous, buildings on the bridge itself, which is 915 ft. long and 72 ft. broad. Before the year 1756 it still had those rows of houses on each side to a depth of 26 ft., so that between them there still remained a 20 ft. broad street. Towards the year 1746 these buildings had become so decayed that the inhabitants of the upper storeys ran the unusual risk of being drowned in the next storm, and the sailors the no less remarkable risk of being killed on board ship by falling bricks and tiles. The leaning of these houses towards the miraculous Hogarth has expressed unmistakably. He did this in 1745, and in the following year Parliament decreed the abolition of these houses. I say decreed, for they were demolished only in 1756. That is how things go in this world. But still Parliament was immeasurably more lucky in its intention with these houses than was Hogarth with the present work. The houses disappeared ultimately; our good man, however, wished to eliminate marriages *à la mode*, but according to the latest news from England they still exist.

According to Mr Nichols' report, Hogarth had also designed a happy marriage series, and even sketched it out in colours. These pictures are said to be now in the possession of Madame Garrick. He did not, however, present them to the public, although he still lived for some time after. Could it be perhaps that he lacked data? Not in his own home, certainly, for he himself, though childless, enjoyed an otherwise very happy marriage. I explain it by the whole genius of the man. Probably his friends gave him to understand in good time that he was in the same position as his great fellow-countryman Milton; Milton lives, as we know, through his lost, and not through his regained, paradise.

151

By an advertisement in the *Daily Advertiser* of 1750, Hogarth put up the original paintings for auction. They were bought by a certain Mr Lane of Hillingdon, near Uxbridge, for 120 guineas, although the frames alone are said to have cost the artist 24 guineas. In March 1792, as I see from the *European Magazine*, April 1792, page 317, they were bought, also in an auction, for 920 guineas, but it is not recorded by whom. The last but one bid was made by the famous Boydell[1] for 900 guineas. Finally, according to a report which I have read in some papers and journals, they were bought in 1797 by a banker named Angerstein for 1,000 guineas. The original engravings were sold by the artist's widow, from whom I also bought my set in 1775, for one pound twelve and sixpence.

[1] John Boydell (1719–1804), an eminent London art dealer. Ed.

Strolling Actresses Dressing in a Barn

A Midnight
Modern Conversation or
The Bacchanalians

Strolling Actresses Dressing
in a Barn

NEVER since the graving tool and the brush were made to serve the cause of satire has so much gay humour been compressed in so little space as here. It would hardly be possible to throw an ombre card on to this picture without concealing with it some characteristic feature or other of the most amusing satire. Every corner of this sanctuary of Ceres announces the presence of the all-powerful Satyr. Now the rogue foots it on the threshing floor, now struts about in the midst, then grins from above out of the clouds—even in a barn. What a pity, one might say, that such abundance of laughter-provoking material should be burning away here almost by itself without a higher purpose. How much might have been warmed at this fire! But perhaps these are only the plaints of poverty. We should not calculate too narrowly where genius is concerned; his gifts are just as little a matter for calculation as those of Heaven itself, for the secret intercourse between the two is probably very far-reaching.[1]

The picture bears the title, 'Strolling Actresses Dressing in a Barn'. Thus only actresses, no actors. How, it has been asked, could Hogarth so entitle it when there are obviously some male figures there? Obviously? Could they not be merely females in disguise? This is a question which everyone who knows this magician should ask himself for a start. We may criticize his draughtsmanship here and there, his frequently poor distribution of light and shade, and his grouping, if we will, but in criticizing his ideas we should be rather cautious, the more obvious such criticism

[1] A finer ear may be reminded of St. John, Ch. 3, v. 8: 'The wind bloweth where it listeth . . .' Ed.

seems. Oh, how often has he not taken me in! Now, if somebody were to tell me: there is a dead fox in front of the hen-coop—it is beginning to smell already, I would always ask first: but are you sure the rascal has not merely perfumed himself and is lying in wait there? There is no doubt that Hogarth had something in mind in choosing that title. But just what he may have meant by it, must and shall be investigated, no matter how delicate such sex investigations may be. Think only of Mamselle d'Eon[1]— what a hue and cry that was! And here we have even three of these Mamselles. However, we shall see. I shall make a frank enquiry for I rely upon a strict, inexorable censor, to whom I show every page before it goes to the printers, and that is—respect for the world of morals. But perhaps the matter is not half so bad as one might suspect. Indeed, before we waste another word over it, we ought to look at the good people somewhat more closely.

Our migrants (it does not matter here whether actresses or actors) are going to produce this evening a little comedy, the announcement of which Hogarth has fortunately preserved for us. Two copies of it are lying there on the bed, directly behind the grill, close to the broken eggs, the chamber pot and the empty pair of trousers. Although these two playbills together would barely cover four square feet of surface, yet they are in immediate contact with the afore-mentioned furniture, clothes and victuals, which in any orderly household would hardly be found simultaneously in as many square rods. It is somewhat cramped here. The top sheet, of which we see only the upper half, reads: 'By a company of Comedians from the London Theatre at the George Inn this present evening will be presented The Devil to Pay in Heaven.'[2] On the second, only the lower end is visible, and this contains the dramatis personae, at least in part. They are: Jupiter, Juno, Diana, Flora, the Night, a Siren, Aurora, an Eagle, Cupid, two Devils, a Ghost and Attendants. As one sees, the order in the programme

[1] The Chevalier d'Eon (1728–1810), a French secret agent, who spent most of his life in female dress. Ed.

[2] The farce, *The Devil to Pay, or The Metamorphosed Wives*, written originally in 1686 by an actor called Jevon, but later transformed into an opera by Coffey and Mottley, has, as is well known, been produced with great success. Was it Hogarth's intention to allude to the metamorphoses in the picture? I should not like to decide. A queer point is that the English have so many comedies in which the Devil appears even in the title. *The Companion of the Playhouse* lists twelve of them. However, he rarely appears in person, but only sends his representatives.

Strolling Actresses Dressing in a Barn

here, just as on the bedstead and in the whole building, is decidedly Bohemian. Here, already, is the devil to pay. The notice contains also a few sad lines: 'Being the last time of acting before the Act commences' (the Act of Parliament against Strolling Players). Thus, all will soon be over, even if they will, as is the custom in Germany, give the final performance three or four times. It is doubtful if anything will be able to save these poor devils, not even the finest hair-splitting of English lawyers. If the Act merely said, as it would perhaps in German, 'against Strolling Actors', they could retort: 'we stroll, to be sure, but we are actresses', and so for the time being they would be as safe in their barns as in their London theatres. But it speaks of strolling *players*, and against that word not even a band of Hermaphrodites could prevail. But who knows what they may do yet? It is true everywhere, and nowhere more than in England, that in order to do right in the world very little knowledge is needed, but to do wrong with confidence, one must know the law. Whoever wishes to examine this Act of Parliament will find it not far from the chamber-pot, lying upon an imperial crown. It has been pushed between that and a hot, sooty pan containing gruel, and so at least they have replaced a lack of reverence for the Act by respect for the crown. So much for the worthy company as a whole. Now we shall present the persons one by one to our readers.

On the extreme left sits obviously Juno, the Queen of Heaven, with a crown upon her head and the book of words before her. She is studying her part, and to utilize the time thoroughly she stretches out her immortal leg upon an overturned wheelbarrow and lets the Goddess of the Night, in star-spangled garment, darn her eternal stockings. That goddess has, out of respect, extinguished her lamp and set it beside her. How kind and considerate of Hogarth—and Night! Holes in the stockings of a Juno should not be brought into the light. She has propped her book against a not particularly new trunk, for time, to be sure, has torn off a part of the skin which, for the benefit of the trunk, has once been torn off a sea-lion. In order to be high enough, it stands upon its small side, and so there is evidently nothing in it. That is just the way with trunks, wine-barrels and such-like—they set themselves up just when they are empty. The book is propped against a salt-cellar, from under whose lifted lid peeps out a rolling-pin. Down in the world these are for kitchen use; here in the antichamber of Heaven they have to serve in the orchestra as well, so as to support the rest of the music with thump and rattle. It is said that these instruments are quite pleasing to the ear, provided the ear is not too dull. Hogarth has made use of them again in his 'Fair at Southwark', where a comedy is being acted too. Thus they seem to belong predominantly to the strolling Muse. They are not too heavy for transport, are inexpensive, and serve at the same time for kitchen and orchestra. On the back of the salt-cellar something is chalked up, probably the amount due to the milk and porter merchants. Immediately behind the salt-cellar stands an earthly tinder-box; steel and stone in a wretched little box, in brotherly proximity to the most august of all tinder-boxes, Jupiter's thunderbolt. What an idea, and what a Jupiter! In addition to his lightning he keeps a common tinder-box as well, so as to be able to strike a light of some kind if in damp weather his electrical experiments should misfire. This thunderbolt is so lightly and precariously balanced upon the trunk that in all probability the next exclamation mark in Juno's role is going to topple it down upon the poor monkey. That little dramatis persona is, for the sentimental pleasure of the English crowd and in honour of the Bourbon line, dressed up in a French hair-bag and Spanish mantle. He holds in front of him nothing less than Alexander's helmet, and quite unimpressed by its plumes, whose proud nodding once made the world tremble, uses it for a domestic purpose which need not be expressed in words. For a monkey the gesture is really philosophical and great. There is something modern in it which is more easily felt than explained. Who, one might ask, would expect under the old Franconian hair-bag so many new Franconian principles? And the face! Oh! let the thunderbolt fall; the mien of the wise remains unshaken,

impavidum ferient ruinae.

Now, another conjecture. How if the wheelbarrow were simultaneously push- and thunder-cart? Loaded with stones and trundled over loose boards on *that* wheel of decidedly unequal radii, it would certainly have a splendid effect. Salt-cellars performing auxiliary service in the orchestra and a wheelbarrow doing likewise on thunder clouds fit equally well into the equipment of theatrical vagabonds. Where the thunderbolt hovers, thunder is surely not far off, never mind where it comes from. If, in addition, the trunk proves to be just the one in which the downpour and the hailstorm have made their journey here, then that group would acquire a dignity and a magnitude whose description would scorn mere prose. That, incidentally, the Goddess of Night is represented by a negress Hogarth has indicated clearly enough by her woolly hair. In this way the good people save their lamp-black, and spare their white linen. An important detail for a household in which, as one sees in the background, washing and drying are, alas! a permanent feature.

In the centre of the picture shines Diana,

velut inter ignes Luna minores.

Her attire is not exactly what is understood by hunting dress. Of all the insignia with which antiquity has invested her, nothing is left but the half-moon. Even the moral ones seem to have vanished. Looking at that figure, one cannot help thinking: Hogarth intended her as a topsy-turvy Diana just as this is here a topsy-turvy world. She who among the ancients was the chaste and unapproachable one stands here almost without fortification. The outer bastions are all falling, and even the inner wall, which in any case was rather lightly built, has a terrific breach on one side, which will give the Goddess of Night something to mend. From her head too there flutters the white flag of capitulation, as some wag once called those white ostrich feathers. Further, the twice-girded (*bis cincta*) is here a nowhere-girded one. All her girdles are discarded: a sad circumstance for a goddess of chastity. And, finally, as is well known, the Diana of antiquity is always represented with legs bare to above the knee, but otherwise carefully covered. Ours, on the other hand, appears almost completely naked except the legs to above the knee, which are even more carefully covered than is usual with the chaste sex. That is very bad. Even the Medusa head down there, which may understand and see all this better than we do, seems to express an antiquarian's surprise at such wholly unmythological be-haviour on the part of the chaste goddess. Nay, more than surprise. It seems as if the sight had made it suffer for the first time that death by petrifaction which it usually dealt out itself.

Diana appears to have been about to step into the crinoline so as not to disturb her coiffure when, in the repetition of her part, she came upon a passage which demanded a rather violent oratorical outburst, and this caused the delay. Or perhaps the crinoline was already fastened in place and the outburst of oratory has also resulted in the outburst of her waistband.

159

Now a few words in defence of that poor creature. It is true Hogarth has dressed her rather badly for a Goddess of Chastity, at least rather un-Diana like. But has Nature done any better for her? Diana was tall and slender; she stood a head higher than everyone else. Ours here is short and plump, and to this constellation of affairs is due a very important circumstance. Head and heart are here a whole span nearer to one another. What the poor warm heart fondly hatches comes here, still poor and warm as it is, to the head, and the geometrical span becomes a moral mile.[1] Oh! how fortunate are those tall, lean damsels in whom the warm machinations of the heart have sufficient time to cool upon the mile-long journey to the head! That is why tall bony frames are said to be more conducive if not to all, at least to some of the virtues, than the more compressed and better covered ones. Her eye, too, and the whole shape of her face strike one as uncouth and vulgar, no matter how many gaze-distractors she has stuck on to interfere with any such close investigation, and altogether she seems to be more stolid than her prototype and probably at some time in the past, upon this or another threshing floor, has threshed something more useful than blank verse. But however little instruction or edification that goddess may offer to the archaeologist, her present bathing attire seems to have specially distracted the eye of a village Acteon who, in the left-hand upper corner, is peeping through the roof. Mr Ireland believes the fellow is perched there because he has to repair the roof; I believe he sits there for his own benefit; that is how interpreters differ.

Immediately in front of Diana sits Flora, the Goddess of Flowers, though as yet without her flowers and cornucopia, about to make her toilet. The candle, with which she is greasing her hair, she has just taken from the clay candlestick which lies on its side in front of her on the floor. In her right hand she holds a dredger from which to sprinkle pollen upon her flowery head. For table she uses a covered basket which could hold at least a measure of corn but which, as we see from the appended label, contains nothing less than the company's jewels. A lighted candle, evidently put ready for kindling the others, is set down there so negligently that its flame has already caught the straw wherein the jewels in the corn-measure jewellery box are packed, and will cause not only the

[1] What the author means here is that the reduction of distance between head and heart has the effect of skipping a moral mile. Ed.

jewels (for, according to the latest experiments, diamonds disappear in fire) but the whole Pantheon with all its splendour to go up in flames, if the goddesses do not notice it in time. Thus, it seems as if the Act of Parliament were taking effect here already, aided by an Act of God. Flora has a mirror in front of her, a mere fragment to be sure, and even that catoptric fragment incomplete, for it has here and there dioptric patches. Close to it lies that well-known instrument which man has learnt to carve from the tooth of the largest animal on terra firma to fight with it the bites of the smallest—an ivory comb. The battle must have been hard, and victory often in doubt, for the comb, as one sees, has lost some of its own teeth in the struggle. But to save the honour of the Goddess of Flowers, one might allow that Hogarth aimed merely at the aphis fly which, as is well known, often resorts to the youthful neck of the Queen of Flowers herself—I mean the rose. By that inevitable intercourse with the first ornament of the garden, that vermin, like the flea and the fly, acquires a sort of dignity. It is vermin of standing. In the oyster shell upon the basket lid there is perhaps salty pomatum-butter, or, as some believe, some colour for the blossom of that little rose.

Behind Diana stands an altar at which a brace of little devils are quarrelling over a jar of porter. That they are devils is clear only from their horns; for, if those were missing on their hoods, a pair of heads like that and an altar would form no contrast at all, at least, nothing out of the ordinary. One would take them for a pair of very commonplace creatures who flourish in all parts of the world, and whose natural history has been given in two excellent works.[1] The group overflows with bitter, almost profane satire, which becomes clear to anybody if he substitutes a chalice for the porter jug. To the honour of Hogarth we must believe that his satire is not aimed at human beings but at devils in human form. Hogarth never had anything against honest people, for he was one himself. Besides, it is not the altar at which he hits out with clenched fist, but at those who officiate there, and, finally, the little table is not an altar proper, but merely an Ara.[2] On top of it stand or lie a medley of objects; a bit of

---

[1]   (i) in *Joannis Physiophili specimen Monachologiae methodo Linnaeana, tabulis tribus aeneis illustratum cum adnexis thesibus e Pansophia* **P.P.P.** Fast., etc., 1783.

   and (ii) in *Histoire naturelle des Moines écrite d'après la méthode de Buffon ornée d'une figure.* Paris 1793. 8vo.

[2] i.e. an altar to the *penates*, or household gods. Ed.

bread, I believe, or something like that; a goblet and some Virginian incense rising from a pipe which the drinker, so as to be able to imbibe with both hands, has just put down. That burning pipe is lying there without a lid, so that if the threatened blow of the fist really materializes, it will no doubt make common cause with the flame on the jewel box.

Further to the left behind the ara, a one-eyed old hag with her scissors is depriving a cat of its most beautiful ornament, evidently to obtain some blood for the misdeed which the dagger that she wears in her cloak is to commit that very evening in the tragi-comedy. The operation appears to please the old woman, and in grinning she reveals a couple of smile-teeth of the utmost charm. Probably they are the sole heirs to the charms of all their departed sisters and brothers. Altogether there is much play of teeth in that group; they are displayed with almost every possible signi-ficance: by the old dame to enhance the sweetness of her smile; by the cat for biting purposes, and by the unhappy tight-rope dancer who holds the victim, to master her pain. She will have a hard task, though, for the cat has not only caught her hand very firmly between its teeth, but has also fastened its hind legs into her scantily-clad *regionem hypogastricam* just above the fig-leaf bloomers which she wears as a fortification over her tights. It is impossible to look at that sufferer without thinking of Laocoon. Not of the Belvedere group, for that would be offending against the highest majesty of art, but of the droll engraving where Laocoon and his sons are parodied by monkeys. It is not quite clear what role the old woman is to play. Hardly a witch, or she would not be cutting off a cat's tail. She might find herself in the same situation. She may be the ghost mentioned in the programme. If that were so, then the dagger would probably indicate suicide. The economy of the old dame deserves a few lines. She cuts off merely the end of the branch and leaves the main stem, despite the Act of Parliament, for future tragic scenes. Here the didactic Trusler[1] would have declared: 'Mark this well, all ye economists!'— always providing he had succeeded in marking it himself. So much for that side of the scene, at least as far as the animate objects are concerned. The inanimate we shall leave for the time being. But they will be resur-rected yet, and we hope not without raising the spirits of the living.

Behind the chaste goddess stands a figure with a crown—in reality a circle of gold paper in the shape of a sun or sunflower—upon his head,

[1] Refers to the Rev. John Trusler, author of *Hogarth Moralized*, London 1768. Ed.

who is instructing a small cupid on a ladder to fetch down, or turn over, a pair of stockings that are being dried in the clouds. That figure is said to be Jupiter. All the interpreters insist upon it, probably because otherwise Jupiter would appear only upon the programme. Among the gods it is usually Phoebus, as everyone knows, who dries the washing, and Jupiter Pluvius who has the job of soaking it. That figure could just as well represent Phoebus. But, of course, the Jupiter of the ancients is difficult to recognize from behind. With him everything lies on the positive side. Even though, when seen from the negative one, he might appear to be a bull, he need only turn his head and the *numen* is immediately there again. Unfortunately, we cannot turn that bull round and so he may pass for a Jupiter. Thus Zeus scorns the washing line and hangs his laundry on a thunder cloud. How grand! It was like that with everything he did. Even for him, however, the washing hangs a little too high up and in order to find out whether it is dry, he despatches his notorious winged servant, who, despite his wings, has to make use of a ladder. In everyday life, too, ladders often take the place of love's wings. Indeed, this cupid's wings are of so little help to him that he only succeeds in reaching up the last three inches through a supreme effort of his toes. However, Hogarth reveals himself to us here in such a clear light that any further elucidation would only obscure him. In keeping with the key in which the whole picture is composed, Cupid is here neither blind nor naked. He sees very well where other people's stockings are, and even wears his own attractively rolled down.

On the right-hand side behind the jewellery box stands a rather pleasant-looking girl, with her hair hanging down. It is probably only the drowsiness of intoxication which somewhat clouds her gaze. This is the Siren, as one sees from the fish tail which is kept in place by a band round her waist.

Desinit in piscem mulier formosa superne.

Her features are typically English, and quite common among healthy English country folk. In her right hand she holds a bottle and is, as one sees, about to dispense a drop of comfort to a Mamselle d'Eon, who complains of a toothache which is shortly to become the object of an *investigation épineuse.* While that water nymph is handing out brandy, a youthful Aurora with brilliant morning star upon her forehead is, with a charming twist of her little gold mouth, busily occupied in squashing some water insects which have been left sticking on the siren's kerchief. The star shines in full splendour. It is still very early; dawn is yet grey in that Aurora face, and Phoebus, to quote from Butler, will have to advance his fire a good deal in order to boil that little lobster red. That a water goddess should serve wine is funny enough. A figure like that would make a good shop-sign for many a tavern, if only it was a wine goddess serving water.[1] But what sort of creature is it that is trying here to assuage its toothache with brandy? We shall answer the most insidious question first. It needs only a cursory inspection to see that it is a woman. The long hair, the beauty spots not yet wiped off, the unmistakable broadness of the hips behind the coat pocket, the whole shape of the legs and knee and the knee posture which everybody recognizes from antique sculpture, render this beyond any doubt. Objection has been raised on account of the shirt. But is it the garment which determines the female sex? A woman who dresses up as a man may also don a man's shirt, if wrist frills and ruffles are needed. Should perhaps these poor devils here, who already lack the space for visible decorum, provide themselves for the sake of an invisible one, with an unimaginable type of shirt, I mean a hermaphroditic one? Before her on the bed lie the trousers which she has to put on. I am almost afraid a fruitless attempt has already been made. The belt is fully drawn out of the buckle, an indication that the greatest possible width was still not enough, or that, provisionally, the greatest possible one was regarded as the only possible one. It is a fact known to everyone, even if he has not studied antique sculpture, that the daintiest woman will find herself uncomfortably compressed about the hips in the trousers of even the most squarely-built man; indeed, the odds are a hundred to one that it will not even be possible for her to squeeze into them without the most violent stretchings, and blanks in the text. With trousers in the figurative sense, since they are the symbol of authority, and hold almost the same place in the household as the *fasces* in the Roman State, it is, of course, a different matter. These are put on by married

[1] The so-called beer sign which in some parts of Germany, especially in country districts, still hangs from houses where wine, or at least brandy, is served, indicates, to be sure, that friendly relation between water and wine. As is well known, an equilateral triangle balanced on one corner is the symbol for water, whereas set on one of its sides it is the symbol for wine; joined together, they are used as the beer sign. Mendelssohn's Thetis embracing Bacchus.

ladies a few weeks after the wedding, often with the greatest of ease, and they fit them splendidly. So much for the first question—but what, or whom, does that figure represent? Mr Ireland believes it is meant to be Ganymede, and I think he is right. Jupiter's bird immediately in front of her rather bears this out, and then the role of Ganymede should always be played by a girl. It is amusing to note, though probably a little too erudite for our artist, that Ganymede's name is commonly derived from two Greek words, γανᾶν and μῆδος, of which the first means 'to show a friendly face', and the second something like 'counsel'. Now it would hardly be possible to show a more unfriendly face than Ganymede's here, or to give worse counsel than he does. Strictly speaking, he does not offer any counsel but, conversely, accepts a very good one. But it may even be possible that Hogarth had something like that in mind. An artist, though he may not be addicted to reading books, even confiscated ones, might for once read a book of myths, or at least consult it, if he thinks of working on a subject of that sort. Here, where a topsy-turvy Heaven was to be presented, he would have found it particularly useful. Though if a man has not properly studied the matter, but only picked up something from the dictionary *pro tempore*, he might easily seize upon the exceptional rather than the established meaning. But this only by the way.

Below in the right-hand corner sits the eagle which is to carry Ganymede over the clouds. This will prove a hard task for him if the unbreeched, and somewhat heavy sufferer behind him really is Ganymede, no matter how low the clouds here are, nor how strong the eagle's wings. But the wings of love in the background there which will make common cause with them, and a good rope of which there is no shortage here, will triumph over all. To what heights can ladder and rope—and the wings of love—not rise? So far, the eagle here is carrying a lighter and more agreeable burden than Ganymede, though in every respect a rather unfriendly counsellor, too. That this eagle is feeding a baby whom he would probably have gobbled up himself were he anything more than cardboard is an excellent touch. It is impossible to look at that trio of heads contrasted here without a smile. In the woman's eye, be she nurse or mother, we read patience and motherly care, in the eagle's a threatening demand for a portion, not of the pap, but of the child itself, and both are directed upon a miserable little lump of damsel-material, whose whole existence seems no more than a dimly felt contrast between his mother and the bird of prey. The eagle here has dainty female feet, not claws. The difference is not so great as it seems. They are both catching instruments; at least the fate of young hares would not be any happier for the change.

Now we have come far enough to make some relevant remarks about the title of the piece. Are these people actors or actresses? About the Ganymede we have already reached a decision. Thus there remain only Cupid, Jupiter and the devils. The latter are obviously not of the fair sex. But Cupid? Oh, he decidedly belongs to it. I believe it is even the custom for the part of Cupid to be played on the stage by a girl, and a very wise custom too. If a boy represents the God of Love with us ('with us' means here 'in our latitude'), then there is as a rule either too much feeling in the role or none at all. I have seen both and there is nothing to choose between empty puppet-play and *amour à la Grenadière*. Little girls, on the other hand, fit perfectly into the role. In matters of nature, where, on the whole, knowledge can be dispensed with, they learn the form long before the substance, and quickly become so sensible that a grown girl a year after her confirmation needs only to assume the hitherto deceptive envelope in spirit and in truth. The boy, provided he is really of the male sex, must always *know* before he *acts*, and how can such a creature who must know what he knows represent love? I should also imagine that with militant forces of this kind, the victory of a mere simulated boy would always be more certain and more general. In the one case he would conquer with what he is, and in the other only with what he represents. Thus our Cupid here might, at least, be a girl. And so all the characters, except Zeus and the devils, would then be women, and Hogarth's title as good as justified. For a Father Confessor and a couple of young tempters surely do not make a monastery out of a nunnery.

Thus, the knot is untied. Here, too, it would have been easier to cut it through. 'Actresses dressing.' Very good, one might say; all who are in the act of dressing here are indeed actresses. And then the whole title would be rather commonplace. It would be the sort of title which one gives to things, or which people let themselves be given—with all sorts of motives. But what could have been the motive here? Oh, I have already talked too long about a minor point. Just ask the village Acteon—he is sure to know.

Before I go any farther, I should like to be permitted a short diversion. Although I have spoken here about Ganymede's sex in very definite terms, this was merely with the intention of saying everything it was possible to say on this side of the question. For some interpreters, Nichols among them, favour the opposite opinion. He perceives in the eye of the little siren something more than mere medico-surgical comfort, namely love. If he is right, it would indeed be amusing to see a lover in such attire standing in front of his love and complaining of toothache, and the service which Aurora renders the girl at the entrevue enhances the situation still more. On the other hand, an anonymous commentator who is, I think, very reliable on the whole, only mentions it in a few words, and these are entirely in favour of my hypothesis. However, I will not sway the reader's judgment in anything. Part of the pleasure afforded by the contemplation of our artist's immortal work depends, just as with the works of Nature, upon the exercise of one's own ingenuity. I at least have been fascinated for many years, not so much by the wholly unmistakable in the artist's wit and mood, but by the easily mistakable and the actually mistaken. He who seeks will always find something. Perhaps it was precisely that attraction, so much to the artist's advantage, which prevented him from writing a commentary to his work himself, although he had often been asked to do so by his friends, and had often promised to as well. It certainly would not have been to his advantage. In order that something should be thought very deep, it should never be known exactly how deep it is.

To the right of the Goddess of Night, where it is in fact rather dark, all sorts of peculiar objects are assembled. Upon a soft cushion, the sort of cushion one finds in English pulpits, a bishop's mitre is taking its rest. The sayings from the Bible and the catechisms which may formerly have resided in it are gone, while comedies and farces have taken their place like sparrows in a swallow's nest, and like them have evidently chased away the first inhabitant. Next to it stands a lantern with a shutter, of the type which in English are called 'dark lanterns'. Above, I associated it with the Goddess of Night, but whether it does not rather belong to the bishop's mitre, alluding to the salubrious mixture of light and darkness which at all times streamed forth from that privileged dark lantern, or whether Diogenes has left his lantern with the bishop, I really do not know. Close by, Night has precipitated a dense fog. It is one of those cosy hair clouds beneath which, in England, the Sun of the Law, when in office, smiles forth with uncommon sweetness. The law, as we see, inhabits it no longer. Perhaps it provides an interim nest for the little kittens, one of which is disporting itself with the orb and the other with the lyre—politics and poetry. It is by no means disageeable to see art and science treated like that, and, fortunately, not so rare either. The little poetess, we observe, is making a blunder. Instead of plucking the strings of the lyre,[1] she only paws and scratches at the sounding box; and how gracefully does the little politician take part in the regimen of the world! Both deserve a place among the printing blocks and to serve as hallmarks on a little poem here, a political Utopia there—in certain journals.

A rope is also to be observed there; it is in fact a halter, and that is why it lies so close to the representative of the law. To a German that explanation might appear forced; to the common people of England it is the most natural in the world. Although in London more is packed, bound, and drawn with ropes than anywhere else in Christendom, even there a rather short one readily suggests the idea of a legal operation. The reason is that with us hanging is seldom done in public, while there it belongs among the Circenses. Finally, there are all kinds of utensils for conjuring tricks lying about there. Are these also professional implements? I think not. For how could Hogarth know that there, too, they perform sleight of hand?

Now a word more about the broken egg on the coverlet. One of the interpreters thinks that the eggs are lying there for the purpose of lubricating and clarifying the voice of the siren. If a misfortune (with which may also be classed unfortunate interpretations) is to happen, the occasion will not be lacking. If the poor girl was not just now swimming in the vicinity of the bedstead, such an association would never have occurred. No! It is obviously intended to illustrate the *cochonnerie* of these good people. What a bedspread upon which there is splashed a contribution to the next meal, and what a meal to which a contribution must be scooped off the bedspread! If in a household like this, where everything is everywhere, separate compartments could be spoken of at all, we might con-

---

[1] I do not know whether all poets and poetesses will know what that lyre originally was. Nothing less than an ox head between whose hollow horns Hermes had stretched four strings. Later, in Greece and Rome, the instrument moved farther and farther from its original form and became the symbol of poetic inspiration and the most beautiful attribute of the Delphic god. But presently it began, in accordance with the incomprehensible will of fate and fashion, to return more and more to its original form, and it is said that in Germany now there are some of these instruments in operation which sound exactly like strings stretched between the horns of an ox.

clude from all sorts of indications that that corner comprises kitchen and larder.

Behind Aurora may be seen a couple of sea waves with turning handles and pivots, just as one might expect, quietly standing in the arsenal between a triumphal arch on the one side and a drum, a trumpet and a worn broom on the other. A *mare pacificum* in the strict sense of the term. The waves which in action will lie horizontally are standing here almost at the vertical, so that the deities should not stumble over them or bark their shins against them. And that good, timid domestic animal, the clucking hen, who usually waits so fearfully if but one of her little step-daughters, a duckling, plunges into the pond, here contemplates with the calmness of a seagull how her true children climb up from wave to wave of the thundering sea, as if it were an ordinary hen-roost. Up above, under the roof, a chariot can be seen drawn by dragons one of which seems to hiss back at our Acteon. On the side hang flags and standards, new and old, British and Roman, with a motto summarizing the whole:

SENATUS POPULUSQUE ROMANUS

Everything else lying about there, such as scaffolding stands, paint or whitewash materials, rural scenes fresh from the brush, these are all easy to understand. Two items, however, deserve our special attention: the dragon chariot, and then the two figures which are sticking out up there from the bundle of straw like household furniture previously stolen or like a pair of lovers about to steal from one another. Of the dragon chariot, Mr Ireland thinks it is Medea's chariot. But why was it stuck up there? One cannot just say, because there was no room below; for, even if there was no room below for a dragon chariot, up above there was room for a droll idea, and surely something of that sort is behind it. If the dragons were spouting fire (and that is what all tragic dragons should do, especially in villages or small towns, or in some large ones too, for that matter) that would have been one reason for Hogarth to pack them so close to the straw and the roof. But they hiss cold. If it were not too pedantic again, I would suggest it was the chariot of Ceres or of her Triptolemus, which, as is well known, was also drawn by dragons. Right at the start I called this barn, quite involuntarily, a sanctuary of Ceres. The expression is quite familiar. How if Ceres at the arrival of so many higher gods had had to dismount and take to the attic, just like many people at the Leipzig Fair when the gods arrive? Corn and threshing flail had to be put on one side, and up above there they really are lying together. Or is that perhaps Ceres with her flail Triptolemus? But enough; perhaps the reader will find some better explanation.

The pair of lovers behind the straw, together with the flag, are the unhappy Oepidus with his Jocasta. That is what is written above them. Trusler, who does not easily surpass anybody, has here at least surpassed himself. He thinks Hogarth alluded by this to the incestuous life of these actresses. What an idea! Whoever has got a general idea of Hogarth will feel how utterly impossible it would be for our artist, in a picture which is all devoted to innocent laughter, to advance an idea which through the abhorrence it arouses would destroy the whole impression in one blow. If these people were incestuous then no one would laugh over them any more; they would be repugnant. They are indeed, as we have seen, shedders of blood, but only very innocent ones, and sinners they may be too, but again very good-natured, poor, sinners. The truth of the matter is that what is stuck behind there is part of the scenery for the Oepidus by Lee. Mr Nichols mentions that in the second Act of this tragedy there appears the following stage directions—'The cloud which surrounds the heads of the figures rises; on it there appear crowns, and above them shine in great golden letters the names, Oepidus and Jocasta.' This part of the scenery has now, for lack of space, been thrown behind there. But since Hogarth never does anything at random, and what he appears to throw away he always throws away with some intention, he has of course somewhat mischievously caused the two good people to hide themselves behind there as if they were ashamed.

If we observe the fluttering of the various garments in that barn, we can easily trace the direction of the toothache-and-snuffle-draught which is flowing here. It appears to make its entry through an opening beside the rosy triumphal arch; changes, after it has made a small detour to the side of Ganymede's toothache, into morning air in Aurora's raiment; in full daylight it behaves somewhat playfully with the chaste goddess and divides itself then into two streams; the left one fans Juno's robe and bosom and thence escapes into the open air; the right one on the other hand dries some laundry in passing and retreats above through the roof.

Since we have now studied this picture with our eyes, it may perhaps be quite instructive to apply an ear to it for a moment. Then it is as if a new world of order and harmony were to open before us. Not counting the rustle of the breeze and the drizzling in Alexander's helmet, there fall here upon our ears the high-pitched blank verses of Juno together with those of Diana, supported by the song of the suffering cat and of the songstress who is holding her. Then the fateful orders of the Thunder God regarding the pair of damp stockings chiming in with the 'damn ye' of the devils at the Ara (if that expletive is indeed a curse for devils), and, finally, the whimpers of toothache again in unison with the plaintive notes of the little nightingale whom the eagle feeds with pap. If the floor were wooden, I would add to that inventory the gay little favourite who is rolling the orb about; it is a very disagreeable matter for eye and ear if the favourite kittens play with the royal insignia.

So much for eye and ear; the third sense we shall leave in peace. Alas! Hogarth has more than once provided very badly for its rest, probably because he wanted at the same time to provide for the entertainment of a class of people whose tastes, and whose definition of the fine arts, differ somewhat from ours. Even this Plate is not entirely free of that mischievousness or, properly speaking, of misbehaviour. I fear the censor, and so will keep silent. My readers do not lose anything thereby. It is only a small island which is concerned, and that may without detriment remain unknown land, like so many other and infinitely larger islands in this world.

The original picture is at present in the possession of a Mr Wood of Littleton, who paid not more than twenty-six guineas for it. Mr Riepenhausen this time has not reversed Hogarth's etching, and, it seems to me, with very good reason. In the first place the light enters again from the left as it should do; secondly, the old woman with the cat now cuts with her right hand; and, thirdly, the Goddess of Night sews with her right. Even if one were inclined to assume that Hogarth has a certain intention with the old woman and purposely put the scissors into her left hand, he was certainly not the man to make use of such a very mediocre device twice in the same picture; and, fourthly, Ganymede's buttonhole appears once more on his left side. If one were now to suggest that the coat had been turned, goodness gracious! what nonsense could not be justified by this type of hermeneutics!

Commonsense gives short shrift to all these insignificant partial hypotheses, and says: Hogarth has not taken the trouble to reverse his copies, thus on some of his Plates there are persons wearing a sword on the right side, etc. But of course one must be careful, for some of them Hogarth has really reversed, or there was no original painting. This is the case with the next Plate: there sits a man who in the original has the sword on his right side; this must be reversed. Also he sometimes had a definite intention; for instance, in his series, Industry and Idleness, a fellow swears an oath in court and puts his left hand on the Bible. This must be intentional since close by a legal official is writing with his right hand.

A Midnight Modern Conversation
or The Bacchanalians

THIS ingenious representation of a company which has drunk itself into a considerable degree of mental dullness is one of the best-known works of our artist, in England as well as in Germany. I myself have found the original engravings in places where works of this kind are not usually met with, and there are a great many copies of them in existence. Among these is a very successful one, smaller in size, with a poem entitled 'The Bac-chanalians or a Midnight Modern Conversation' dedicated to Mr Hogarth, evidently with his permission. In addition, a certain poet by name of Bankes[1] has attached a copy of this Plate, reduced in size, to one of his leaden poems, like a swimming bladder, so as to keep it afloat upon the stream of Time, and has achieved his purpose; it may have kept the whole volume afloat as well. About this time, too, there appeared a pamphlet with the same title as the engraving, and its content was made into a scene for the stage. Finally, it is known that some of the groups were transformed into life-size wax models and publicly exhibited.

It is surely the universal comprehensibility of that picture, at least when viewed as a whole, which has made it so popular. It is, in fact, a picture of common human nature caught at a moment when it pleased creation's masterpiece to forget his rank somewhat, and through drunkenness to descend a couple of rungs towards the beasts, or even to allow the beasts to ascend a couple of rungs above him. It would hardly be possible to imagine a company without women more mixed than this one. Here we

[1] Probably John Bankes, a miscellaneous writer. He first set up a bookstall in Spitalfields, and later entered the service of a bookseller, and published poems by subscription. Ed.

173

find not only members of all the four Faculties distinctly portrayed, but even the farmers and the military have their representatives. And then a fellow has stolen in whom one does not quite know how to describe: lampooner, riot-preacher, poetaster or rogue; perhaps a little of all four, according to the requirements of his purse and of the occasion. We find here the most diverse effects of drunkenness in their different gradations, represented in a masterly way, from the clergyman who still holds his vigils with some self-possession, to the officer who lies prone upon the battlefield. The only missing characters are the quarrelsome and the over-liberal; people who must be deprived of knife and sword, or of their purse, if they are not to commit murder or to make presents to the whole world. All is executed without exaggeration, and this is one of the main reasons for the permanence of Hogarth's works, and perhaps of all works of art which have survived the years. Caricatures proper usually owe their short life to some party spirit or, if they are granted a slightly longer one, to lack of taste. Under the patronage of the former, many of Hogarth's caricatures have perished, and the few which still remain only live through the precarious protection of the latter.

The clock here says 'four', and bright daylight is reflected from the bottles, the goblets and at least one out of eleven pairs of eyes. It is four o'clock in the morning according to the sun. That is what everybody must think when they look at the picture, but Hogarth certainly had something else in mind. It is in fact really midnight here, and the good people are determined to sit, or at all events to lie, until morning, and there are still four or five hours to go until then. The explanation is this: in England, by which we understand for the most part London, they keep time by the sun as in the rest of the world, and set their clocks accordingly. But in addition there is another entirely different sort of time; one might call it the wrong-time, and that is the time by which the population really lives. Quite a few activities are governed by it, especially all those connected with 'Bed and Board'. With these one is united, and from these separated by the wrong time. Thus Hogarth means to say that in the year 1745, when this engraving appeared, the true sun was four hours in advance of the sun of the wrong-time. At four o'clock in the afternoon it was mid-day, and thus at four o'clock in the morning midnight. Since that date, the two suns have moved farther apart still. The so-called luncheon has moved far beyond the true mid-day, and similarly dinner far into the night. Since,

A Midnight Modern Conversation or The Bacchanalians

however, there will always be some people to observe a better time in their activities, this occasionally gives rise to the queerest contrasts. The following anecdote has been told me by a friend who was in London at the time. The present Pitt, a great admirer of the true time and the old style of reason and sanity, wherever it was possible for a minister to preserve it, was invited to dinner one evening by the Duchess of D— at ten o'clock true time. The Minister regretted that on this occasion he could not have the honour of attending, as he already had a supper engagement on the same day at nine o'clock. That sort of thing hits its mark; such a cut could hardly have been parried by the combined wit of Fox and Sheridan. So much for the time which regulated affairs in this picture. Now something of the executives, and the affairs in space.

What first strikes the eye, like bold black Hebrew amid profane Latin, printed in Didot's[1] type, is the parson, probably more pharisee than theologian, since he did not even refrain from appearing at this midnight entertainment in his cassock. However, he is now absolutely ready, spick and span, as one might say, for the morning sermon. It is not displeasing to note how Hogarth spares that man's profession even here. A bungler would certainly have supplied something more humorous, that is, something in a much lighter vein, and more open to contempt. But there is even more to it. I cannot recall a single classical work of art in which majesty and seriousness, combined with circumstances which seem entirely incompatible with either, have been expressed so impeccably as here, except perhaps in the head of Jupiter represented in carved stone as Europa's lover. No Pope or Archbishop, provided he was not ashamed of drunkenness as such, would need to feel ashamed of being drunk like that Chosen One. With what dignity and how quietly he sits and ladles and mixes and smokes! Oh, there is some advantage to be gained from compelling face and body to preserve decency and decorum for a few hours every day, while the spirit either does quite the opposite or is missing altogether! In the end they[2] learn to perform the service by themselves, like well-trained dragoon horses who continue to go through all their evolutions while their riders are already lying behind in the ditch.

It is generally affirmed that most of the heads in this picture are

[1] A French printer in eighteenth-century Paris. Ed.
[2] Face and body.

175

portraits, and I am prepared to believe this, especially since Hogarth expressly states that it is not so.[1]

Two people claim some resemblance to that cleric: a certain parson, Ford, and one Henley, also known as Orator Henley. The former was for some time chaplain to Lord Chesterfield when he was English Ambassador at The Hague, and Dr Johnson, whose acquaintance and relation he was, speaks of him as a man of great talents but of the most abandoned morals.[2] He had applied a well-known economic rule to his good name: with much one can make a show, with little one can also exist. However, according to Sir John Hawkins, the well-known author of a *Life of Dr Johnson*, this is a likeness of the so-called Orator Henley, a well-known and very popular preacher at the time; a sort of Sackmann,[3] who, in low, almost vulgar, language managed not infrequently to say quite good things, and won much applause. Sir John's opinion is supported by a portrait of Henley where he is represented baptizing a child, and clearly has just this face. But this is of very little concern to us here. What is indeed queer is that to the picture of a clergyman who in full pontificals at four o'clock in the morning is rowing in punch, two resemblances should have been found in England, although the face, far from being concealed, shines rather in full light, as if it were the centre stone of the first water in the diamond ring around the table, nay, the glory of the ring itself. This presupposes at least that had the face been covered, quite a tidy queue of claimants would have formed up.

Next on his right stands (for the moment at least) the leading chorister and—drinker, a latere; in the present circumstances a sort of parish clerk. He has taken off his own wig and is crowning with it the crown of his

---

[1] He expresses this in verses which he put under the original; but it is well to note that they were added some time after the original publication, when the interpretations began to worry him. The first two lines are:
'Think not to find one *meant resemblance* here;
We lash the *vices* but the *persons* spare.'

[2] Boswell's *Life of Dr Johnson*, Vol. 2, p. 263. In that passage it is taken for granted that Ford was the man who appears in this picture. It is also affirmed there, though not with absolute certainty, that after his death he twice appeared to a Tavern attendant. The words in which Johnson describes Ford's character are entirely appropriate to this otherwise decent bigot. 'I have been told he was a man of *great parts*; *very profligate*, but I never heard he was *impious*.' This, especially if said of a parson, sounds almost like: 'I have heard that though he was a wolf, he never went about without sheep's clothing.'

[3] *Jacobus Sackmann* (1645–1718), Hanover, famous for his original sermons. Ed.

worthy master. The double wig evidently symbolizes the similar dual aspect of a bishop's mitre, and thus the toast proposed here might be: to an early bishopric for the parson! Next to him sits obviously the English *marchant de droit*. The *Jus utriumque*,[1] if only as right and wrong, gleams still out of his differently centred eyes, and his wig, too, looks as double and two-fold as a single thing can possibly be; yet the left side seems to be the right one, as can be demonstrated by putting a finger over the right side. In one hand he holds a snuff box, and in the other a glass of punch, but Buridan's ass[2] seems here in favour of the right side. It looks at least as if his stereotyped smile had some reference to a speech of his neighbour on the right who is perhaps putting a case to him in which there is some profit to be made. But he is beyond thinking, or if he thinks at all it is only as people who have some feeling in their toes long after their legs have been amputated. To this portrait also, funnily enough, two people have claimed a resemblance. In such a country, it is worth while drawing satires. The one was the young Lord Northington, who afterwards became Lord Chancellor, and the other a certain Kettleby, a well-known advocate and noisy busybody at the London Bar. But the former withdrew his claim and the latter came into its undisputed possession; he could have had this face framed as his portrait had he wished. The reputation of that double-faced fellow acquired such notoriety that he was also accorded a not unimportant role in *The Causidicade*, a widely-read satire of the time which deserves to be adapted to German conditions in Vienna or Wetzlar, and to be printed in Germany or Altona.

These represented two of the Faculties. Now by a little jump round the table we come immediately upon the third in rank.

This is represented here by a creature who hangs over the chairback or floats or walks or stands—one cannot rightly say which. He evidently believes that he is standing on a rolling ship, whereas his neighbour has happily reached terra firma before him. That this is the doctor is the unanimous verdict of all interpreters, a testimony borne out by the two knots in his wig, of which only one has still preserved its dignity; the other has come undone and the hair hangs over his chest. If these two knots portray

[1] Church and Civil Law. Ed.

[2] An ass who, standing between equal and equally distant bundles of hay, must die of hunger, because he cannot decide which to eat (first mentioned in connection with the freedom of the will in the writings of the scholastic philosopher, Johann Buridan). Ed.

the two branches of the healing art, medicine and surgery, as I once heard, then the unfastened one probably stands for medicine, for in truth what still holds sway in that individual, in whom hardly anything else still holds its ground, is, to some extent, surgery. Acting on the instinct always to pour something over suspected contusion, he is pouring a bottle of wine over the bald head of the officer who has tumbled down in front of him. The remedy, it is true, does not reach the place for which it had been prescribed, but this does no harm to the truth of the representation. By far the greater part of all medicines is more correctly addressed than delivered. On the roads which they have to travel, the Post Stations, with the exception perhaps of the very first, are not nearly so well predetermined as one might wish. I have called the man who lies here upon the battlefield (no *memento mori*, but a mere *hic jacit*) an officer, and so he is, not on account of the battlefield but of the badge which he appears to wear on his hat. In England, badges always denote the officer, whatever the colour of his coat, black or green, and no matter how queer the cut, as for example the facings here which are of the type known in my fatherland as Roman-months. Some years ago, when badges were worn at our universities by almost all the students, an English traveller paid me a visit a few hours after his arrival and expressed his surprise and satisfaction that so many young officers should be studying here. He was just about to base a reflection upon his observation, which would evidently have been very much to the disparagement of the English military, when I interrupted him and explained that, although he was not entirely mistaken, since many officers were in fact studying here, possibly more than in any other country, he had perhaps been led astray by their badges to take many students for officers, who were anything but. In London, therefore, it is quite possible to cheat by means of badges, but then the wearer would before long be reproved by the profession which he simulated, as well as the one which he intended to dissimulate.[1] In the tumble the conquered hero loses

[1] A case like this has been preserved in the following delightful story: It is known that English judges enjoy great privileges when sitting in court as interpreters and propounders of the law. It is on record that one of them once had the Prince of Wales, later King Henry V, promptly arrested because he had given him a blow while carrying out his duties, and we know, to the redounding honour of the hot-headed but excellent Prince, that he himself afterwards approved of the proceeding and asked the judge's forgiveness. Now some years ago it happened that an individual who must have looked very much like a soldier sat down in the Criminal Court of the Old Bailey on a bench not intended for the mere spectator he was.

hat and wig, and a couple of scars *pour le mérite* appear together with their beauty patches which this hero on half-pay might well have acquired upon a similar bed of dishonour. Little though both doctor and officer may know of their professions now, yet in their latest actions which they are here doing or suffering is a little touch of their professions. The officer falls and the surgeon anoints, the one with the wrong weapon, the other with the wrong bottle in his fist. They have only seized the wrong implements. Before the officer withdrew, he hastily threw a bridge by means of a chair leg over a not inconsiderable stream which the affluent heiress of the bottle and the punchbowl, the river goddess Cloacina, has here poured out of her urn. He really got across the main stream quite well; the rest will be mopped up by the Roman-months. If the officer were to stretch his legs a little more he would trample upon politics whose worthy representative is sitting here. A remarkable head, enjoying his peace and letting others enjoy theirs. Everything in that statesman's expression is so calm and reliable; he is certain of his cause, but whatever he tries to do is not worth a hangman's rope. In his head he has formed the project of lighting his pipe, but in fact is about to set fire to his ruffles which will quickly ignite the neckerchief, and this will then do the same to the great hair magazine not far away. Indeed, he seems in his meditations to take the right frill for the flame itself and tries to light his pipe with it. What politics and what a way to execute a good idea! Out of his pocket peep two political journals of different colour, *The London Journal* and *The Craftsman*, here, at least, peacefully united. They rest significantly upon a sword, which even the officer lacks.

To the right of the armed politician sits an old coxcomb with hair-bag and solitaire. He seems to be a foreigner. He could hardly be a German; for if he were, being as near as that to the Church, he would be on better terms with her. Or else, what he is about to give utterance to here will not be a requiem but merely something incidental between the fourth and fifth acts; and that will make him join in the chorus somehow. How a man's appearance is improved by a good degree of tipsiness, especially if he is

---

When the judge noticed this he said to the beadle in a somewhat loud though friendly voice: 'Would you tell that soldier over there to be so good as to sit somewhere else?' The man took offence at this and replied in a fury: 'I'm not a soldier, I'm an officer', and pointed to his badge. The judge now, without in the least losing his composure, said very loudly to the beadle: 'Remove that officer over there who is not a soldier!'

of a certain age. Even the wine-paralysed hand resting on the table beside him speaks volumes, while the mouth is still searching for words which it will probably find before long. For it could not remain like that indefinitely. Such a crater does not close up without some eruption or other. I am afraid politics is coming between two fires. Daylight has just extinguished a tallow candle; the column of smoke from the morning sacrifice rises to Heaven; but it seems as if the finest and therefore invisible part of it may have drawn rather more to the right and thus may be accelerating the ferment in that volcano. But I must confess that though the delineation of that dandy is very strikingly done, the sex for which he most likely did *not* don all his finery the day before will soon have enough of him. We will leave him therefore to Nature and turn our attention to a more agreeable object—I mean the beautiful sleeper on the opposite side of the table. Here at least we need have no apprehension of anything harmful issuing from that gaping mouth.

I believe it is well-nigh impossible to look at that marvellous object without thinking of Endymion, although it is not Phoebe here but Phoebus who shines upon his face and clothing. How lovely he looks sitting and sprawling there, his wig upon the chair and his head upon the wig! If one does not actually hear him snore, I am sure one can see him do it. A nose like that, half of it apparently of transparent horn, a proper clarinet mouthpiece, could not possibly remain indifferent to the gentle alternation of breath; it must vibrate. Everything obeys the eternal laws of Nature! What a happy being he is. He no longer sees the wolf in lamb's clothing, no longer hears the stroke of the punch ladle nor the collapse of the military, not the rumbling of the bridge; he no longer observes the blunders of diplomacy which burns itself with its own projects; nor is he any longer disturbed by the news in the papers, and he neither knows nor even guesses that the slightest tremor of the table will precipitate his badly balanced punch on to his trousers—from the outside. Here I cannot refrain from quoting over that lucky creature those exquisite verses of Meibom's[1] which have lulled me many a time to sleep. If the reader falls asleep over them too, well and good; this time at least the reader's sleep would do honour to the author. The ladies may have it translated to them first before sleeping.

[1] Probably *Heinrich Meibom* (1555–1629), historian who also wrote Latin verse; made poet laureate at Prague in 1590. Ed.

Somne levis (quamquam certissima mortis imago):
Consortem cupio te tamen esse tori:
Alma quies optata veni, nam sic sine vita
Vivere quam suave est, sic sine morte mori.

Good night!

Further to the left of that burnt-out pastille just in front of the clock, Hogarth has put two more such objects who are still alight, and still fuming in more than one sense. The little group has something about it which is more clearly and better felt than described. The one has averted his face from the world and is smoking towards its boundary. The other gazes into time, though with a somewhat inward look. They are sitting back to back and each makes the other's chairback. If in some future edition of the *Orbis Pictus* the souls of two courtiers whose bodies embrace and kiss one another are to be engraved (the soul of natural man is already represented there), then I would highly recommend this group for a model. If it happens that two people of the same sex take to one another, it is usually with a polarity of this kind. The outward-looking man seems to be clever and calculating; I'll wager he is the soberest in the whole company. One need only observe how quietly he has settled himself between table and chairback, even his forefinger taking care that corkscrew and pipe-filler should not fall down. He has brought his night-cap with him, and the objects hanging there on the wall, as if on the gallows, are his hat and wig. He seems to be meditating and turning over some scheme in his head. It can hardly be a poem, or if it should prove to be something metrical, it would surely be some part of the multiplication table: six times six are thirty-six. In a word, that man knows what he is about, and I should conclude from his sitting here all night long, and also from his churchy attire, that there is no Stock Exchange today, but that it is Sunday; and then in England a man could let himself go a little, provided he did not proclaim it from the housetops. The English Sunday appears to serve a double purpose: it provides an opportunity for doing penance and for collecting material for future penance, so long as one does not do it to a fiddle accompaniment. For music leads to dancing, and dancing and gaiety makes it more difficult to do the collecting without giving offence. This is how I have always interpreted that figure, and still do, although Mr Ireland, who in the text of his commentary claimed he was a J.P., a sort of magistrate, says in a footnote that this is believed to be the portrait of Hogarth's bookbinder, a stone-deaf person named Chandler, to whom that head is said to bear a striking resemblance. There is no harm in that. I cannot see why a bookbinder and a J.P. should not also look like a scheming merchant. The one, in addition to his main occupation as craftsman, is really a tradesman, and the other may even make his main occupation into a trade. And then it is well known that the shell only too often promises more than the kernel warrants; a statement of whose truth and usefulness nobody in the world has better opportunity of finding out daily than—the bookbinder.

What the black wig at the back there means and does is not quite clear. However, for the comfort of interpreters it very probably does not know itself. A creature so utterly turned away from the world, disdaining everything empirical, sucking so completely for itself its pittance of breath from an unknown world and blowing the choking smoke into the known world, might symbolize philosophy. If that were so, then thanks be to Heaven that it still leans with its earthly pole at least on the Six-times-six-is-thirty-six—and must lean if it is not in the end to be buried under the human One-times-one-is-one.[1]

Provided the forward-looking member of that group, the meditative one, is not deaf, which one would hardly wish him to be, there would be something rather comforting in the idea that both were conversing with one another—by mouth, but also at times by their chairbacks. This type of joke reminds me of a scene which I would immortalize if I knew how to immortalize anything; however, I will describe it for the time being, at least.

Two Jews were conversing with one another in a public street, but I am sure one will not often see people carrying on a conversation as they did. Both of them were over fifty, both very affluent and with unmistakable business instincts. Whenever they spun out a single thread, they would instantly catch a number of flies in the web. They were not standing close to the houses, but in the middle of the road; more precisely in the middle of a cross-roads. They really deserved to be cast in bronze and set up there

[1] A clue to the explanation may be that the two contrasting heads are placed on each side of the clock, and thus seem to have something to do with the time. The pair might symbolize in black and white what the clock shows in figures, the passing of night into day. The black wig is the end of the previous day and thus black midnight; the white turban upon whom the rising sun shines represents the new day. Ed.

in perpetuity. They stood so close together that they actually touched one another, but only with their upper arms—the right arm of the one pressed against the right of the other, so that if one faced south the other faced north. Neither of them saw the other's face, and could not see it—did not wish to see it, being afraid of showing his own face. They held their arms akimbo. Each listened, gazing slightly upwards, talked in a low voice, and from time to time nodded briefly towards that part of the sky which lay opposite him, and at which he was gazing. They must have meditated a great deal to be sure, but probably saw little or nothing. They often leaned gently towards one another, as if they wanted to rub their deltoid muscles, and they really rubbed them slightly. Whether this gentle nudging represented brain waves or a sign of ratification or a signal that they understood one another completely, so much is certain that it must have had some importance, for half their conversation and mutual information passed through their upper arms. What a scene for a play! It was too good for words. The discussion evidently concerned a plan for a very profitable enterprise, from which each hoped to draw the greatest possible advantage. The profit, however, was in the end probably divided into equal parts, not so much out of fairness but because the opposition was equally strong on both sides. They evidently wanted to outwit a third party, but one friend would have liked to hoodwink the other a little as well. For friends they were, as far as merchants trading in a small town in the same wares can be friends. This is just what makes the scene so valuable to a moralist. Each gave his contribution to the plan transposed into mere words and signs, in the dark, and was unwilling to let the other see how much of his conscience had been compromised as well. The eye understands and is understood, suddenly, like lightning. There is no time for a protest, no matter how small the security; with the ear and the deltoid muscle, on the other hand, it is quite different, there always remain *res integra* and time for an objection. With the former, sentence and execution are simultaneous; with the latter, there is still time to ask oneself before the execution—are we not all poor sinners?

And now there is only one left of the eleven here who, quite apart from what they may have consumed in punch, have emptied twenty-five bottles of wines and spirits, that is counting the bottle on the table which is not yet out of office, and another in the hand of the surgeon who is using it *ad pias causas*. Twenty-five bottles! A terrific broadside upon a picket of eleven men, and yet only one of them is quite dead and two wounded at the utmost. That eleventh about whom I am going to say a few words now is the creature whom from the outset I conceived as doubly crooked. He puts his hand to his breast, not on the spot where the *point d'honneur* is situated in a man, but against the right side of his chest where there is nothing but the right lung. It is an ill-mannered gesture, the way he crooks his arm up backwards like a grasshopper's leg. It seems to indicate the assurance with which this good-for-nothing panders to himself. Some people are good at doing this with their hands just as some monkeys can grasp things much better with their tail. He is crying and, since this does not go very well with smoking, he has taken his pipe out of his mouth for the time being. What a vulgar mouth compared with the sweet mouth of the advocate! It looks as if he were complaining about the lack of right and justice in the world. I have known people who sometimes get rid of their wine by way of the eyes, and then with a world of self-pity start complaining about the government and the lack of justice; yet the majority of them were just the people who had that lack of strict justice to thank for their very existence.

In the place where the officer was standing when he was still upright, we see part of his martial equipment in picturesque confusion; a tobacco pipe sticking into the air and being prevented by an empty bottle, itself not much steadier, from hurling itself into the abyss, whither its master has so gloriously descended. It certainly belongs to his armaments which Hogarth has suspended here above the corpse. Beside it lies a scrap of paper: Freeman's Best. This might be a tobacco wrapper: *Freemanni Optimum subter Solem*, or a political pamphlet, or both together, like many in Germany. But here it lies brazenly as the motto on a coat-of-arms: *Summum bonum* of freeborn Britons (tobacco and wine and to be drunk like a lord!).

Tobacco smoking, however, has much diminished in England now, at least in the higher strata of society. Nowadays it is more often dice that keep company with the bottle. Dr Johnson, according to Sir John Hawkins who wrote his life, often remarked that suicide had increased in England among the higher classes since smoking was abandoned. This much is certain: if someone is playing for high stakes, or if his life is at stake, he cannot smoke at the same time; the pipe will go out at every moment. If the company here had played at dice, many a member would do to himself at home what the bookbinder has done with his hat and wig there on the wall. Hogarth has in fact painted a gambling scene of that sort in a masterly fashion, as we shall see later.

To finish with, a small but rather droll touch which all the interpreters have overlooked, and which incidentally has happened more than once in every Plate of the series we propose to put before the public. What, namely, is the meaning of the bright spot on the clock dial? Apparently this. The sun is already shining into the room as we can tell from the sharp shadows of the fallen candlestick and of the martial equipment, and from the high-lights on the convex as well as the concave sides of the punch bowl. It seems, therefore, as if the bright spot up there is sunlight at second hand, reflected from some sort of fluid or other, of which there is no lack here. It can hardly come from the great lake in the hemisphere, since that is undulating; it must come therefore from some smaller inland lake. How if it was from Cloacina's urn! It really is a little brushed by the sun. But whatever the source of that spot of light, even supposing it came from one of the static fluids here, the angle which the ray makes with the horizon would in any case be too great for four o'clock in the morning, even on the longest day in London. It may be that Hogarth wanted to show by this that according to the sun it was ten o'clock. At least that would be just in his manner, and expressed completely in the language of which he was master, and where he is so much more difficult to understand than even in his most complex heads. Thus the clock shows neither true time nor wrong time, just as with human beings. And how could a clock possibly be right in a room where so many people have assembled whose ways are so wrong?

A Rake's Progress

A Rake's Progress

I

BEFORE applying myself to the interpretation of these Plates, overflowing with wit, humour and knowledge of the world, it will not be out of place to say something about the word 'Rake'.[1] It is as a rule translated in German as *Liederlicher* (Good-for-nothing), and this work of Hogarth's is generally known in Germany under the title *Der Weg des Liederlichen*. But although, as a general rule, every Rake is a Good-for-nothing, every Good-for-nothing is not a Rake. Good-for-nothing-ness has its classes, like poetry, and, strangely enough, very similar ones. In the Rake's life there is something definitely lyrical, especially if we share Sulzer's[2] opinion that lyricism is essentially due to passionate temper; whereas imagination and reason are merely accidental to it.

The true Rake (of the male sex, of course) drinks, gambles, whores, talks of French pills and bougies as we of candied aniseed and barley sugar; turns night into day and day into night. Thence arise his eternal

---

[1] Dr Johnson defines the word as 'a loose, disorderly, vicious, wild, gay, thoughtless fellow' and refers to the Dutch *rekel*, a sheep-dog or a dog in a derogatory sense, which in Germany, too, is still in use as a slang expression, especially among people to whom the name would best apply. In French, we have *recaille*, just like *canaille* from *canis*. The German expression, *liederlicher Hund*, combines both terms. In the year 1735 there appeared in London *The Rake of Taste*, a poem dedicated to Alex. Pope; and, in the same year, a pamphlet, *The female rake, a modern fine Lady, an Epistle from Libertina to Sylvia*. Pope even says:
'. . . every woman is at heart a *rake*'.
Otherwise, a rake usually means a gardening instrument; to rake in the sense of 'to gather together' is a meaning that should also be borne in mind here, since Hogarth is alluding to it in the name of his hero, or rather in that of his hero's father.

[2] J. G. Sulzer, author of a general theory of art (1771-1774). Ed.

war with street lamp-posts and his active and passive thrashings of and by the Watch; he ruins innocent creatures who have fallen in love with him, and fights duels with people whose honour he has offended; he squanders money everywhere and whatever money can buy, his own and other people's, and not infrequently himself into the bargain, and in all this he is seeking honour. Thus it may sometimes happen that he becomes a good and useful citizen in the end, provided that his idea of honour undergoes a change before his energy has evaporated; whereas the out-and-out good-for-nothing has no conception of honour at all. The latter does not tell many tales, or at least fewer than he enacts; the former acts primarily for the historical Muse, which he himself represents as a rule in his own circle, and alters events as it suits him, just like the . . . Newspapers. It is said that since the invention of brandy (Brown's wine, *Spiritus Brunonis*) which for sixpence enables a man to attain a transitory happiness that will make him forget the whole world, the last named class is very much on the increase. Hogarth's Rake has a little of each.

The father of our young hero, an old, wealthy, stinking miser, was named Rakewell. The word is composed of 'to rake' (to gather, to scrape together) and 'well' (heartily, stoutly). The name, together with his scraped-together riches, he has bequeathed to his descendant Rakewell the Second, the youth with the milksop face, who is here being measured for a pair of trousers. The heir interpreted his name differently, understanding by 'Rake' a bon-vivant and spendthrift, though the word 'well' again betokened 'thoroughly, heartily', and in this way the old treasures were scattered according to the new etymology. Such interpretations of legacies do exist, even outside the fairy story of the barrel. From this point of view, the name is not badly composed, and is at least a tolerable specimen of wit, though of a type which, in general, does not amount to much. In German it would be difficult to invent a family name which would be as expressive as that, nor is it called for in a country where there are so many actual names which express the relation between father and son. They are easy to find in all three States of the Diet. In the *ora-et-labora* State as well as in the *ora-et-non-labora* one (provided the denizens are allowed to marry) and in that of *neque-ora-neque-labora*. In each of them it would be easy to find Et cetera II,[1] who would chase through the

---

[1] An expression by Swift which means something like So-and-So.

A Rake's Progress Plate I

gullet and associated parts of the anatomy what Et cetera I had laboriously scraped together.

The occasion which Hogarth has chosen for the first Plate is immediately after the old man's death, when the young gentleman has for the first time obtained free access to the departed's Holiest of Holies, I mean his treasures and his lumber, his Lombard[1] and his Archives (for it has something of all these four). At least it cannot be long since he who had tucked so much away here has been tucked away himself, for they are only just beginning to mourn him. Probably he is not even buried yet, and consequently the upholsterer on the ladder there is employed in draping with black the room in which the corpse is to be displayed, while another, on his knees, is taking the measure of the mourning drapery in which the young heir is to show himself beside the corpse. On a heavy, somewhat antiquated chair, a piece of sacristy furniture, lies a roll of black cloth, presumably only for the upholsterer on the ladder, for the scatterbrained heir to so many thousands would hardly mourn for the testator in material which is rolled like that. Thus the tomb in which noble riches and civic plunder had slept together in churchyard-like mixture for perhaps half a century, awaiting their redemption, and the heir who in painful expectation had long awaited their resurrection, are both today simultaneously draped in black. They are mourning on the resurrection day. The Trump has sounded everywhere, and not a moment too soon; every coffer has burst and every door opened. Gold and silver and old iron and purses bulging with coins peep out of their cages and rejoice in the new day; documents of parchment and paper, inventories, savings, IOUs, rent contracts and shares with content of great import roll to the feet of their liberator, flutter around his ankles and crawl under his shoes. Even gold, which had its abode in the ceiling of that room, hears the mighty call and is raining down to the Judgment. Only some old wigs, boots and shoes, broken jars and bowls and bottles, a hat-case and a street lantern, an overcoat in Doctor Johnson's style, a tombstone and so on, perhaps conscious of their damnation, keep a timid distance. But today is only the rehearsal.

Here he stands now, our hero, Thomas Rakewell, with a youthful, still healthy but rather empty face; obviously more dupe than fripon one would say, to judge only from the head; but *vis-à-vis* those two women

[1] *Financial Matters*, from Lombard Street, where the Banks are situated in London. Ed.

the matter looks somewhat different. *Duo cum facient idem, non est idem.* The story is as follows: the young fellow comes from Oxford where he had carried on and had done everything that in Universities goes under the general term, 'studying'. With the call of the Last Trumpet summoning the parchments, there arrived also a couple of aprons with documents, more properly speaking with *opuscula academica*. They are both portrayed here. One of them belongs to a mother and the other to her daughter. The former, as we can see, really contains manuscripts, and the latter, to which the mother points, covers the forms to which they refer, and in particular an important outline from which may evolve in the end a Rakewell III *in linea directa*. The poor and, as we shall see, extremely good-natured, honest and sincere creature who stands there crying near the door had been got into trouble through the 'studies' of our good-for-nothing. The girl's mood is well brought out. What is not altogether pleasing is that she is already oldish, and could and should be more beautiful; but the delineation of beauty was never the object of its analyser.[1] She is crying in the proper sense of the word, when the most intense pain and the highest degree of inner suffering seek rather than find alleviation in tears. Her face is not childishly distorted, but relaxed and disfigured as if by the onset of a deadly disease. Oh! how much is going on in that wounded heart. The scoundrel!

I said, she is crying in the proper sense of the word, for as one knows, that sex can produce quite another type of tears which serves not so much to give relief from pain, as to bring on the pain itself, if it is not readily forthcoming. Here we are not concerned with that type of tears.

The girl's name is Sarah Young. This we gather from the considerable collection of love letters which the mother is carrying in her apron there. The romance must have been long, or at least carried on very ardently. All that can be read of it is, first, the Oxford address, then the formula 'Dearest Life', a mere *praemissis praemittendis* instead of Sir, or My Lord, and finally, 'to marry you'. The artist has expressed the rest by empty space; in the originals the words were evidently of similar weight. Thus the rascal has promised the girl marriage. One sees, in fact, a ring in her

[1] As is well known, Hogarth wrote an *Analysis of Beauty*. Nichols says that face came out better in the first prints. Hogarth tried to improve it, but made it worse—as we might say, 'improved it for the worse'. This type of correcting, which is not infrequent in works of satire by the best exponents, well deserves a name of its own because such faults, far from being the fruit of negligence, are rather the result of too anxious effort.

192

hand, which she had evidently held up to him with outstretched arm to remind him, by this also, of his promise. But—it was too late to have any effect, and so the arm sank down limp against the body so faithlessly abandoned. The apron full of bills of exchange which that fellow had formerly drawn upon his heart in his own handwriting, he is now, since the heart has refused payment, anxious to honour with his purse, and he offers her, together with the protest, a handful of guineas. 'I am sorry my dear ("dearest life") to see you in other circumstances, but then so am I, as you can see. Here is something for your trouble and kindness. There are more young chaps in Oxford—You never know—Just take that. If you don't want it—very well then, I'll give it to the lawyer and then you won't get a thing.'—Something like that must have issued from the little open mouth. However, the money is spurned; at least by the daughter. For her all is over. She is as little likely to grasp the money as would a marble statue in church, weeping over the urn of a Saint, grasp the tip intended for the sexton who is explaining the tomb to the sightseers. The mother, though very much in the flesh, perhaps even too much so, also refuses it. Fists clenched like hers and supported by such a face do not accept money; still less does such an elbow, the very image of repulsion. 'You scoundrel, is it on these scales that you weigh my daughter's honour?', she demands, and to judge from her furious look and her whole attitude, probably accompanies the question with a little storm of blessings and good wishes which for once, to the satisfaction of morals and virtue, will be punctually brought to consummation. Three of that woman's fingers out of the four which are visible are adorned with rings. Perhaps she has put them on specially for the purpose of this visit, whose outcome was unpredictable, so as to show that they were not so destitute as to come for the money's sake.[1]

The young gentleman listens to all this and looks on, stiff, with arm stretched out like a signpost, and probably with just as much feeling. He who could forget honour and offended innocence does not, however, forget to render small services to his tailor, carefully holding back his coat-tails so as to enable him to take his measurements.

[1] In the third Plate of Hogarth's 'Marriage-à-la-Mode', we find a similar face in similar mood and with similar expression. There it is not a mother's face. Rings on the fingers might there be thought somewhat remote mediators between seduced innocence and its seducer.

I have often heard it said that the more a tailor looks like a shoe-maker, the worse a tailor he is. If that observation is correct, this one must be a most miserable bungler, for he looks exactly like a cobbler. If I am not mistaken, the fellow is really more than half calf-leather. It also seems to me as if a sort of theosophical-apocalyptical light were playing on the brow and lips as he kneels, and this kind of beatification, even if it sometimes occurs somewhat *ultra crepidam* in other Guilds, rarely, as far as I know, visits a tailor's face.[1] Evidently that creature belongs to the small circle of persons who obtained from the housekeeping money of the deceased whatever they had earned, with 50 per cent rebate; maybe even in specimens from the lumber room. It is by no means impossible that he who, as we shall see, used to repair his own shoes, had, by way of compensation, appointed the family cobbler as his tailor, who then followed that trade as an amateur. To serve up a pair of trousers or a dressing-gown for the third or fourth time, as many a German writer will know without my reminding him, does not call for great skill, and then amateurs do not charge much. Our Thomas, who is sending away even his 'dearest life', keeps Theosophus as his tailor, for the present at least, out of childlike respect. Of course it is the clothes which make the man. But Thomas is not to be 'made' here, only to be draped, *pro tempore*, in black.

Immediately behind our hero, and in direct contact with his upturned coat-tails, stands a table decked with documents, and with an ink-bottle and purse served up on it. Both are dishes which a certain customer, being at the time alone at the table, knows only too well. He therefore takes advantage of the little quarrel about honour and shame between the host and his 'dearest life' by making for the best dish. He cannot be sure of being offered it once the meal has begun. That cunning guest is undoubtedly one of the most eloquent heads which Hogarth has ever delineated. He is not a Valuer, as Gilpin believes,[2] nor, as he thinks, does he just finger the money. Evidently this is a relation of the Law, a latere at least, an attorney, or something like a solicitor and notary. Under his right arm he has the green baize bag which quite unmistakably denotes that class of persons. They carry their papers in it, and sometimes also they carry home in

---

[1] Lichtenberg evidently alludes here to the greatest German mystic, Jakob Böhme, who was a shoemaker by trade. Ed.

[2] Treatise on copper-plate engravings. Frankfurt and Leipzig, 1768, p. 171 f.

it some little trifle out of the dishes served at repasts like these, to which nobody has invited them. How could Gilpin have believed that the hand which belongs to such a head would only finger money, or that his secret castles in the air could be supported merely by the ravishing sound of guineas in other people's purses? The idea in itself is beautiful, even striking, but much too finely spun for our Hogarth whose feelings were true and strong, but not tender, especially for an a latere relative of the Law, who has no feelings at all. No! the fellow is a rogue. If it was merely a platonic fingering, his expression would be more poetic. Here, however, the Rabulistic eyes are evidently on guard, while the hand is filching. He steals, but, as one can well believe, with juridical security, advancing outwardly with caution, and keeping subtle hermeneutic[1] in reserve. I would wager that if Thomas were to turn round and see with his very eyes how his guest was slipping half a dozen guineas into the baize bag, he would only run the risk of having to pay a dozen guineas tomorrow for having seen it.

Although the old man is dead, he it is, mainly, with whom the artist makes us acquainted in this Plate. He lives here in his portrait above the fireplace, and in his dirty deeds throughout the whole room: everything that is going on here, one might say, still moves in him and through him. The portrait is excellently placed, and how subtly has Hogarth indicated by a small touch, which at first seems quite unimportant, that this is in fact a likeness of the old man! On the mantelpiece lies the original of the fur cap in the painting, and that hint at once throws light on the whole subject. The spectacles hanging there belonged on the face of the man weighing gold, and the crutches standing there were his front legs. They are of unequal length, evidently designed for hemiplegia.[2] On old buildings props of different lengths are used; also the smaller one might sometimes have served as sceptre and Commander's baton for securing respect in the household or, prompted by the spirit of discovery, as a probing instrument for use in wardrobes, or for exploring other dark corners. Here, then, Hogarth wants to say, he used to sit, here he put away his front legs when resting and here he hung his eye-crutches when weighing money in his head. He illuminated his nights when necessary by candle-ends stuck into 'save-alls', which we see here upon the mantelpiece, one

[1] Interpretation, usually of Scriptures. Ed.
[2] Paralysis of one side. Ed.

195

completely burnt down and one kept in reserve. Probably these little lights when burning on chilly evenings represented not only the most brilliant but also the warmest part of that hearth, which here, somewhat ominously, wears a fur cap. The garment too, which the old man is wearing in the portrait, looks more like a warmth-gatherer for an open Mail-coach than a dressing-gown for comfort. Everything in that household that could burn was burnt in 'save-alls', even the little flames of life of two miserable domestic animals which we shall meet presently. Perhaps even the life of the old chap had burnt down in this cold place. There was no doctor at hand to stick up the reserve candle-end, and death thus quietly took possession of the remaining half.

People versed in allegory or in the stone language of monuments will find, without my prompting, how much Hogarth has enriched both by the arrangement round that cold hearth. Just imagine such a monument with its candle-ends in marble; the portrait of course in bas-relief elaborately worked out and displayed in some church, and then ask yourself whether any words would still be needed to describe the deceased who lay beneath, or the heir who erected it in his memory.

The upholsterer by hammering in his nails has broken off a bit of cornice, or a part has come adrift which had not been fixed firmly enough. It seems to have served for hiding treasure which had the inaccessibility of the place to thank for its security rather than its having been firmly locked away. A very good, though not a new, idea generated by the desire for safety. Dispersed money cannot be stolen so easily all at once. Besides, subtle concealment has a secret attraction for this sort of person, and capital tucked away in a warm nest, even if it comes no nearer to hatching, is often more attractive than some other sort which, though hatching dutifully every year, lies in the open where it is more easily exposed to a watchful eye, whether of the righteous or the unrighteous. What I have called concealment behind the cornice might also have been a burial on the upper floor, since money, and especially gold, as we know, has a way of moving.[1] The golden rain is going to fall this time past the gold scales and the 'save-all' on to an old Danae's[2] humped back, which no doubt is better acquainted with other burdens, with the attentions of the small

[1] According to a superstition of the Middle Ages, buried gold would come to the surface by itself. Ed.

[2] Punished for some crime to fill a leaky barrel; a symbol of unending labour. Ed.

crutch and the old man's hail of words, than with this type of rain. This poor domestic animal which not so long ago in Germany, on account of its honest face, would have been treated as fuel,[1] is here carrying an armful of faggots. A new wind is blowing. The present régime has decreed, as one sees, that there should be a fire in the fireplace where under the previous régime the air was always in conformity with the season outside. From now on money is no longer to be counted out with stiff fingers. However, gold is still moving slowly here, and there is still no Scottish coal.[2] An elegant and typically London grate, which should properly be fed only with such coal, is about to be replenished with rural fare, with remnants of hop poles and palings.

Beside the strong box in which gold coins are lying in their thousands, and in whose uncoined metal the day of redemption is reflected, stands the other domestic animal, the starved cat, miaowing over the chilly look of the silver. Its footstool is a book, probably a Prayer Book, and its left fore-paw rests on little bags full of guineas, marked '2000' and '3000'. Poor Ribs! Looking at you, who could help thinking of the Arab who, like you, was about to die of starvation in the desert where he had lost his way, when he unexpectedly came upon a tightly-filled bag. He fingered his find. 'A thousand thanks to Allah!' he exclaimed, 'Rice, rice!' Then he undid the string to find only a priceless treasure—pearls! Alas, only pearls! he sighed, and in despair threw away the useless plunder. 'Absolutely nothing of value in these boxes,' Ribs seems to sigh, *'ne musculus quidem!'* You are quite right, my good creature, but have patience! Your friend the meat-jack is still alive up there, and is freed. Its prison, where it had languished for half a century, has been thrown open as you see. It can see daylight again and soon it will survey and rule over the kitchen fires; and under a mechanical minister of that sort servants of your cloth and your honest skill have their livelihood secured.

To the side of the cat, in the left lower corner of the picture, a pair of old shoes is to be seen, one of which has been soled by the deceased himself, and though not quite finished, is lying there as an *opus posthumus*. The thread still hangs out of it, and one can clearly see its end where the Goddess of Fate had got hold of it, together with a certain other thread, and had inexorably cut off both. Upon the sole is a coat-of-arms stamped

[1] Burnt as a witch. Ed.
[2] The best but also the most expensive fuel in London.

in gold, which properly belongs to the binding of an old Bible lying beside it, and out of which the sole has evidently been cut. That can only mean: to trample on the word of God. That this should happen in such a household does not surprise me, since the true niggard will not tread upon anything else. But that his own god, gold, should be trampled upon, that does surprise me. Can it be perhaps that soles cut from Bible covers provide protection against something? Gout or corns? Or were they intended for pilgrimage shoes? I do not know, but what I do know is that a certain person who held religion and money in equal esteem, and highly at that, once frankly confessed that he felt the braid of his Sunday hat and what it had cost him, right down to his shoulders, even when going to church. But now such magnificence, a golden coat-of-arms, in a place like that, so utterly cast before swine! It could draw blisters on such a person! And it is not in keeping with a miser's character. Had he patched his shoes with an Evangelist printed on parchment, and his leathern breeches with the Book of Wisdom itself, I should not have wasted a word on it. But here we have evidently a case of *lèse-majesté* towards the only being he worships. That is unthinkable. It is said that on the earliest prints this queer touch is missing. I am too little acquainted with English heraldry, and with the book-plates of English book-collectors, to decide whether our unfathomable satirist intended by this feature to pay a compliment to some aristocrat, of the kind made to the well-known Mr Tw. . . in Ireland, after he had spoken disparagingly of that country in his published Travels. Dainty sacrificial bowls for the service of Cloacina were made with a picture of the offender inside upon the bottom, and the inscription:

> Come let us p . . .
> On Mr Tw . . .

On the floor in front of the young gentleman's feet, being thereby already profaned and no doubt in expectation of even greater profanation, lies another book. It is the old man's Journal (Memorandum book). By chance it has so opened that we can read quite clearly some entries of May 1721. They are all truthful memoranda, or so-called curious epoch-making events in the monarchy. None of the entries are of the type which somebody once found in the note-book of a universal patron—who also happened to be his patron—under the heading:

with underneath, his own humble, and, as he thought, already half-granted petition.

1. 'May 3rd, my son Tom came from Oxford.' Where they have been fattening up his latin. It would be funny if *per nefas* the arrival of the young gentleman had been a mere visit, and the 3rd of May that year been within the so-called Term, during which one has to be in the stable. We observe in passing that this is the point from which we learn that the youth's name is Thomas. An excellent use which Hogarth has made of that piece of information in the second Plate renders it worthy of remark.

2. '4th. Dine at y French Ordinary.' Most excellent. Evidently to give the young visitor a meal at which even the 'place where?', the *ubi*, had something tasty about it; with a French cook. For although the common people in England, and even many from the comfortable middle-classes, were of the opinion (1721) that it was impossible for a sensible man to eat his fill in France, and that the whole of French cooking consisted in fried frogs' legs and a *soupe maigre* upon which they scatter a few drops of grease, a belief to which our good artist almost fanatically subscribed, yet a French cook meant a great deal to the upper classes; almost as much as the upper classes themselves. But perhaps here, too, the name was everything, and the French cook-shop was just the one house in the whole of London which, by a certain law of continuity, ranked closest in quality to the Rakewell house, where not only did they not cook well, but did not cook at all; where the meat-jack sat in prison and the cats starved because the mice had emigrated.

3. '5th. Put off my Bad Shilling.' An incomparably beautiful touch whose excellence hardly needs further emphasis. *My* bad shilling! What intimacy between him and the bad shilling! How long may not this single false shilling have embittered his possession of millions, the mental pleasure of all his genuine, full-value gold! Perhaps he had been taken in by it once, or had got it in exchange, at a huge discount, in order to defraud with it—without having been able to do so. Thus selfishness and self-love were long and equally strongly offended by that intruder. At last, on the 5th of May, 1721, he succeeded in getting rid of it, and the event was entered in the annals of the house with deep satisfaction, like the death of a wicked wife. A single such touch would, I think, be enough

to impart to the stale brew of a modish tale of chivalry a flavour of wine, and to invite its consumption.

In mourning chambers where bodies lie in state, the escutcheon of the deceased is hung up. Here we see two of them already nailed up with a candelabra in between, without save-all. The deceased, as we see, had three firmly screwed-down vices in his escutcheon with the motto 'Beware, keep what you have' (except bad shillings, of course). He had lived up to his motto. With the heir, if he keeps this rubbish at all, the motto will soon be reduced to the importance and value which such maxims on family escutcheons usually have. Family escutcheons contain only too often merely obsolete claims to virtues and talents which the forebears had possessed, just as coats-of-arms in their fields contain obsolete claims to terrain. This sort of tool is called, in English, 'a vice' and, therefore, the word means in an extended sense what can be gripped with the hand, a handful, sometimes also a paw- or talon-ful. All this is very much to the point. But it also means viciousness, and here I leave it to the reader's feeling whether Hogarth also had that meaning in mind. It is quite possible. The natural disposition of a people for wit, where those people are without proper culture, usually finds expression in puns. The common people of London, therefore, are specially rich in punsters. If, for example, Colonel Charters[1] had driven through the streets with that coat-of-arms upon his carriage, he would surely have found a moralist at every street corner who would as little have thought of interpreting the three vices as symbols of his miserliness, as of Faith, Hope and Charity.

What has that man not hoarded up in his lumber-room and in the box standing in front of it! It is all money in some form, but of a somewhat high specific lightness. Here in a single bag lie 3,000 guineas, and there a closet and a box are needed to house a few shillings-worth. (With a ducat, so the saying goes, one might gild a strong horse, and a little shilling may be a heavy load for it.) He kept raking in without caring very much what it was. If it proved unsuitable for his little Eden, it was consigned to the manure heap, without which no Eden can thrive nowadays. The position of the old boot in the box at the door is rather curious. It looks as if it was the lower end of an English coffin in which had been deposited *ad interim* among the rubbish some old knight or other who was somewhat too long for it, or even the old miser himself in the bedroom slippers in

---

[1] See Plate I of 'A Harlot's Progress'.

which death had surprised him, until the proper coffin had been made ready and the room appropriately draped. Now some questions to end with:

1. What is the meaning of the letters PC (according to the original they might be PG) marked on the box? Do they merely stand for a name, or do they denote the erstwhile contents which would form a contrast with the present ones, an opposite example of which we had in the jewellery basket of the actresses?[1]

2. Just what is it that is lying jumbled up in the box? Is the perforated piece an old finger-plate, or the folded cross of a yarn-winder? And is the object hanging out there a one-legged tripod, or something else that has lost its legs? The English interpreters who could so easily have found out do not trouble about these items at all. And yet it could not have escaped them that our artist has often concealed much fine satire behind such apparent trivialities. Only think of the comedy texts in the Bishop's mitre.[2]

[1] Strolling Actresses, p. 160.
[2] Strolling Actresses, p. 167.

II

THIS Chapter could well be entitled: 'The finishing touches.' As we can see, the crude block which was sent to Oxford to be polished into Latin[1] has already passed the coarse chisel, and comes now under the finer one. The bearing is still, of course, somewhat awkward, and the mouth still that of a lout; but in the former the line of beauty is not entirely lacking, and the latter is rattling on already over his shoulder, and that is much for so short a time. Soon everything will improve.

Our young gentleman has just risen, thrown on a light casaquin with gold tassels, put on some slippers and is holding his levee. But in order not to miss Aurora's genial influence, he snatches her last but most potent rays, I mean those that shine between 11 and 1, avidly and in all haste, and takes five lessons at once—in the French horn, the piano, fencing, dancing and pugilism.[2] At the same time he attends to some important domestic business and, in general, gives audience.

Whatever the sceptic may say or think about this style of education, it certainly cannot be said to lack encyclopaedicity; nor is it, after all, so rare as one might think. One only has to look at it from the right angle. Hogarth, who in presenting the truth had to employ the language of pictures, could hardly have achieved his object otherwise if he wanted

[1] A certain John Clarke, rector of a college at Hull, has actually written 'An Introduction to the *making* of Latin'.

[2] Since boxing has been classified as one of the fine arts, and is practised by persons of standing, one no longer speaks of a man as a great boxer, but a great pugilist. The words 'pugilistic' and 'pugilistical' are also used. Athletics reminds one of heavy bones; pugilistic is more akin to the grace of figure of those who indulge in athletics, and it is for this reason that the word has been coined.

A Rake's Progress Plate II

to express clearly what happens in many a scholar's head every day, although invisibly, yet all the more encyclopaedically. A Jacob asleep is easily painted; if, however, one wants to paint him dreaming of the ladder to Heaven, I cannot see any other way out of the difficulty than, as in Weigel's *Illustrated Bible*, to stand the ladder beside him, let it lean upon the clouds above, and thus to let the angels climb it up and down. What I really want to say is this: if many a head which appears to be silently following instruction were to be depicted with all the little angels that were occupying it at the time, and to whom it was giving audience, the result would be not like Jacob's ladder, but—like *Rakewell's Levée*.

There are eight people in the Audience Chamber who enjoy the favour of his immediate presence, and behind are six others *in limbo*. Thus there are fourteen people altogether whom we shall now examine more closely; for they really deserve it, and we shall identify them as far as we can.[1]

The man in the (probably) dark brown overcoat with whom Rakewell is conversing and at the sight of whom it is almost impossible to avoid thinking of cannons or powder and lead, is a so-called Bravo, a fire-eater, who against a small consideration strikes blows for others and occasionally, as we see from the plaster on his nose, receives them too. The letter which Rakewell has in his hand is a letter of recommendation which that man has just handed to him, and whose content is as follows:

'The Capt is a Man of Honour; his sword may serve you.' 'Are you the Captain?' Rakewell seems to ask. 'Yes,' is the reply; 'I, I am the man,' upon which he puts his right hand to his sword, and his left upon what is assumed to be the seat of honour, in whose cause alone he would draw it, as well as the source of the courage and strength with which he would wield it once it was drawn. It is, however, worth noting that the letter is signed *William Stab*, which is about the equivalent of William Knife-thrust. From this one would be inclined to conclude that the Captain was a man who, to save his employers' honour, sometimes used other blades which were not quite so long as the one hanging by his side, and not worn so low either, but somewhat nearer the seat of courage and below overcoats. Roucquet[2] in his booklet finds fault with our artist for

---

[1] Nichols, who has it from a good source, says (*Biographical Anecdotes of Hogarth*, 3rd Ed., p. 17) that most of the heads on this Plate were portraits of contemporaries.

[2] A French enameller in London, author of *Lettres de Mr . . . à un de ses amis à Paris, pour lui expliquer les estampes de Mr Hogarth*, Paris, 1746. Roucquet was a neighbour of Hogarth, who probably knew about these letters. Ed.

introducing this character here, since he is not an English type, but an Italian, and it seems to me Roucquet was right. In the peculiar character of the English nation there is nothing of the bandit, be he employer or employed, even in the lowest stratum of the people; though there are of course people everywhere who will do a special job for money on occasion. But evidently Hogarth's meaning was not as sinister as all that. He probably only wanted to say: the young fellow here in his nightcap and slippers counts poltroonery among his other manly virtues; his honour has recently received a blemish which must be erased by the sword, and in such a predicament a Second who, for a small consideration, would do something special, or who in the guise of a father or guardian would take the whole matter upon himself, would indeed be of value. In a word, our hero appears to have received from Nature, together with his womanish face, that charming need for protection of the defenceless sex, so that his heart is impressed by nothing more easily than by the insignia of protection and security, sash and ruff, together with whiskers. Thus the scene between Rakewell and the Jingo which at the first glance looked so bandit-like becomes at once a sort of marriage pact. Why should not two hearts of the same sex unite for protection and attack, and become one whole, just as two of opposite sex unite for protection and love; *deux courages comme deux coeurs?* An interpreter must halt when he comes as far as this with a difficult locum—enough of it.

Behind the Bravo stands the French-horn player, with his left hand in his trouser pocket. The Captain's letter of recommendation is certainly enhanced by the heroic hunting call which the horn player produces. Music acts on the relationship of souls like warmth on the physical body. It expands and refines through expansion; those who had hitherto repulsed one another or had lain beside one another in lifeless contact begin to mingle their more subtle matter, and in the end the whole flows together. Marriages are made in Heaven, so they say; one should say— in Heaven, but if it does not come off there, in dance-halls and music-halls. That horn-player is certainly drawn from Nature. Hogarth must have seen a man blowing his horn just like that, keeping his hand in his trousers, and having the lower part of his coat buttoned up to hide this. Perhaps Hogarth did not know himself the reason for that attitude. But I remember having seen in my youth a horn-player standing just like that when he was blowing, and I knew for certain that he did so in order not to rupture himself. The purpose of the position of his hand was unmistakable; for if he altered it when playing *piano*, he would always return to it again at the next *forte*.

The man in the centre of the picture who seems about to parade before Rakewell in a sort of turkey strut with outspread tail is a French dancing-master of those days, and undoubtedly some grand and eccentric personage.[1] As one can see, he is uplifted by the enthusiasm and the inflammable temper of his nation, and only just touches the ground with his toes. Some consider the figure exaggerated, and wrongly drawn as well. But where is the dancing master, especially if he is, like this one, so utterly lost in the spiritual enjoyment of his own being, who would not occasionally exaggerate and draw himself wrongly? It may happen to a master of the language of gesture, as it happens to many masters of the Latin language: they can no longer express themselves naturally, through a surfeit of *syntaxis ornata*. That the left leg looks so utterly like a right one may be, partly, the fault of the chair which was less willing to yield to the fine, undulating lines of movement of his body or his dress than the air for which those movements were meant. The greater the refinement, the more easily can it be wrecked. Over a little straw which the normal pedestrian does not even feel, a dancing master may break his neck. This happy mortal (and that he is happy, everything in that beatific face declares that is capable of so doing; the eye closed to the outer world, and open merely to the images of Fancy, and ah! the little honey-mouth slit across with contentment), this happy mortal, I say, is

[1] Mr Nichols, in the quoted passage, says expressly that this man was the famous dancing master, Essex. On p. 210, however, where he names the persons he recognizes among the portraits given here, he makes no mention of this one. Mr Ireland believes him to be a Frenchman, and that is what I think too. But Essex is certainly not a French name, nor is it likely that Hogarth would have depicted one of his compatriots with hair-bag and beauty spot, or that a compatriot of his would have used such adornments. Thus the whole figure is not that of an Englishman, at least not of a person brought up in England. But, of course, one must always take into consideration the relations between our artist and Essex. It is quite possible that something of the face belonged to that man, and that Hogarth intentionally gave him a Frenchman's body. Fielding (*Tom Jones*, Book 14, Chap. I) says of that Essex that had Homer and Virgil, Aristotle and Cicero, Thucydides and Livy, combined all their talents, he did not believe they would have been able to describe the art of dancing with such mastery as had Essex under the title *Rudiments of Genteel Education*. The dainty head gains not a little here if we imagine it enjoying such a triumph over those great writers of antiquity, and if we assume that he either regards them all as having been, or pities them for not having been, dancing masters.

executing bodily a *pas frisé*, which, however, his inner being, unencumbered by shoe and shoe-buckle, and under the purest form of never realized lines of beauty, contemplates with inexpressible satisfaction. What peace of soul! To be sure, Truth itself must be amazed when it sees here a pair of feet carrying their volatile possessor to the goal which he might have missed a dozen times, even with Wisdom's own head upon his shoulders.

Behind the dancing master stands Dubois, a French fencing master; a portrait. He is about to venture a lively pass with his rapier into the air, and therewith to challenge that opponent. The man is remarkable for his tragic end; on May 11, 1734, he was run through in a duel with an Irishman of the same name, also a fencing master; he walked home from the field of battle, but died a few days later from the wound he had received. Of course, the same name, the same profession, and such a profession as that, in one and the same town, may well have given rise to all kinds of bitter and offensive confusions and nicknames. Since they were both privileged dispensers of the specific remedy against offended honour, each prescribed it for the other in a brotherly fashion, and in this way the evil was happily removed, to their mutual advantage.

Although this man has here no adversary before him whose thrust he could parry, yet he has one behind him who casts at him such a glance as a world of Dubois could not parry, namely a glance of calm, quiet contempt based upon a clear consciousness of his own lofty superiority. This quiet adversary is the man behind there close to the wall, who with a pair of considerable cudgels under his arm looks more or less like a third himself. His name was Figg, and he was one of the greatest rowdies of his time, and without quibbling over words, really a great man.[1] With his fist he could have felled an ox, and with his quarter-staff a whole menagerie of Dubois at one blow.[2] This quiet combination of the British athlete and

[1] He died in the year 1734. A portrait of him exists, painted by Ellis, engraved by Faber, and printed by Overton. In Mr Samuel Ireland's (the frequently mentioned interpreter of Hogarth was a John) *Graphic Illustrations of Hogarth from Pictures, Drawings and Scarce Prints, etc.*, London, 1794, quarto, with 52 engravings, there are many anecdotes about him, and also the copy of a decoration from his visiting card which Hogarth had designed for him. He is shown there in his theatre addressing the spectators. Writers who mention that artist regard him as a miracle. His power lay especially in wielding the broadsword and the quarter-staff.

[2] Quarter-staff: this is a crude cudgel of somewhat more than a man's height. The name is apparently derived from the fact that when the staff is wielded, the right hand grips it in the middle, and the left in the middle of the lower half, so that it appears quartered.

the French fencing master is certainly one of the happiest: the British firm, enduring oak opposite the trembling French aspen, the cudgel of Hercules beside the rapier, and the lion beside the crowing cock. How the strong-fisted Figg leans there against the wall and looks down upon the droll fencing solo of Dubois, with an expression on his broad, placid face which leads one to believe that not only is he man enough to cut Dubois in pieces, but that, should it be required of him, he would be quite prepared to devour them afterwards!

On Figg's left, and in conjunction with the Venus on the wall, stands the old landscape gardener, Bridgeman, with the plans of a garden which he is about to lay before Rakewell who, however, is much too occupied at present with the *utile* to pay much attention to the *dulce*. This head, it seems to me, is clearly a portrait. How honest and genuine he looks! Perhaps the most honest person in the whole picture, and on that account he is being treated by the master of the house to his backside. A face like that is really an annuity, though, of course, by now nearing its end. In nature we could well imagine a little deafness or paralytic shaking of the head to go with it. The artist has been reproached for putting here into the hand of that famous beautifier of gardens and the first to banish from them the cold symmetry of the Dutch, a plan which bears witness to exactly the contrary. But how if it were just to indicate the young master's lack of taste; perhaps he has already turned down a better one, or what is still more probable, suppose Mr Bridgeman, who is evidently holding more than one plan here, wanted to put his employer to the test? But this is perhaps too far-fetched. For the purpose of a hieroglyph, the Dutch type is really more suitable than the English, and the description 'Garden Plan' was not so necessary here as it would have been under many a genuinely English one. Incidentally this excellent man is also said to have been the first to banish the topiary treatment of trees and hedges and to have invented the so-called Ha-ha's.[1]

[1] Walpole's *Anecdotes of Painting in England*, Vol. IV, p. 136. Ha-ha is the name given in England to the fencing in of a garden with steep, dry ditches which sometimes have a brick lining, but sometimes also, where they are less steep, contain an ordinary fence of palings. They have the advantage that the view from the garden into the fields and country beyond is not lost, as it is with walls and hedges when they are raised noticeably above the ground level. Somebody walking in the garden and not knowing this might often be astonished, when seeing strangers walking quite near, that the garden should have been left open like that. After closer examination and on discovering his mistake, many a man may have exclaimed 'Ha-ha!'

In front of our hero kneels a jockey who in his service and with his horses has won a heavy silver bowl which he here presents on his knees, probably because, on account of its great weight, this is the easiest way for him to hold it until his master has finished with his more important business. The father would perhaps have forgotten his immortal soul for the hundredth part of such a trophy. Upon the bowl itself are engraved the pictures of the horse and jockey. Above are the words 'Won at Epsom', and underneath 'Silly Tom', the name of the horse. This is the application which Hogarth makes of Rakewell's Christian name, to which we have alluded earlier, p. 199. His horse is called Little Thomas, and so is he; it is ridden by other people to their advantage, and so is he; it would not allow that if it were cleverer, and suffers it merely because it is a bit silly, like him. By the word 'silly' the English denote good, simple-minded fellows with whom one can do what one likes, and who do not know how to look after themselves; thus are somewhat foolish. In some parts of Germany the Thomases are called by the common people *Tumme*. According to this, Silly Tom could be construed *Dumme-Tumme*, which does not sound unlike Dun-Don, the name of an excellent race-horse which the writer himself saw in October 1774 win against five or six others. Don denotes the breed and dun the colour. Whether in that name Silly Tom there is not perhaps the faint sound of 'filly', at least from afar, can only be decided by an English ear. Of course, 'filly' means a young mare, and thus does not suit the name Tom, but in horse-racing fillies are so often spoken of, and the name appears so often upon the programmes, so many fillies are running in a race, and the name is so often found on engravings that I have twice already known it happen that an Englishman trying to read that inscription read 'filly' at the first attempt, being misled by the picture of the horse. Nobody would readily imagine the name 'Silly' under the picture of an English race-horse, so noble and lovely a creature which, in the scale of animal perfection, activity, and sensibility, stands certainly a number of rungs higher than other horses, and sometimes than the master himself. The animal only seems to have been debased here somewhat by the artist for his master's moral instruction. But I shall cut short this

---

Hence the name. Sometimes they are arranged so as to separate the garden proper from the deer park. It once happened to the writer himself that when wishing to approach the deer he suddenly came upon such a Ha-ha. He said something when he found himself so deceived, but though he does not quite remember what it was, it certainly was not 'Ha-ha!'

tirade lest the word 'filly' should begin to resound in the reader's ear, at least from afar.

Rakewell keeps race-horses, and, as we see from the two portraits of combatants on the wall, fighting cocks as well. Were he in addition to distribute golden apples to such fighting hens as Paris on the wall there has before him, then the history of our young gentleman would become thoroughly intelligible.

At the piano sits a man, no longer young apparently, and quite respectable-looking, from behind at least. He has before him the music of a new Opera, *The Rape of the Sabines*. Upon the right-hand page stand the names of the actors, beginning with Romulus Sen. Far.—no doubt Signor Farinelli, a famous Bistoury-tuned singer of that time, of whom we shall hear more presently. Then follow the Ravishers, very funnily numbered like violinists: first, second, third Ravisher, with their abbreviated names following, in which surely no one is interested. What gives relish to this idea of Hogarth's is, first, that these terrible ravishers were probably all artificial sopranos, and second that in English the word 'ravish' has the secondary meaning of 'rape', whereas the German word expresses rather a forced abduction which might also lead to a happy ending. To an English ear, the expression would sound rather like, 'first Raper, second Raper', and so on. One might also think of a third meaning, but one which Hogarth would hardly have hit upon. Namely, 'to ravish' has in English the same meaning as *ravir* in French, to overpower with delight, and in this sense Farinelli with his voice was a great Ravisher and Ravisseur, especially of ladies' hearts, a quite definite expression of which we shall find upon this Plate. These were the ravishers, now come the Virgins: Signora Str . . . dr, Signora Ne.gr. and so on, although natural sopranos yet false virgins and great ravisseuses in more senses than one. They all belong to the well-known order of the Sabines who wander through Europe singing and, in addition, blackmailing the male sex into paying fines because of the lost innocence of their female forebears, which they requite with a miserable imitation of the unhappy story, and in the end carry everything back to the *Agro Sabino*.

From the pianist's chair-back hangs a long scroll covered with close writing. From a cursory glance one would almost take it for a petition addressed to somebody, and the assembled company as a Press Gang for obtaining subscribers to it. It is nothing of the kind, however, but something much more real, namely an inventory of presents made to the ravisher Farinelli, who at that time had almost acquired a ducal estate through his voice. It runs as follows:

'A List of the rich Presents Signor Farinelli the Italian singer conde-scended to accept of the English Nobility and Gentry for one Night's Performance in the Opera *Artaxerxes*.

A Pair of Diamond Knee Buckles Presented by . . .

A Diamond Ring by . . .

A Bank Note enclosed in a Rich Gold Case by . . .

A Gold Snuff Box Chased with the story of Orpheus charming the Brutes by T. Rakewell Esq.' (Bravo! So among the charmed brutes there was also an animal called 'Silly Tom').

These are merely the Pretiosa; now comes the cash money, first 100, then 200, and again 100, evidently guineas. The remainder is rolled up.[1]

Under the roll lies an engraving attached to a eulogy upon Farinelli, which the poet, according to the inscription, has dedicated to our Rake-well. Thus race-horses, fighting cocks, whores, and poets; they could get through something in a year.

The engraving itself represents Farinelli above an altar on which hearts are burning. Before it stand and kneel ladies who have brought burning hearts as an offering to him. A queer sacrifice for such a deity who could never properly understand the meaning of these night-lights. The High Priestess exclaims: 'One G–d, one Farinelli.' It is said that some lady in a fit of the then rampant Tarantism,[2] enraptured by the singing of the castrate, shouted these words aloud from her Box in the Theatre. Such a creature would really have deserved the punishment of Midas; everything she touched ought to have been changed—into worshipped gold. However, all the ladies hold their hearts in their hands (one of them even grips hers at the top, right in the flame) and this circumstance makes the sacrifice understandable. They were mere Sunday hearts which some may even raise to Heaven without incommoding their real heart in the least. The satire is directed, as one sees, against the rage for Italian opera, and is therefore very proper, only not nearly sharp enough, and

[1] That this Farinelli really received presents of tremendous value after his performance of *Artaxerxes* is confirmed in the newspapers of that time. Mr Ireland confirms it too, not in this passage of his Commentaries, but, on another occasion, in the fourth Plate of 'Marriage-à-la-Mode.'

[2] Dancing mania. Ed.

quite incommensurate with the genius of our artist. There is really nothing to choose between a strip of paper with writing hanging down from the back of a chair like a towel, or rising like tobacco smoke in front out of a mouth.[1] If after a contemplation of these ingeniously drawn heads one happens on so heterogeneous a device, one has a curious sensation, almost as if (I beg pardon of the Fine Arts for this simile) with a substantial roast the gravy were to be read out of a cookery book.

But who now is the man sitting there in the chair, if the figure is intended to represent some one then living? Opinions on this are divided, even among the English interpreters, and no foreigner could decide it. It is certainly not Farinelli himself. To such a figure no young lady would sacrifice her heart, not even her Sunday one. It is impossible to find any in such a creature. Put whatever you like on the altar for them, marble or wood, but for goodness sake only youth, youth! And Farinelli as he sits over there in Heaven really seems to possess that, since even in the microscopic representation one can see that the head-gear is of a man not yet thirty. A fairly common interpretation is that the figure is our great countryman Handel. Trusler affirms this, and only a few weeks ago obtained a written assurance, supposedly based upon the statement of a man who claims to have known our artist personally, that it is indeed Handel. Nichols is against this, but he bases his opinion purely upon an *argumentum a priori* which Sir John Hawkins once expressed to him: 'Handel,' said Sir John, 'had far too high a sense of his own value ever to have put himself into such a position. That being so, the artist could hardly have had the idea of putting him into the picture. He must have meant some other composer of operas.' The same argument is repeated by Mr Ireland. Of course, it may well be that the figure is not Handel, and as the matter now stands, it will hardly be possible to decide it until Hogarth's own notes appear, which, as I see from the papers, are now said to have been found. But this much, I believe, can be said, that Sir John Hawkins's proof that it could not be Handel is no proof at all. It shows but a poor acquaintance with the spirit of satire in general, and Hogarth's in particular, to credit it with so much conscience. Handel's figure, which our artist and a thousand others may have seen more often from behind, seated at the piano, than from in front, may have appealed to him. And therefore, just because it was familiar to the public, it could

[1] The cartoonist's device for indicating speech. Ed.

stand as a sort of generally recognizable symbol for music, like Bridge-man's head for the art of Horticulture. I readily admit it would have been contemptible flippancy to have portrayed Handel's face in such a scene, but as it is—it is Handel's art which sits here and not Handel's noble and lofty character. The greater facility for depicting the likeness of a man in that position, combined with the probability that many must have seen him from that angle, deprives the idea of the character of a studied intention which alone could make it appear malicious. But if it is indeed Handel, then Hogarth has made ample amends, through the trailing manifesto, for whatever offence he might have given. 'To this man here', the in-scription appears to say, 'is due what you, my country, are wasting on miserable sycophants. If you would reward a foreigner, at least reward him whose melodies do not enervate your manly feelings, but enhance them through their magic power, and incite you to deeds which are worthy of you. As to the others—

Give them brickbats for bread.'[1]

So much for that figure if indeed it does represent Handel, and for the evidence that, despite Sir John Hawkins's opinion, it might represent him. However, that it really is Handel seems to me somewhat unlikely after all, since I have read that Handel was a big man and was specially re-markable for his large hands and thick fingers. Now for a brief glance into the ante-chamber.

The second complement for these morning hours is assembled there already, waiting for the bell to ring. A milliner waits with great resigna-tion, listening to some man's rather violent remarks. From the gestures he makes with his hat we conclude that it is only a petty quarrel, possibly about precedence. He is afraid of being number six at the presentation. Had the girl not come, he might have been the fifth. He may be a shoe-maker. Next to him, according to Gilpin, stands a French tailor, and beside him a French wig-maker; the one with a new evening suit upon his arm, the other with a new wig in the box. What a tailor compared with the village Theosoph who took the measure of the mourning suit! But then, this one here carries the garment for the festival day of resur-rection in the great world. Just as the other smelt utterly of cobbler, this one here, despite some slight similarities in their faces, is every inch

[1] Handel's 'Give them hailstones for bread' is well known.

the titular Acting Counsellor. Evidently both tailor and wig-maker have made their way hither in a carriage. Who might that long figure be beside the mirror? It appears to be a creature on half-pay, or even an unemployed. He certainly has nothing to bring with him, except perhaps a few claims to benevolence, and he utilizes the isolation which he has to endure among these people for putting them into the best possible form. But now the poet! The poet with the Epistle to Rakewell in his hand! He who cannot taste and feel the bliss of that man who reads his own verse aloud, perhaps for the hundredth time, has certainly never been himself a begetter of verses, and consequently is a stranger to one of the greatest domestic joys with which Heaven has thought fit to brighten the lives of all those who write in rhythm and rhyme, whether in a garret or at Ferney or Twickenham.[1] Only see how tenderly and with what paternal joy he gazes on his beloved metric progeny, lisping childishly back to him. The right hand rests on his heart and begs it to bear witness to the truth of his feeling; hand and mouth do everything in their power, and so does the wig, for it is the very spit of the late Voltaire's. Did we not already know that Hogarth wrote verses, we might guess it from that lightly drawn poetaster's head. Otherwise he could not possibly have known that among all those in this world who offer sacrifices, the poet is the only creature who mirrors himself in his sacrificial wine, even at the moment when he pours it on the altar. However, what may seem difficult to anyone else is often easy for the genius. The best comfort in such depressing experiences is to believe that one has achievements of one's own which other honest people would find very difficult to attain, be it only the gift for writing such wise notes as these to interpret a caricature.

One the wall between the two fighting cocks hangs the Judgement of Paris. The arrangement of the pictures testifies to the owner's taste, or perhaps only his steward's, or maybe the steward was a sly fox and the fighting cocks are a subtle pass at poor Paris. Really the two animals stand there, one opposite the other, as if the three goddesses were three hens, and Paris as if he were another cock. Is this picture supposed to be a copy of the one in the possession of King Francis I, and which our Rakewell has been sold for the original? *Francois I, Roi de France, avait un tableau, que l'on disait être sans défauts; il permit à tout le monde de le venir con-sidérer et ordonna qu'on lui fit parler tous ceux qui y trouveraient des*

[1] As is well known, the homes of Voltaire and Pope.

défauts; ce tableau représentait Junon, Venus, Pallas et Paris, nus. Rabelais après l'avoir examiné longtemps, dit qu'il y trouvait un grand défaut de jugement: on le fit parler au Roi, qui lui demanda quel était ce défaut; il répondit à sa Majesté que Paris, étant au milieu des trois plus belles Déesses du Ciel, ne devait pas être représenté d'un si sang-froid, et que c'etait se tromper lourdement, que de penser que ce Prince, jeune et vigoureux, fût ainsi demeuré, sans donner quelque signe qu'il était homme, devant trois Déesses nues qui tachaient à l'envie de lui plaire.[1]

That passage has been adopted by the anonymous interpreter of Hogarth, and Ireland has it from him. It may therefore stand here also. But how did it come about that neither of them remembered how their great fellow-countryman, Burke, solved the puzzle with the philosophical acuity so characteristic of him? The passage is in his *Philosophical Enquiry into the Origin of our Ideas of the Sublime and Beautiful*, Part IV, Sect. 19, 7th Edition, p. 286, etc. One must read the passage there. If brought into juxtaposition with the one just quoted, it would give rise through affinity to a third, which by its form might do harm. Chemistry provides many similar examples, and Cupid upon the picture there is a clever Cupid.

On the front of the piano is the name of the instrument maker, and if I am not mistaken, for it is almost unreadable in the original, it is J. Makoon *fecit*. Probably this is another allusion to the owner's thriftlessness or lack of taste. The English interpreters are completely silent about such features, although it ought to have occurred to them that what would have been easy enough for them to ascertain at the time would be no longer so for posterity. Since Hogarth elected to engrave the name of an artist there, it is certain he must have chosen the best and most relevant for his story.

---

[1] Francis I, King of France, had a picture which was said to be faultless; he invited everybody to come and examine it, and gave orders that anybody who found fault with it should tell him; the picture represented Juno, Venus, Pallas and Paris, naked. Rabelais, after having studied the picture for a long time, declared that he had discovered a great fault of judgment in it; he was made to speak with the King who asked him what this fault was. He replied to His Majesty that Paris being in the midst of the three most beautiful goddesses of Heaven ought not to have been represented with so much *sang-froid*, and that it was a grave error to think that this Prince, young and vigorous, would have remained like that without giving some sign that he was a man, before three naked goddesses who were all intent on pleasing him.

III

THE greatest scientists, and in particular chemists, have held the view that man, and everything that draws breath and wishes to do so for an appreciable time, would do best to draw it from a mixture of one part life-giving and three parts death-giving air. This is very remarkable. For if a human being is put into the latter alone, he will no longer be good for anything—it would be all over with him. If, however, he is put into the former unadulterated, oh, then life blazes up with six-fold brilliance, his cheeks glow with youth, and his stomach digests with six-fold power, but the rate of consumption is very rapid, and if he goes on like that one grows apprehensive of—eternal life. How wise was it, therefore, of Heaven to mix with the air of life eternal in our atmosphere, a three-fold portion of the air of death! Without that damper, most plants would probably, through all-too-rapid growth, yield more straw than corn on the harvest day. I believe, therefore, that a profound treatise on the Damper would be of immense advantage to our modern hot-house system of education. At present there is too much forcing-matter in it. How does Heaven rear us? If we consisted of soul only we should all shoot up as male and female bigots, who in the end would be of no use in either Earth or Heaven, but the well-known five dampers have the effect that the spirit grows somewhat slower, with the result that in the end it need not feel ashamed of being seen in either climate. But why all this? Why? I should think the application is clear enough. In the second Plate, Rake-well stood in a hot-house, and now here he sits under the influence of the damper. Today he has fought, danced—though only with the dancing

215

master—has taken a piano lesson, another on the French horn, and another in the art of boxing. He has listened to a lecture and has dealt with a good amount of domestic business. So much work requires rest wherein the mind may gain time to brace itself again for the morning, and this he finds here; of course, in a somewhat curious way, but that is none of our business—it is a matter of taste. In former times there were men who sought recreation in this way from the most difficult of all occupations, that of government, and by this means regained their capacity for ministering to whole countries.

Here then the busy man takes his rest at an Inn. Whether it is a permanent brothel, or one created by himself *ex tempore*, I do not know. Nor does it matter; but the latter is more likely. With money one can make anything out of a room in London: library, picture-gallery, museum, or harem, and in less than no time. Rakewell here has chosen the last for himself and a friend. The composition is, as we see, of almost oriental proportions, that is, apart from the little toad with the ballad near the door, who evidently does not belong to it, ten females to two males, or more precisely now—two men.[1] There must have been frightful goings-on, and that for a good long time, for the light which shines here cannot come from the four little flames in the background. Day has dawned and mirrors itself in the bottles, and that is very lucky for us, since without its help we should barely be able to distinguish half of the reign of terror which has held and still holds sway here. This Plate could serve as a warning to those who know country life only from pastoral poetry.

There he sits now, or rather the little which still remains of him; very little to be sure. Of the six senses which he brought with him, hardly a single one remains, and the traces of those not yet completely departed are no longer worthy of mention. His clothes hang loosely around him and on him, merely following the law of gravitation, just like his limbs. The left stocking has already reached the lowest point and with the least jerk the right will follow its example, and then no doubt the master himself will follow suit. There is every indication that he has already had a slight conflict with the law of gravitation, in which the chair behind him had its back broken. What bliss there is in that face! The whole feeble residue of gesture-language which still hovers about those lips seems to

---

[1] It is hardly necessary to remind the reader that, in dealing with human beings, one must sharply distinguish between two men and two males.

A Rake's Progress Plate III

have assembled merely to convey to the observer the indescribable joy of senselessness. At his side hangs his sword across its sheath, thus already in the position in which it is to lie over the corpse of our hero, in sign of honour, as soon as he has accomplished his own destruction.

We cannot possibly let him sink to rest like that without casting a glance at his actions, and this leads us to a closer investigation of the battlefield. Beside him on the floor lie the trophies of victory, the lantern of the night-watchman, more properly of the watch, together with his official quarter-staff, and this is as creditable as if the watch himself were to lie stretched out there. Figg's pupil has done well. In the immediate vicinity and almost under the point of the sword, apparently felled by it, lies the noblest object that could have fallen by the sword of a hero—Julius Caesar's head. A second Caesarian (*sectio Caesarea*) has here stretched the master of the world in the dust amidst broken glasses, clandestine pills, and horn-lantern fragments. Rakewell in his intoxication (and that is the best time for it) has hit upon the idea of restoring the Roman Republic and has attacked with his Jacobin the Imperial Zodiac of the first century who adorned the wall up there. The order of the zodiacal signs there is, as one sees, quite in conformity with the system of the place and its furniture and movables.

Sunt: Aries, Cancer, Virgo, Gemini, Leo, Taurus, etc. The tyrants are really beheaded, as far as one can see, with the exception of Nero; here was a boon companion, a perfect devil of a fellow, who had a head on his shoulders, and so he shall keep it there. As for the others, in place of the tiresome heads of office which they possessed, Hogarth seems to have endowed them with some giddier ones for private use. It looks as if the empty spaces were heads, or the other way round. That might often have chanced in Rome too. Augustus puts out quite a considerable piece of tongue, perhaps at the poor Republic; Vitellius (Hogarth writes Vitelius) by virtue of wig and ruff looks, on our copy at least, really respectable, and the honest Vespasian carries a pig's head. Did Hogarth take him perhaps for the destroyer of Jerusalem?[1]

[1] The assumption that Hogarth, by these holes, wished to express not only empty heads but also a certain characteristic, of which even emptiness is not completely void, I have already put forward in the Taschenbuch for 1785 (second edition, p. 139), thus really already in 1784. It was applauded at the time by an expert, but another, an Englishman, declared it improbable. But in 1799, thus eight years later, in England itself, the anonymous interpreter hit upon a very similar idea, only he believed Vespasian's head to be a fox's head and adduces

In Caesar's place (and in the first copies of this Plate, it was really Caesar who hung there) a solid, stout man of the world has been inserted, who *fills* his place. With such a figure, the *orbis terrarum* surely has something on which to support itself. The man's name was Pontac, and he was, as Mr Ireland assures us, an eminent cook. A German would rather have taken him for a beer-brewer. Perhaps a lower Saxony Pontac-brewer. The anonymous interpreter does not quite know what to make of the paunch, but thinks he may have been an infamous brothel-keeper of the time. So maybe it is even the landlord of that Inn whom Rakewell has put in Caesar's place:

Tyran, descends du trône, et fais place à ton maître.

In an illustrated book of fairy tales it might also represent Clod I which Jupiter threw into a pond when he was asked to provide a King; upon this followed Stork I, Stork II, etc., about which Suetonius tells us more.

The mirror, the universal portrait of all present, is also slashed through; perhaps it was a suicide *in effigie* performed by Rakewell's sword. The larder has been relegated in haste and in the general tumult to the left-hand corner, which, as one sees, was already engaged. That sort of thing never does any good. Here, too, it has given rise to confusion. The first occupant, a pot which in general is treated with scant ceremony, and which itself very often does not stand on any at all, inexorably pours its whole abundance over roast chickens with the fork still in the breast, over torn off chicken legs, and plates and lemons and liqueur glasses, and remains master of the field. The master's Spanish cane lies broken with its strap beside it, and holds sway no longer. In the foreground lie female garments from the deepest layers (they have made themselves thoroughly comfortable here); they reach as far as the Emperors' heads, and past these to mingle with the vulgar pills; and so on. All the chairbacks within sight are broken.

This is a brief survey of the devastation of inanimate Nature. Now for a

---

a passage where somebody says of that Emperor who not even as Emperor could abandon the miserliness to which he was addicted despite his other sterling qualities: I can see the fox changes his hair but not his character. However much this little piece of mischief may accord with Hogarth's mood, he would surely have expressed it clearer and better if he had really had that intention. With some imagination one can easily find a torso in every summer cloud, and a silhouette in every ink blot. And so I no longer put much store by that idea.

few glances at the plight of the living. Indolence and relaxation have here, as usual, something of the outward appearance of sobriety, and in the general arrangement of the bodies there is at least some picturesque system. A line drawn through the heads hovering round the table ascends gradually from right to left, and from the turning point of a shorn head descends again towards the left with equal inclination towards the horizon. Thus one returns more or less to the starting point. But this is the only sort of plan to be found here, and even this is merely consequent upon the shape of the table. Tables may well have such an effect; they arrange in an orderly way what would otherwise have defied arrangement, they enhance physical distance, and through their stiff neutrality offer protection to those who sit around them, whereas a few inches less wood might have led to murder and manslaughter. It is the same everywhere. One could demonstrate it with a geographical map.

The black-feathered hat of our hero is rather intimately approached by a white-feathered one. Of course, they are only hats. But the girl certainly had this rapprochement to thank for her victory over so many of her sisters. Probably all goes into one kitty, but she was the one to achieve it. Rakewell loves feathered hats, and if one of these girls put one on, with a white feather versus his black feather, this surely means for anybody who can read: 'I and Thou', and that is more than half the battle. With her right hand she feels for his heart, and thus for his pulse at its source. But the attack is a feint. The real attack was directed at another pulse, his watch, and that is safely delivered to the rear under the girl's watchful eye. The hands of the watch point to three o'clock. This, even in the height of summer, would be somewhat too early for so much light as blazes here, and which can have no other source but the day. But there is really no difficulty here. It is a well-known fact that if human beings no longer order their lives by following their clocks, then their clocks follow them. Disorder has this advantage, that one can explain everything by it. The composure with which the *arrière-garde* receives the spoils is marvellously expressed. Behind that face one would hardly suspect so much acquaintance with crime. With her elbow leaning on the chair-back of the vanquished she catches the watch with her right hand as if it were a soap-bubble, and before handing it over to the treasure-chest it amuses her to toy with it a little, and quite near Rakewell's ears at that. She must certainly have a good idea of how *such* ears in *such* heads work. That

Hogarth must have been rather proud of that face can be seen from his use of contrast by which he has thrown it into relief. Here again are English milk-and-blood on a background of African pine-soot.[1] How the little black Satan behind there is lit up! Hers are the liveliest eyes in the whole Plate. They are really directed towards the shiny dish near the door where a girl in the attitude of the trumpeter in the second Plate blares out a very indecent ballad, 'The Black Joke'. The witch seems to find amusement in this song. Of course she too is black, and apart from that is fond of a joke, in any colour. She puts her finger to her mouth; probably she had intended to hide behind her whole hand as an expression of female modesty, but decided half-way that it would be unnecessary in this company.

In her immediate vicinity are two little female dragon-heads, one of whom is spitting fire, and the other foul wine. Up till now they had evidently been duelling with tongues only, or had had their pistols loaded merely with invectives; but now since all the linguistic ammunition has been used up, they have adopted more substantial weapons, the one a knife and the other a fire-extinguisher. Maybe the burning damsel had merely begged the extinguisher, the Nymph of the well, for a drink, of which she was in need; this the other is sending her in the form of a jet, while securing the well with both hands. A few inches less table-wood might have produced interesting results. Between that warlike pair, just where the pyramid of the group reaches its peak, is a rather peaceful couple. In the striking face of the girl even the fumes of wine can hardly obscure the faint glimmer of another fire. She seems to have the intention of ensnaring an indolent lap-dog fellow on her own account, and evidently with poor success. The scene lies outside the limit of our Plate. The two remaining figures at the table are very easy to understand. They represent the technical side of the art of drinking, upon the first rung of its ladder and upon the last. The one, quick and lively, still drinks with the left hand alone, holding the right, which is hanging down but not relaxed, with considerable dignity. She holds her glass with that well-known air of refinement in which the little finger is outstretched, as if one were taking a pinch of something. The other drinks in a state of exhaustion, grasping the overflowing vessel with both fists, and is at the end

[1] See p. 159, 'Strolling Actresses'.

of her tether. The first reminds one of the Greek poet who imbibes soul-giving *Chier* and enthusiasm in strong draughts, but always with grace. The second, on the other hand, resembles one of our poets who puts the heavy bucket of his publisher's demands with hopeful flourish to his lips but, happily for his readers, empties half the heavy stout into his trousers.

In the background we see a girl engaged upon a significant procedure. In her hand she holds a light, and is evidently about to set fire to something, and that something is nothing less than the one-time property of the bright heads up there on the wall, the *Orbis terrarum* itself: TOTUS MUNDUS. That Hogarth has chosen a whore for that business is evidence of his great familiarity with ancient history and the earliest relics of lofty poetry. Perhaps there is more to it still. One of Hogarth's commentators made short work of it. He believes the girl had felt herself slighted by the company and in her rage she sets the world alight, despite the fact that she would thereby share the fate of all the others. What a joke to be sure, and what a gift for divining and sharing Hogarth's mood! Why not rather set fire straightaway to Mr Pontac's house by applying the light to the staircase? No! If that action is to have a meaning, as I believe it has, beyond the utterly senseless craving of the drunkard for destruction, in order to relieve his feelings, it must surely be a deeper one. Perhaps the following interpretation, if not the true one, is at least more commensurate with Hogarth's genius. Whoever intends to set fire to a map (of the countries themselves there is no question here), quite unallegorically, will begin *in dubio*, if the map is hanging on the wall, with the lower edge. This, however, is not what the poor girl is doing; indeed, she seems rather to be searching for some particular spot, employing some bodily exertion and probably standing on tiptoe. Now if I am not mistaken that spot is just in front of the East coast of America, whence, as is well known, the Spaniards brought a certain product to Europe with which girls of that type carry on a sort of smugglers' trade, up to this day. Therefore, what one might here take for inflammation, may it not be a mere illumination or search for the main storehouse, prompted by mercantile-geographical curiosity? Certainly not! There is no doubt that because she has become bankrupt in the trade she is setting fire to the world *in effigie* just on that spot where the former American Company first started a conflagration *in natura* and lit a fire which they now try to extinguish by Amalgama-

221

tion.[1] Hogarth accompanies this world-conflagration with a mischievous touch, partly concealed and thus deniable if need be, which is all the more dangerous for an interpreter. Behind the door there stands a blind harpist upon whose harp, funnily enough, King David, whom Hogarth enjoys bringing into bad company,[2] is displayed also with a harp. Here he sits immediately in front of Nero, and one cannot avoid the suspicion, knowing something of Hogarth's roguery, that he has been placed just there to make music for the conflagration of the world, as did Nero for the burning of Rome.

The damsel who in the foreground there seems to be making her toilet is a rather notorious figure of that time, known as the posture-woman. Her name, so Trusler declares, was Aratine (or Aretine). She really is stripping. She is prepared to show her art, and for that purpose to let herself be served up at table in the guise of a chicken, with a fork in the breast, as a living dish. The dish which is being brought in over there at the door, and which the baboon who carries it illuminates so as to advertise the spectacle, is to be the revolving stage upon which she will perform. This is really abominable. But would the human race be greatly benefited were it deprived of the faculty to descend sometimes like that below the beasts? That here and there, in the shadiest corners of great towns, vermin is generated which finds its amusement in such bestialities is much less to the disgrace of human nature than the verdict of the inner judge, who uncorruptly dwells in the breast of millions and condemns that vermin to eternal infamy, is to its honour. A certain Englishman, Mr Pawson, has edited *Joe Miller's Jests* with Greek notes, which is not a jot better than a *Till Eulenspiegel* with Hebrew ones. I always remind myself of that book when I am tempted to become too serious in these Commentaries. However, since I have already mentioned one Greek note, I cannot refrain from adding a second as balm for the trauma which Aretine's story may perhaps have inflicted upon some tender organ. Hers is a shameful story, it is true, but it is not only the desire of the assembled company to revolve the plucked chicken on its dish, it is the desire of the chicken itself to let itself be revolved. It glories in it, it lives by it, and through it can buy itself new feathers. But how if in little social circles in

[1] Certain objections which might be raised against this on account of the Plate's being drawn in reverse, I will discuss at the end of the chapter.
[2] See 'A Harlot's Progress', p. 23.

many a devoutly Christian provincial town, in rooms where perhaps instead of Pontac an 'Ecce Homo' looks down from the walls, the absent neighbour, nay even the absent friend herself, is deprived of every cover for her human weakness and is served up upon the coffee tray for the entertainment of the company, and is there displayed to the accompaniment of giggles from the ladies and pious humbugs, what about that?— Oh, at least take away the 'Ecce Homo' and hang up old Pontac!

Round the dish are the words: 'John Bonvine (*bon Vin*) at the Rose Tavern, Drurylane', whereby Street and Inn are identified wherein such orgies were celebrated in those days. The name Bonvin justifies our assumption about Pontac. The baboon is also a portrait of a notorious waiter at the Rose Inn, who was known by the name of Leather-coat. He must have distinguished himself considerably since already in 1732 Fielding had shown him on the stage in his *Covent Garden Tragedy* under the name of Leathersides. He is said to have had an incredible familiarity with this type of trade; whoever wished to acquire American products would be certain to obtain the best addresses through him. Rakewell is sure to have consulted him.

I do not quite understand what the servant on the stairs is bringing in on his dish, or why he is there at all, but he is certainly not put there for nothing. Does it mean that on the other floors there are similar goings-on at this early hour, or does it indicate that this room is perhaps in the basement and more properly is a so-called cellar? For as a rule food is carried from English kitchens upwards and not downwards.

Nichols rightly reminds us that these are no longer the morals of the present time. Perhaps the priests and the idols are still the same, and it is merely the liturgy which has changed, or perhaps we agree with Dr Johnson's very clever remark:[1] 'It is a good thing,' he says, 'for our young people, if they want to be dissolute, to be so at least outside their own country; then when they return they may start a new life with a new character.' Rakewell does not seem to envisage anything like this; he only thought to himself: 'stay in the country and earn an honest living', or he is quite willing to settle down abroad. Where? That we shall discover.

Herr Riepenhausen has drawn this Plate in reverse, and in this I think he was right. Since Hogarth's engravings are mainly copies of

[1] Boswell's *Life of Dr Johnson*, Vol. II, p. 265.

larger pictures, he himself did not take the trouble, unless there was a special reason for it, to reverse them; and therefore many well-known places and streets in London often appear in quite the wrong direction. In our picture the light enters from the left as it should do, Rakewell's sword hangs on the proper side, although of course the sword–belt hangs here as if it had turned round. The spitfire grips the knife with her right hand, and the coat buttons of the man at the head of the group are also on the right. But had there been any carelessness here, the greatest loss, for the interpreter at least, would have been the East coast of America. For on the original engraving the girl lights up the Eastern Paniglobium, and thus the Old World. But this is also true. Only the inspection of the original painting can here decide.

IV

HERE is our hero at his zenith—in his greatest glory. He will never rise higher than this. As we see him now in the fourth Plate, he is also entering the fourth stage of his path through life. In the course of the sun, this stage is called Cancer, and it means something like that here for our meteor. From now on, our hero moves steadily on the downward path, and in fact Leo has an eye on him already. The scene is at the corner of the street leading to the main entrance of St James's Palace (St James's Street), whose gateway we glimpse between the two venerable towers in the background. Before it appears a huge carriage-sedan-chair-and-lackey crowd. It is a great crowd of faithful subjects swarming and pressing around St James's like bees around the hive of the Queen. Here too it is for the Queen's sake. Today is the 1st of March, the birthday of Queen Caroline,[1] thus a political Sunday, to celebrate which they are crowding to the Temple and the *praesens numen*. That it is no other day but the 1st of March has been as clearly expressed by Hogarth, at least to his own countrymen, as that there is a thunderstorm here. For to the right paces an elderly gentleman with somewhat heightened gravity and inflated self-esteem. In his hat he wears a badge of deep significance: it is a leek, the day is Saint David's Day (the 1st of March) and the man himself a Welshman. He wears the leek in memory of the deeds of his forefathers,[2] regards himself as one of those heroes of old, and accepts, as one

[1] Wife of George II, born March 1, 1683.
[2] On this day, March 1, 633, so the legend goes, the Welsh, led by their King Cadwallawn, won a great victory over the Saxons and, since there was a field of leeks nearby, the victors

sees, in their name, the admiration of the world and the *Dicier Hic est* with profound dignity, although at the moment there does not appear to be anybody to offer it to him. What wonders may be worked by a badge and a warm imagination! He offers his breast to the early March air, of which only his fingers seem to be afraid, though they cannot really be so, for his muff looks more like a cold air bellows than a warmth accumulator. In this way Hogarth indicates the birthday of his Queen. This preliminary explanation of the scene was necessary in order to understand why Rakewell arrives here with so much splendour.

The hatter's box as well as the wig-maker's in the second Plate have opened, and the tailor's work has unfolded in order to adorn the artistic product of Figg, Essex, Dubois, Pontac and Co for the festive day. The fellow wants to go to Court; to mix with the swarm of bees—the wasp! He does not appear to have a carriage of his own (remember the sign of the Lion), he chose therefore for the transport of his noble self the cheaper four-legged domestic animal, the porte-chaise. Concealed in it, he believed he would come warm and safe to St James's, there to gaze upon the light of the great world in quite a natural way, like hundreds of others, merely by getting out of his vehicle. But he has miscalculated. Certain events intervene. It is a difficult birth; the dandy is fetched out with forceps on the public highway. One has incurred debts which one is unable to pay and one is arrested. That this event involves not an active but an exceedingly passive descent from the vehicle can be seen from the fact that the foremost bearer is still holding the two poles, and is only unable to proceed because his hindmost colleague with leek in hat is already occupied in raising the roof of the post-chaise so that Rakewell—should not ruin his coiffure. Excellent! A police officer is presenting to him a strip of paper, hardly a few inches long, but also, simultaneously, a cudgel which is somewhat longer, and that strip of paper acts on our hero as if it were the heavenly beam itself which flashes so brilliantly over there to the

---

stuck leaves of it in their hats. Nowadays little bunches of leek, sometimes decorated with silver, are sold on this day in the streets of London, and are worn by many in honour of that brave people. Shakespeare (*Henry V*, Act IV, Scene 1) alludes to it when the Welshman, Fluellen, is mentioned:

Pistol: Know'st thou Fluellen?
King Henry: Yes.
Pistol: Tell him I'll knock his *leek* about his pate,
  Upon *St David's Day*.

A Rake's Progress Plate IV

accompaniment of thunder. Indeed it is no mean weapon which strikes here, but one of the *foudres de poche* of English Justice which unfailingly find their man, a warrant of arrest; awe-inspiring at any time, but here, introduced by Heaven with a peal of thunder, even terrible! Hamlet, if the ghost had appeared to him when he was leaving a *porte-chaise*, could hardly have been more petrified than Rakewell here. It looks as if the lightning of Heaven had struck him in the literal sense of the word. Electricity-wise persons will find everything they seek here. The hair-bag rises off his shoulders as if standing on end, the fingers are spread like spikes, the eye stares without seeing. He is really struck and knocked out, for the vermin notice it and fall upon him. The mischievous lamplighter intentionally overfills the lamp, and the surplus streams on to Rakewell's festive clothes. That he does this purposely can be surmised from his lower lip, and his eye looking where there is less to see than is below him.[1] However, he does damage like an honest man, without deriving any advantage from it. Not quite so honest as this satirist upon the ladder is a member of the small club which here upon the pavement of a public street is holding its sessions, without any proper seats. He is stealing a handkerchief from the poor all-but-prisoner's pocket. This is how that action is usually interpreted. I too have nothing against it, but I should humbly like to advise people to be rather careful in the use of the word 'steal', and in too hastily declaring as theft every means of acquisition without compensation, thereby reducing the number of honest people in the world by half. The incredible legerdemain of the English so-called pick-pocket really does not deserve the name of stealing. In fact the boy here does no more than any thorn-bush in a hedge along the way; he robs not by pulling but by being pulled, and to plunder by mere reaction is *eo ipso* no longer plunder. After all, it is the officer of the law who is depriving the handkerchief of its master. Londoners are familiar with this sort of thing. If the tiniest bit of a handkerchief is hanging out of somebody's pocket, the very first man who meets him will say: 'Sir, you'll lose your handkerchief,' and not 'Your handkerchief will be stolen.' For shame! who would say such a thing? Indeed, handkerchiefs are not stolen out of pockets there; they are only lost to responsive fingers on the road. It is the constellation of events that matters.

[1] Actually he looks at the lightning, the light from heaven, which makes him spill the source of his own. Ed.

Misfortunes seldom come singly; even the comfort which he un-expectedly encounters here, and which otherwise would have warmed him like a ray of sunshine, has the form of lightning and humiliation for him. It is impossible to fall any deeper. Rakewell falls in the eyes of the world, and even—in his own. That is the very depths. Sarah Young,[1] the girl who on the first Plate he so light-heartedly turned away, has in the meantime earned a living as a milliner. She passes this way, sees the danger which threatens her faithless seducer, and hastens with her little all to buy the freedom of the scoundrel who had regarded the thousandth part of his income as too dear a price for her honour and faithfulness. She tenders her purse to the officer of the law in such haste that she forgets everything else, and her little bundle of goods falls from under her arm. That sort of thing may help. Even if the dandy cannot attend at St James's, which after the anointing he has suffered he could not very well do, he may at least be able to chew his nails again in his own chair of sorrow till better times! That the girl should be passing here just at this moment seems to me to happen quite naturally. She still loves him, she has followed his movements from afar, and wanted perhaps today to see him once in all his glory. One cannot but heartily forgive this faithful creature who, as we shall see, is to visit him still where gala clothes are never displayed. Besides, days like this, and in this part of the town, are for milliners like blossom time for the bees. They swarm from one Court flower to the other, which on such occasions arrive by the hundred to deck the rich flowerbeds of St James's with their colours. The eye wanders from one to the other, gathering material for the imagination which thus laden with the finest stuff of ideas returns to the working cell. Thus the reasons why little Sarah should be here are poetically valid and good, and so surely will be the moral feelings which our good-hearted gatherer will this time bring back instead of ideas, no matter how despicable was the little nettle which provided the substance for them.

Rakewell surrenders apparently without resistance; perhaps what in-duced him to it, apart from the sight of the well filled purse, is the all-too-clearly displayed second cudgel which a sort of Figg with an already patched up face holds there in his hand. The cudgel as well as the fellow who carries it, and who, even while discharging official duties, is chewing tobacco, seem both to be as coarse and cold as nature made them, each

[1] That it is she can be seen from the name on the falling box.

228

possessing about an equal amount of feeling. It would be just as impossible to fight against the cudgel with kid gloves as against its owner with academic eloquence. In that position the most reasonable thing one can do is to compose carefully all wayward extremities and to make oneself in words and actions as pliant and compact as possible so that nothing should tear or break while one is arrested.

This is the part of the Plate which continues the story proper. We now come to the side strokes. One would hardly suspect them here, yet a Plate by Hogarth in which these were missing would really be like a picture by Wouvermann without a horse, and therefore of just as little value. Not only are they not missing here, but Hogarth has dealt them with unusual force and bitter roguery, and has wielded the lash so that it is felt through ceremonial wigs, decoration-ribbons and stars.

In the background to the right there hangs from one of the houses a little white signboard inscribed with the name 'White'. This is White's notorious Coffee House, of which every one of our readers must have heard, slight though his acquaintance with English authors may be. This is the very establishment in whose honour the white lightning up there in the sky has been hung out. May the lightning strike you! Hogarth seems to say, and indeed the inmates really deserve something like lightning. It is in fact the house where the value of a whole Estate is often staked upon a card or upon dice, and if that goes, houses follow suit, and after them the gold shirt buttons—we had a famous example of this a few years ago—and then—FINIS; it is the place where wealth and beggary change places in a second; the source of thousand-fold misfortunes and misery, of duels, of despair, of incurable madness, of raving mania and suicide. It is for this den that Hogarth intended the lightning with its basilisk-tail. But why did he not bring it right into the house through the window, or more scientifically by the high chimney or the lightning-attractor, the protruding rod?[1] As it is, it hangs in the air just as un-naturally as Sarah Young's millinery box. Surely, it can be in no doubt as to where it ought to go here! That would only be excusable if the slinger of its fire were a mortal. Many a London house might be under the same sentence for similar crimes, so that in its execution the choice may

[1] The commentator is not committing an anachronism here, for although in the year 1735 when these Plates first appeared lightning conductors were not yet in existence, lightning attractors had long been in use.

sometimes be rather difficult. Besides, the zig-zag is really the line of indecision, and I cannot therefore entirely blame a certain good lady for thinking that the reason why lightning went zig-zag, and changed its course so often, was that it again and again turned away from regions where people had repented in a hurry.

It almost looks as if while the lightning shoots towards the Coffee House, the sun is shining upon St James's Palace. Such a distribution of storm and sunshine between buildings in the same street is not only possible but even quite common. If Hogarth really had some intention with this, it may have been to offer his congratulations on that day of national rejoicing to his Queen in perhaps a subtler form than did any of those big-wigs down in the street who are about to be disgorged from their vehicles. But if this was not his intention, or he had something else in mind with his distribution of light, the interpreter of these Plates craves his readers' forgiveness if an assumption which then, of course, could not be valued as a special proof of his acuity, is left standing as an expression of his opinion, at least, of St James's and White's Coffee House.

The lightning strikes towards White's Coffee House. Now let us see how Hogarth strikes at the very same house, or rather at its inmates— it is a real joy to watch him.

Almost opposite to Mr White's Gambling-and-Coffee House he has put a little Gambling-and-Brandy House, outwardly somewhat different, inwardly and essentially, however, of one and the same type. This is Mr Black's House. Since it has neither walls nor roof, the landlord cannot hang out his signboard, much less so brilliant a one as Mr White's; he is satisfied with painting his name 'Black' upon a post, which together with the tables, chairs, seats and arm-chairs of the house forms one single *continuum*. To this remarkable openness of the building, however, we are indebted for the benefit of being able to see the customers sitting around, and for being able to read, on account of the complete similarity of morals and Club regulations, as if in a convex mirror, what is going on over there behind the thick walls of Mr White's. Anybody raising the smallest claim to poetic feeling must admire Hogarth's art in this, and I really cannot call to mind any trait in the works of antiquity comparable with it, except perhaps in Virgil where the poet lets Aeneas see upon his shield, through the thick mists of the future, the deeds of his descendants, almost down to

Pope Peter I. It is *mutatis mutandis* just the same. What White has dark and walled in over there, Black shows here illuminated and under the open sky. Thus to read straight off here what is happening over there calls for nothing but eyes and a little knowledge of plus and minus and black and white in which all colours disappear. The following hints, classified under the headings, Black and White, will certainly guide the reader through the whole story. Thus what appears here under Black would be something like Aeneas's shield, and under White like the Roman history relating to it.

Black
Here sits a little chimney-sweep with a black wig; he has a leathern strap over his shoulder and plays last trump.

White
There will be very clean gentlemen with white wigs. They have nothing in common with the chimney-sweep except their habit of climbing by clinging, and through very dirty channels too. Across their shoulders they sometimes wear broad silken Orders, and they play Faro.

Black
The black boy has no shirt to his back, and even his jacket is only there in part, but the Sovereign Lord of the part which is still there is the black boy himself.

White
Here only the finest shirts and the most elegant attire will be seen, but those whose bodies they clothe are not always the Sovereign Lords themselves, but often a sublime sort of livery-servant to their creditors to whom they belong.

Black
Here the shoe-black boy is throwing dice and has already succeeded in dicing himself right back to the door of Paradise, into the style of dress first fashionable in the world. His only cover is hardly worth mentioning. With the present throw he stakes the implements of his craft, the only source of his precarious living. If he loses, then his *noblesse* will be pure.

Precisely as with Black, only there are no occupations here, no tools for making a living, and therefore much purer *noblesse*.

BLACK

Here the dice-thrower has a star upon his breast, a black one though, albeit fixed upon the breast in the strict sense of the word. Such stars provide no warmth but they ennoble, and the blood which they ennoble is warming them. They are never worn for the sake of display, but only display themselves in the state of innocence. No gold embroiderer has worked them, but for that matter no thief can steal them.

WHITE

There, too, they are throwing dice, with stars on the breast; with shooting stars one ought to say, for they are as little fixed upon the breast as are those upon the sky. There is little relation between the symbol of honour and honour itself; they are not dependent upon one another. Each may be doffed separately and, in order to make oneself entirely comfortable, both together.

After that hint on a method of interpretation, it will suffice to sum up the rest in a few words. One sees that by Black's Coffee House Hogarth merely wished to say:

Here too soup is being cooked.[1]

The two dice-players stake their belongings against one another, and lo! the dice are hanging in mid-air like Sarah Young's hat-box and Mr White's lightning. Hogarth has put much into that Plate which might— and ought to—hang. The scoundrel with the white wig who is on the point of becoming a shoe-black with two sets of instruments, as he has already two sets of clothes, is said to be the portrait of a French boy who cleaned shoes at the corner of Hog Lane, where it was doubtless very necessary. The sly fox had chosen the right stand, just as he chose here the right man. Under his right knee are more dice; perhaps he has even succeeded in making the tipsy Baron believe he could only play with his own dice. The strap which is lying there upon his lap may be used for

---

[1] A translation of the Low German saying, *Hier wird ok Seepe gesaden*. Ed.

some game, but perhaps it is only an Order ribbon which the Baron has lost.

Behind him sits a player whose face, elsewhere, might make one think it was hanging. In his hat, whose whole brim has been snipped off, sticks a note which compensates ten-fold for that loss; a real pearl in the crown. 'Your vote and interest' it reads, meaning: 'I beg for your vote and whatever else you can do for me.' The boy is an Election canvasser, but the main vocal organ by which he makes his living hangs at his side—a little trumpet; he is a Post-boy who with that instrument does much trumpeting, and (translated into White) such a *votum* may be useful. Clinging to the canvasser from behind sits a spy who indicates to the man with the sash how many Honours his opponent holds in his hand. That item we shall leave entirely black.

Almost directly under the pole of the *porte-chaise* sits the little politician, his dram beside him, studying his Penny-Moniteur, and smoking his little pipe whose heat serves also to protect its small neighbour, the nose, against the March air. There is an inexpressible warmth and domesticity about that little statesman; he does not hear the thunder in the heavens, he does not see the lightning of the London police as it strikes close to Black's Coffee House. Is it possible to look with greater complaisance into the politics of one's country? All must be well with England, or at least with the nobility to whom the little person belongs. The remainder of White's Coffee House, which is not shown us in the mirror, we shall soon investigate when Hogarth himself takes us there, as he does in fact in the sixth Plate.

The little dog who belongs either to the Welshman or to Sarah Young (we shall have more to say about this later) seems to find so much disorder here in the street among reasonable beings very unreasonable, and to express his disapproval with evident signs of astonishment. That is what dogs do; when they are brought into society they often disapprove of many of its vices, especially the noisier ones, but as a rule only make matters worse by their objections, because of the way they express themselves.

Behind the lamplighter stands a *statua equestris* without a rider. Down below lives a saddler who has erected that horse to show by way of example what a miserable object is a horse without a saddle. With a similar intention a famous Paris dressmaker chose for her signboard a picture of the Venus de Medici to make it quite clear what contemptible creatures women are if they have no clothes on.

Among the swarm of bees before the Palace entrance stands a queer figure; it almost seems to have something like a beehive perched upon its head. An anonymous commentator remarks that it bears a resemblance, though a very remote one, to the small figure in the Plate 'Noon', who is leaving the French Chapel. The similarity is indeed very remote; more properly speaking there is none at all, for the object there was evidently a wig, whether made of human or goat's or sheep's hair, or carved or formed from plaster of Paris, whereas here it is evidently a basket perched upon a somewhat short female figure. The anonymous gentleman did not take into account that it is raining slightly here, and that in the first prints it is said to have rained much more, and thus it is easy to understand why a girl should dive underneath an empty basket. It is said that the storm on this picture gave our artist a lot of trouble. He touched it up so often that it became worse than before and he had to let another storm blow up whose production he left to a completely strange hand.

What is the meaning of the 41 on the *porte-chaise*? That it is a hackney chair, that our hero cannot even afford his own *porte-chaise* and that he could not let himself be carried quite to the gateway of St James's in this vehicle, all that is clear. But why just 41? That Hogarth should have chosen that number without a reason is unlikely, indeed I think it impossible. Mr Ireland conjectures, but with the misgiving and even disapproval which such a doubtful and forced idea deserves, that it might mean 'four to one', because Rakewell is here attacked by four persons, two officers of the law, a thorn bush and a joker with an oil can. This is somewhat crude. But what can it be? The Queen was born in 1683; Hogarth in 1698; these Plates appeared in 1735, and they are not even the forty-first of his works. It may be therefore that such *porte-chaises* have their definite stands in the town and Hogarth here may have indicated something which only a few of his friends would have understood.

V

Our hero continues his way through the zodiac of his life. He appears to have made a fortunate escape from the jaws of the British Lion of Justice, and here he is entering the sign of the Virgin (Virgo). The sign itself is depicted, but requires some explanation. Rakewell's paternal fortune has gone, and the whole conglomeration of boxes and cupboards and corners which we saw on the first Plate may still contain many a little trifle for pussy, but alas! no longer anything for him. To fill that terrible void he has opened up in the East End a small bartering business with his manly figure, and this has prospered so delightfully that everything filled up once more. To understand that business thoroughly, one should know that in the orient of London live the true money-planters who concentrate specially upon cultivating its seeds; in the occident, on the other hand, they are more occupied with the enjoyment of the plant itself, and have so little thought for the future that families often find themselves compelled to obtain fresh seeds from the orient, on stringent terms. It is just such a bargain whose contract is being concluded here; only the conditions are not too strict; he merely has to marry, and the wedding is now being solemnized. Bride and bridegroom have found what they each sought: she a handsome young man, he a rich wife; what more does one want? That neither of them found what they did not seek is nobody's business, least of all a motive for rejoicing in another's misfortune, as I have sometimes found it among people to whom I have shown that wedding scene. But they were quite wrong in this. A sensible man will express his enjoyment of other people's misfortune only if he perceives that they have been deceived in their hopes; but where is anything of that kind here? She did not look for riches and did not find any. And he? He did not look for beauty, and so he found none. On the contrary, he found debts to Nature into the bargain. This is the theme.

That the bride does not, and cannot hope to, find any fortune has been excellently expressed by Hogarth. But how does he show that the bridegroom did not find beauty? For poetic justice to his hero requires this at least. Come, dear reader, and look at the friendly angel who stands beside him; that is what he has found. Now do you complain of the lack of poetic justice? On the contrary, I am afraid your verdict may be: *Summum jus, summa injuria*. There will hardly be a pair of hungry eyes in the world, even if they were specially trained to look for precious metals, that would not recoil at the sight of that little treasure, just as another pair of eyes on the first Plate flinched before another little treasure box— Ugh! Only guineas! It is too bad. But we shall see.

It has been observed long ago that it would be much better for ladies' adornments, and consequently for the ladies themselves, if they were more intent upon the subordination between their two great dressmakers, Nature and Art. But as a rule the latter, an amiable, ingratiating witch, is mistress of the house, and thus it is not surprising if the other completely withdraws sometimes, or else, when the former has finished with her flimsy work, uncovers with one jerk, but with infinite subtlety, a little spot of contrast, and thereby puts all art to shame. Thus, for instance, the head of the bride would not have been at all bad if she had only let Nature have her way. For though chance has deprived the poor creature of an eye, that in itself would not have rendered her ugly, but now comes the above-mentioned busybody and to improve matters she puts that omission, by means of a few stuck-on beauty-spots, so obviously among the errata, that nobody can fail to detect it at once. I challenge the world to tell me whether the pair of natural eyes that stand there in the face of the bride like an iambus ($\cup -$) is one whit more disagreeable than the sly, artificial spondeus ($- -$) in the face of the bridegroom? Apart from this, one might apply to the remaining eye what the English Aristophanes[1] says about the eye of Lady Pentweazle's great-aunt: 'Although it stands alone, it is a genuine piercer, and procures her three husbands for one.'[2]

[1] Foote in his 'Taste'. (Samuel Foote, 1720–77, a comedy playwright and actor. Ed.)

[2] Since Hogarth is here poking fun at a natural deficiency or misfortune, or at least appears

A Rake's Progress Plate V

Also, as it seems to me, Art could have been better advised to leave her mouth as it was, without the quite purposeless ∪-shape. This is the sign for short syllables. All right; but a mouth cut to the pattern of the sign for short syllables is for that matter not yet a short cut. The whole symbol is no use anyway. Had the first poets understood geometry they would surely not have denoted the long by the natural symbol for the short, nor the short by the symbol for the curved and the roundabout.[1]

Although, in some respects, Art has been somewhat niggardly in its dealings with that bride, in others it has not treated her quite so badly, and this deserves honourable mention. Thus, for instance, the circumstance that the lady is almost two feet shorter than her bridegroom, and only four fingers taller than her chambermaid who kneels behind her, is a natural deficiency which has as far as possible been counteracted by Art. It is only a pity that the ceremonial height with which it has endowed the lady is not designed for the still, stuffy air of a village church, but rather for a Zephyr in the Park, or the whirlwind of a waltz at the Ball. We observe that she has the peacock adornment of her lovelier part, I mean the feathered tail of her head-dress, swept backwards. In a storm or a whirlwind she would float along like a Juno. But though she may add to her stature, thereby, this is neither the time nor the place for it. The words of thunder 'And he shall be thy master' could fold up all the splendour of the world, as could rain the loveliest peacock's tail. Some people have

---

to do so, the commentator had to adopt the same tone, but for the sake of the artist's feeling as well as his own he must make the observation on behalf of certain people that the ridiculous does not lie here in the natural deficiency, but in the whole behaviour of that unmistakable fool of a woman. That, at her years, she is marrying a young voluptuary renders her the more ridiculous in that, on account of certain secret considerations, it makes her contemptible as well, to which her embellishments make their own contribution. Whether even vulgar people ought to make fun of somebody on account of a lost eye depends mainly on the behaviour of the remaining one.

[1] That the chord is shorter than the corresponding arc is, I think, just as clear as it is incomprehensible why, despite this, short syllables have up to now been denoted by the arc, and the long by the chord. How much a correct terminology or sign language can contribute to the progress of science has been so clearly demonstrated recently by certain scientists that I cannot avoid the hypothesis that the poor development of the poetic art with us may perhaps have its roots in that utterly nonsensical language of prosody. Since reason nowadays seems to carry on its ancient family lawsuit against her administrators, I could wish that a separate claim would be made to the effect that in future the dactyli be denoted no longer by —∪∪ but by ∪——.

found fault with Art for having left the bride's ear so unbecomingly un-covered. Now I cannot see anything in this. I rather find fault with Rake-well's peruquier for having so completely covered up his. At a wedding ceremony ears are more needful than eyes; and then I find the little touch of vanity in a half-blind person, especially one blessed with a some-what suspect physiognomy, in wanting to show that she has at least both her ears, very natural and human.

But now we come to a major question: is the bride still a virgin?—or more properly, is the bride there a widow or not? A matter which nobody else in the world would trouble about is often of paramount importance to an author, and that is the case with us here. Were she neither virgin nor widow, I would at least have to ask the reader to cut out a line from the beginning of this Chapter where it was said that Rakewell was enter-ing the sign of Virgo. But it can quietly stay where it is. For the benefit of the doubters in such a delicate question a miracle has come to pass, so beautiful that if it is genuine, which nobody could well doubt since it is so beautiful, Madame Rakewell's name would deserve to be honoured in red letters. On the pulpit behind her are the well-known arms of the Jesuits, a sun with the letters I.H.S.,[1] which have this in common with the Jesuits themselves, that one can make out of them what one will, provided it is something good. That sign stands here, in full conformity with its meaning, just above the head of injured innocence and thus becomes the Virgin's crown. Yet, what renders this miracle wonderful even as a miracle is that the connection is evident only from the side where we, the doubters and sneerers unfortunately, stand! Just as ghosts are known to appear, in the largest gatherings, only to those whom to convert or to frighten they have left their graves. To believe and hold one's peace is to be wise.

Rakewell's figure is not utterly devoid of grace. One sees that Essex can achieve something when he tries, so can the proposition: 'Quarter of a century younger and two feet taller.' In his eye gleams a sense of superi-ority coupled with an easy contempt and dissimulation, with a touch of the lover's roguery. Without that touch we could have spoken of Jesuit signs here too. The ears we cannot see and the eyes—only just! But they

[1] The usual interpretation of these letters is well known. Sometimes the S stands for Salvator, sometimes Socius, and in conjunction with the †: In Hoc Signo (vinces); In Hoc Salvaberis. Very, very true! United to that domestic cross; In *Hac* Salvabere, poor Rakewell!

themselves are keenly focused. Their glance passes right through the bride's halo, without disturbing it, on to a little item from the bride's Inventory, the chamber-maid, who, compounded with the rest of the Capital, has evidently contributed to the completion of the bargain. The girl is occupied in improving something in her mistress's *Culotte*,[1] the *Seraphin* being beyond improvement. In the girl's face we notice the trace of a hidden smile, which leads us to think, not without reason, that the parson, in order to make the bride a compliment, has refrained from eliminating certain words from the wedding formula which are usually omitted when the bride is a quarter of a century older than the bridegroom, who is just entering his second quarter.

Before the bridal pair, like two liturgical clocks, stand the parson and the parish clerk; they are both set at 'Wedding', the former being the regulator, the latter the chimer. The English institution of parish clerk is one which will certainly disappear as soon as Herr von Kempelen has succeeded in constructing his talking machine; even now, one would think, a clock that could strike 'Amen' would not be more difficult to construct than one calling 'Cuckoo'. One can almost hear the man bleating his tedious 'Amen'. However, beneath that cold official mien one can still discover a little glimmer of mischief. I fear it is about the semi-secular feast which is here solemnized as if it were a Day of Dedication. About the Pastor, Mr Gilpin observes, quite excellently, that everybody who looks at him thinks that he has somewhere seen such a face and such a wig, but cannot for the moment say where. It would be impossible to praise our artist more highly in so few words. Eyebrows, eye, mouth (*sit venia verbo*), nay everything down to the very thumbs are cut as if out of one piece. The boy in front of the bride who is occupied in pushing a hassock before her, since the kneeling down is imminent, belongs, as we can see from his little collar, to the Charity School of the parish. His miserable clothes demonstrate that the Director so manages matters that the children do not forget how to beg. One never knows whether they may not need to again. Jacket and stockings are torn, and from the shoes peep not only the feet of the stockings, but the toes themselves. Since, as we shall hear soon, this Church, and consequently the parish, are very clearly

[1] In France, it was the custom formerly to carve a roast pigeon at table in dissimilar halves, the piece with the legs being called *culotte*, and the other piece not *sans-culotte*, but *seraphin*. Nowadays Egalité carves so that everybody gets something of the *sans-culotte*.

indicated, Hogarth must have known whom he had before him when he dealt such blows.

If we let our eyes wander over the whole of this scene, it almost calls to mind the prospect of a harbour on a rough day, where in the foreground ships of all kinds lie peacefully at anchor, whereas near the entrance waves are beating high, making entry difficult for newcomers and dealing blows which, if the ships do not quickly succeed in reaching the open sea, not uncommonly end with the loss of the rigging or even of the cargo and the ship itself.

My readers will have noticed that a violent storm is really raging in the background here. The trouble is briefly this. Sarah Young has saved her abominable seducer by sacrificing her little all. He promised her marriage for the second time and—here for the second time betrays her. She appears here with the child, this time in her arms, to protest against the union of her seducer with another woman.[1] Probably she did all this on the advice of her mother who, to judge from her physiognomy, holds somewhat different views about the ways of Heaven than does her good-natured daughter. The latter surrenders to its will in the hope of a better future; the former, on the other hand, is in favour of at least trying whether, by the use of the fists which Heaven has granted her, something might not be done already upon earth. She thus arrives here with her daughter at the harbour, but as she is about to enter, and is already making headway, they are met by such terrific breakers that the daughter is immediately driven out again. The mother, though she tries to battle with the waves, and throws out a five-pronged anchor, finds that such measures cannot help much here and, as we shall see, they have in fact not helped at all. The Sexton's wife, or some other aged pew-opener, well versed in the law of the Church, who may be apprehensive of the Power of the Keys and of the loss of the stole-fees, seizes a bundle of Church keys and, entirely contrary to reason and equity (and specially the *compelle intrare*), starts hitting out against the two protesting women. The daughter, gentle and yielding and more concerned for her child and her mother than for her own rights, compromisingly withdraws. The mother, on the other hand, takes up arms and defends herself desperately to the last with

[1] The jolly pair here are thus married rather grandly by special licence, in which case the banns in the parish of the bridegroom, as well as of the bride, are dispensed with. Without that circumstance, the protest would perhaps have been raised somewhere else.

large and small, though always natural, guns. To understand this classification of natural arms, one must know that in England when men quarrel, they carefully draw in their nails and endeavour with clenched fist, by weight and swing alone, to fell their adversary. But the women on such occasions leave their nails out and try not so much to down the enemy as to bleed him with a ten-bladed scarifier. Madame Young, however, fights here like an Amazon, combining the scarifier with the cudgel, and yet victory is not for her; she has the clergy against her! If from that storm one turns one's thoughts again to Rakewell's face, it almost seems as if he heard and not a little feared its roaring. Apart from him nobody in the whole Assembly seems to pay much attention to it, except perhaps the sole 'dearly beloved brother', the pious listener, up in the Gallery.

From the creatures endowed with reason, of whom we can count here precisely ten, provided, as is only fair, the young child in arms and the old woman in front of the priest, labelled with the I.H.S., are lumped together as one, the transition to inanimate nature is effected most becomingly through the animals not possessing the gift of reason. Moreover, through special circumstances, the gradation here is almost unnoticeable. In the so-called inanimate nature Hogarth's immortal spirit lives and works, and the animals are of a kind whose sagacity would do honour to many a human subject in that congregation—the almost-thinking dog and the geometrizing spider.

On the left-hand side, immediately behind the hassock, is a small *tête-à-tête* which stands to the main group in this picture in almost the same relation as the Assembly of Black Patricians on the pavement, described above, to that in White's Coffee House. Hogarth's immortal pug-dog[1] called Trump, a lively male, is observed in secret conversation with an elderly creature of his species but of the opposite sex, which deserves our attention for the reason that it is carried on with three eyes only. If we examine the group a little more closely we cannot help arriving at some

---

[1] Hogarth has also immortalized his dog elsewhere. For example, in a Plate against the poet Churchill, where he leaves it to him to censor a poem which that biting satirist had written against Hogarth, the notorious 'Epistle to Hogarth'. The dog perceives the fire of the satire, takes steps to extinguish it, and does so. Also, in a list of statues, busts, etc., offered for sale by the sculptor Richard Parker, of the Strand, Hogarth's pug-dog is included.

rather queer ideas, for does it not look as if the little bitch[1] were boasting of her white breast, of the little shiny bells round her neck, and of something which looks very much like a small metal plate? And there is really something hanging down behind which would be more suitably paraded in the open air, or at a so-called Wedding procession in the street, than in here. All that is missing is a little bitch to occupy itself with the culotte of the amiable lady, in which case Trump would probably also squint that way, over the head of his beloved, whereby a certain similarity, which we must not proclaim too loudly, would be complete. But no! Trump is honest, and as one can see from his whole attitude, which he has not learnt from an Essex, does not ask for anything to be thrown in.

Close beside the symbolic group we have just described is the Poors' Box, attached to one of the pews. The box must be very poor, or at least visited more by flies than charitable fingers, for a cross-spider has spread its net over it, as one of the safest spots for her in the whole building, and evidently the Elders of the church have let it stay there to save themselves the trouble of fruitlessly opening a box which cannot be rattled in order to verify every morning that none of the contents was missing. This is the only object in the church which would lead us to think that its wardens were still capable of doing something, if they had a mind to. This idea of Hogarth's has become famous, at least I had already heard about it when I was very young. It must have really mattered to the artist that he should be understood, in this case, and that is why he has drawn the threads of the web so strongly that even the most cursory glance remains hanging in the web of that satire lurking in the corner there.

Behind the clergy of the establishment are the Tables of the Law, one of which has a strong crack running through the ninth Commandment (our eighth): 'Thou shalt not bear false witness against thy neighbour.' For the Anglican Church makes two Commandments out of our second, and by way of compensation, one out of our ninth and tenth. From that

[1] There is some similarity between this little dog and the one in the fourth Plate. If that is really so, it might be Sarah Young's dog which has come in here and found a better reception in this temple than she did. I do not set much store by this suggestion, and not only on account of the missing left eye. But if Hogarth's pug-dog is here, where is Hogarth? If he is wandering somewhere looking for faces to draw, it was very wrong of him not to show himself to us in this Plate. I would certainly have counted him as two in the list of rational beings, and so made up the dozen.

apparently negligible, theoretical alteration, however, arises a great difference in practice. Every crime in *pto. sexti*, for which, in the greater part of Germany (where it refers to the relations between parents and children), nobody gives a damn, is in England inevitably punished by hanging, for there it refers to murder. By way of compensation, however, we in Germany, provided nothing untoward happens, hang the trespasser against the seventh (stealing), whereas in England the thief can marry his accomplice (in adultery) and go where he likes.

Next to the Tables of the Law, just behind the Parish Clerk, is a spot where something had once hung which must have been of importance, not because it was behind the clerk's place, nor because a knight's helmet with a lion still hangs above it like an emblem of the knight's virtues, nor because a cherub's head floats above it, but because it had hung next to the Tables of the Law. Luckily for the interpreter, Time's tooth, or more likely Wantonness' claw, or whatever it may have been, has left just enough of it for us to see what it was. There are still upon the precious relic the words 'I believe, etc.' It was thus the creed which used to hang there where nothing hangs any longer. This could be interpreted as: I believe nothing whatsoever, or everything which may be hung there again in the future. It is a pity that the vacuum of faith there has such a very indefinite, frayed edge. In a frame, polished, beautifully gilded, and decorated with all the insignia of philosophy, it would provide the most eloquent symbol of tolerance imaginable. Taking everything together, one could conceive of no church which would combine so little outer charm with so much inner charm for one and all, as this one. It demands nothing but faith without caring in what. This alone would be certain to bring to her every honest person in the whole world; furthermore, her Tables of the Law, starting from the Sixth Commandment (our fifth), are broken, and therefore it will also enjoy the patronage of rogues, lechers and adulterers. Also the pillar which rises between the chamber-maid and the bride, slightly towards the pulpit, is not quite of the order used in the First Church, and the pulpit itself completely resembles an ancient Chair of Philosophy, which is really what every pulpit should be. A couple of suns, with or without tonsure, one above for the pastor, and another for the congregation, could easily be painted upon it, as here, without making any difference in the matter. On the back of the pulpit one sees a dark circle which is much too clear to be just accidental. It seems to be some-

243

thing blotted out; a stain on a curtain which apart from its being of one piece with the rest of the cleanliness in the church may be a symbol of how much light is coming from there. I do not know. . . .

Taking all in all, one can well see that the physical aspect of this good Church of St Mary[1] is not in a very good state, wherefore they have tried today to deck out the old lady, in honour of the occasion, with all kinds of foliage and green branches. Yes, it even looks to me as if that whole pillar were nothing but a crutch which they have given her today, for the sake of her noble customers, so that she might hold herself erect during the wedding ceremony at least. Thus, old, decked out and *pro nunc* renovated, *Notre Dame*, the church, reminds one somehow of notre dame, the bride. Yes, I almost think that part of the decoration here appertains to both ladies simultaneously. Our readers will notice that the boughs are not specially remarkable for their flowers, though they are usually very generous with these in England on such occasions, and in general on all occasions. There is merely the greenery with which the year adorns itself even while growing old, winter-green. Out of politeness it is also called evergreen, just as black clothes are called best clothes. Nevergreen[2] and mourning coats would be more appropriate. What about thy fees, though, good Amen-chimer, if the piece of wintergreen that stands before thee knew the meaning of thy branches!

But how do we know that this is the Church of Mary-le-Bone? It is inscribed up there on the gallery: 'This church of St Mary-le-Bone was beautified in the year 1725. Tho. Sice et Tho. Horn Churchwardens.' Here thus are the names not only of the church but also of the churchwardens who in the year 1725 so intensely beautified it that in the year 1735 it looked as it did. Nichols makes a point of remarking that these are not fictitious names, but they really are the names of the churchwardens of that year. A parochial inspection could not have done more. The church was in fact demolished and a new one erected into which this barn here could be fitted, even more comfortably than the one at Loretto, in its casing. The old church really was as small as this, and thus indeed very small, not more than the width of three crinolines; also the pews seem more in

---

[1] It is in fact the Church of Mary-le-Bone, a village on the outskirts of London, which at that time was distant enough from the city for such a wedding to be solemnized in it. Today, however, it has, together with other villages, good hopes of being incorporated in the City itself.

[2] An idea of Pope's, who called evergreen plants nevergreens.

proportion with the church than with the human body. In the double-bed on the left-hand side, people could not possibly have been awake, certainly not standing. Even Trump, who stands here next to his little winter-green, reaches up to the key-hole. That it was indeed a pew, however, and not perhaps a relic or a holy wardrobe, is proved by the inscription. We give that here to save our readers the trouble of deciphering it for themselves. It is remarkable for the 'spelink' and diction.[1]

THESE: PEWES: UNSCRU'D: AND: TAN: INSUNDER:
IN: STONE: THERS: GRAVEN: WHAT: IS: UNDER:
TO: WIT: A: VALT: FOR: BURIAL: THERE: IS:
WHICH: EDWARD: FORSET: MADE: FOR: HIM: AND: HIS.

Thus it is a private church pew and not a wardrobe. However, since there is a burial vault beneath, the matter is to some extent explained. Perhaps the pew is half below ground and level with the ancestors, and would thus as temporal sleeping accommodation provide communication with the eternal through the *memento mori* or as a reminder of the Resurrection.

Mr Gilpin has gone sadly astray as an art critic in this picture. This often happens to critics in practice. 'The perspective,' he says, 'deserves praise, only the church appears to be too small, and the wooden pillar which serves no special purpose divides the picture in a rather unsuitable way.' Mr Gilpin, usually so subtle, has not taken into consideration that the Creed and the Tables of the Law on the wall there and the face of Rakewell's sweetheart have been still more unhappily divided. Had he enquired from the churchwardens, he could perhaps have discovered the uses of the pillar. It served as a prop for the church and in addition was quite indispensable for people who have a propensity for putting the revenues of the church into their own pocket. The whole thing is drawn from life and with a purpose which, if Hogarth really had the intention of expressing ideas thereby, would conform only with a debasing and not an elevation of the subject.

---

[1] Nichols says the inscription is faithfully copied, the letters are cut in relief and can be found in the new church, because the Bishop under whom this was built took care to preserve these memorials as much as possible. Since the family Fawcett died out, the vault reverted to the owner of the land, the Duke of Portland. Also the little bas-relief of gilt lead which we can see at the back under the window, and which commemorates the tomb of a family Taylor, is still there.

VI

HERE is White's Coffee House from within. A fire broke out in this house on May 3, 1733, and Hogarth makes use of this event to identify the place for the London public of his time. Why, indeed, did he not use lightning? The company, as we shall see, would have deserved it.

Rakewell has not had much success with his fighting cocks and race-horses, or else his winnings from them, together with his other means, have all gone to feed the gaily-coloured poultry in Pontac's menagerie. By the barter in Mary-le-Bone Church he raked in a fair amount at least of what he lacked, but of course not nearly enough. *Caetera desunt*, he thought and, in order to be consistent, availed himself of the means of earning a living which accorded best with his capacities and his philosophy, that is, games of chance. How one world has arisen, other worlds can arise, and thus through mere chance a structure of fortune arises for our hero which cannot compare more fittingly with anything than with the ward-robe of the Knight of the Star *sur le pavé*.

The expressions in the faces and figures of that company are beyond everything, so varied are they, ranging over almost the whole scale of human emotions. Indolent vacuity on the lowest step, a proper moral nihilism; wary, constitutional gravity, and gravity of a callous sort through acquired insensitivity; ill-humour deeply and quietly introspective, and ill-humour with expressions of incipient despair; gnashing, raging despair as it raves against itself and fate, or armed with a murderous weapon turns suspiciously on others; cool-bloodedness if fortune smiles and comfortable joy while it lasts amid a roaring tumult of malediction from the luck-

A Rake's Progress Plate VI

less ones upon whose ruin it has been built; fear, terror in all its forms, everything in a degree which renders a man insensible to anything but what is here at stake; all this is to be observed here in motley mixture. It is terrible! If now in addition we could listen, even for a moment, in front of the door there to the crashing of chairs, the chinking of guineas paid up one by one, and the heavy rustling of money dragged across the table in masses; curses and oaths ejaculated with all the power of language and of the human voice; the barking of dogs joining in, and all that amid shouts of murder and fire! What should we suppose it was? A gambling party? Surely, if it were not for the chinking of money, we would take it rather to be a worldly dispute about human rights? Or a spiritual one about precedence for eternal bliss? Or, to hazard the mildest guess, a lively discussion in the realm of the civic dead—the lunatic asylum? But it is really so—they are gambling. From that box on the table they await the verdict of chance on the possession of their fortunes, and Rakewell has lost everything! His treasures are gone and nothing is left to him but—his little treasure! He throws himself upon his knees, he grinds his teeth, and with epileptic, staring eye and threatening fist calls upon Heaven that is guiltless of all this. His right foot rises tremblingly upon the toes, his right arm rises too, and so does the left opposite it, like outspread wings. It is too late! Were they the wings of Aurora, punishment would still hover over him. What sort of angels' voices can they be to which he listens, or is it the jangling of prison keys or the rattling chains of Bedlam which he hears?—There lies the torn out hair, the empty wig beside the empty purse, and between the two the poor pigtail, the handle by which it was flung down; a pitiful exclamation mark and at the same time a sign of the cross†. Miserable wretch! If only thy Captain were here.[1] 'His sword may serve thee.' His chair collapses with him, and behind it a dog from Covent Garden expresses his sympathy with so profound a fall. A change of fortune must be very great before poodles observe it.

On the right the man whom the dog has not yet noticed turns his back on fortune because he finds it unbearable to look on fortune's backside any longer. He came here in deep mourning, even with weepers, and probably with a legacy in his pocket, over which now the toad-like shape of a strange hand squats upon the table. Before, he was mourning the loss of a relative, and now, much more deeply, the loss of his legacy. There is a curious

[1] See p. 203.

contrast in the convulsive expression of despair at the sudden loss of money acquired by our hero through marriage, and by his neighbour through inheritance. The former, as if filled with explosive air and set on fire, bursts through excess of tension; the latter like a pricked bubble collapses. There is really in the attitude of each something that reminds one of a wedding and a funeral. The one has at least the explosive force of the man *in jubilo,* and the other the shrivelled attitude of the mourner, reminiscent of sackcloth and ashes. Perhaps in the painting Rakewell's garment even has the wedding-like white and silver. The contrast between these two gamblers has been intentionally exaggerated by our artist. For Rakewell's scheming head even the wig is too tight; everything makes for expansion. With his neighbour everything shrinks within, and in addition he even presses hat and wig inwards with both hands; and while the former raises his right arm with great force, it seems almost as if the latter had used the little raising power which was left to him for raising his left leg.

On both sides of that group are two other more peaceful, or at least quieter, ones.

Just in front of the mourner sits an old usurer who out of goodwill is just lending £500 (probably half capital and half interest) to a Lord Cogg[1] (thus not incog.) whose sleeve, ornamented with gold and silver, shares the light in front of it. Behind our newly-wed, a highwayman twiddles his thumbs in deep thought. He intends neither to borrow nor lend here, but he carries in his pocket the tools for a compulsory loan on the highway—a pistol and a mask. Quite excellent is the head of the old man who, in the midst of fire and bloodshed and the bellow of despair which makes even the dog chime in, sits quietly by his little candle and with careful quill notes down and rounds off every little item. But of course it is easy to win something off such a frog-physiognomy as my Lord Cogg's. There is really something intolerable in the labial and brachial system of my lord, whose lips stretch in equal width like a jet around his mouth, and whose arms are bent like a pair of swimming legs. However, both sides are content, and what more does one want? They are happy.

> The pleasure, sure, must be as great
> Of being cheated as to cheat. (Butler)

[1] From to cog, flatter, swindle, etc. Hence a Cogger.

248

The highwayman has apparently lost here through dice everything which he had acquired that evening on the highway with his pistol, and now his conscience also calls him to account, and the balance is rather terrifying for him. His meditation here is really an execution by conscience; very understandable. From the gallows side the outlook is always the same; the crime has been committed, it can never be undone; from now on he is for the gallows as soon as he is discovered, and even his own horse may betray him. From the other side the outlook is no better. What he had hoped to acquire by crime, and had in fact acquired, is lost, gone for ever; he is again as poor and destitute as he was a few hours ago, and then he was perhaps still innocent; now the gallows will be ever before him, ready to receive him; the hateful Greek letter Π will from now on form the frame to every plan of the intellect and every picture of the imagination. With such a Calculus and a prospect like this it is small wonder if a complete physical paralysis sets in. He no longer sees or hears or feels. The boy standing in front of him, calling him loudly and even shaking him, simply does not exist for him. With smell and taste it is probably no better, for even the refreshing draught he ordered gets no attention. He has even forgotten to hide the pistol and the mask. Luckily for him, the boy, the only reasonable being in the whole company who is still capable of observation, is not standing on that side, otherwise the above-drawn frame around the vision in that hero's imagination might quickly become the frame around the hero himself. I do not quite understand the meaning of the white stroke between the pistol and the floor: is it a lace from his garment, or is he perhaps even a tailor?[1] He sits in front of the hearth which is protected by a wire netting. This is not a *garde-feu* but a *garde-fou*.[2] It is to prevent the clever people here from throwing dice-box, cards, hats, precious purses (when they are empty of course) and wigs, together with their exclamation mark, into the fire. Fortune's priests are said to be rather inclined to offer their goddesses such additional sacrifices of the negative kind, and she again is said to be just as ready, with as gracious

[1] Most likely, Hogarth wanted to indicate what the man was pondering on: whether to end his life by a bullet from his own pistol or to wait for the hangman's rope. Ed.

[2] In England, the fireplaces still have no *garde-Madame*. For it can easily happen that in one winter more females are burned alive in England than young widows in Bengal. They have, though, some dainty fences which are called fenders, but they only protect the floor and the carpet; they are as little protection to petticoats and aprons as many a moral 'fender' which is supposed to act as a shield in one's way through the world.

a face as she can muster, to accept such sacrifices. Not far from the fire-place is a niche with a similar fencing around it. What could that be? Perhaps a table stands there with glasses or refreshments which should not be exposed to collisions with wigs. If every keyhole, as they say, represents a lampoon upon the nobility of human nature, what about such wire netting? We can see we are here in the ante-room of a madhouse.

Behind the little boy, leaning against the wall, stands a seriously wounded victim. He has surely been hit in a tender place. What he holds here so pointedly in front of his mouth does not seem to be the part of his person on which he really gnaws; he is taking a bigger bite inwardly. Are his eyes perhaps directed upon the heavy, double-backed gentleman at the table who is raking in the money, and does perhaps envy mingle with incipient despair? In that event he deserves double compassion. To be obliged to look on in cold blood while our lost money is being raked in is in itself hard enough, but to see it gathered up by the warm, puffy, broad hand of a well-fed, carefree fellow like that, slowly, and with quiet secret satisfaction, is unendurable. Although it is difficult to explain, there is really something extremely mortifying when in a game the lean, or even the moderately plump, lose to the corpulent. Whether those think themselves cleverer because they are more agile, or whether, on a completely opposite principle, they reckon the temporal fact of corpulence as a temporal good in itself and mere superfluity, or whether they believe that he is more deserving of money who earns it with a sanguine impetuosity, than he who sets it before himself phlegmatically like a roasted goose, I do not know. But the fact is undeniable.

Behind the mourner sits a creature of whom one cannot exactly say what is the matter, but one almost feels like mourning for him. A perfect vacuum; mere space for a human head. 'As if painted,' one might say, if one wished to praise that figure. God save all human beings from looking like that wax-work! How did this dandy come to be here with his gaze into the blue, and his sheep's eyes at the air? He is certainly the most despicable object in the whole company, and Hogarth probably only brought him here to serve as a foil to the others. He seems to be one of the cowards who without sufficient energy for active debauchery still think it necessary to give themselves the air of it occasionally: 'We were at White's yesterday; played for damned high stakes!' The little gaping mouth is longing to boast of it, and is perhaps at it already.

The division of booty behind the highwayman is excellently done. Around the lips of the blissful, hatless creature there hovers an almost infectious satisfaction. All the same, that happy soul should take good care; the man in the hat divides somewhat summarily, and almost intentionally with more jingle than weight. In the familiarity of his manner there is something very rhetorical as well, apparently to give the jingling coins still more sound, and thereby to give that roundness to the figure which it lacked in reality. To judge from the apparel of the two partners they are not of equal rank, and in such a case the humbler half readily takes a word, administered at the right moment, for cash down, especially when such jingling is going on in front of him, and gracious pats are gently administered behind.

Opposite that sober little group, nearer the door, a wig is missing, and doubtlessly much which had been in the head underneath. The creature has a close resemblance to Rakewell. All is lost. Only unlike Rakewell, he does not search for it above the clouds:

> *quod petis, hic est:*
> *Est Ulubris.*[1]

(at White's), so he thinks, and makes a terrific thrust at a poor devil, possibly quite innocent, whom he takes for a cheat. Even that means looking much too far. Luckily he wields his sword just as clumsily as the dice, otherwise the game could have cost him very dear. And then a good-hearted mediator lends him some of his own reason—one might almost say, of his own wig. The latter is quite a natural consequence of the former. For since in difficult cases like this it would be impossible for heads to understand each other indirectly through words, the best they can do is to talk and at the same time let their arguments, together with the skulls under which they lie, run tilt against one another. The method is excellent and we have reason to believe that many controversies in this world, especially the learned ones, would not have gone so far if one had tried to settle them by this method. For in the first place, all verbal quarrels would, *eo ipso*, be cut short at one blow, and consequently nine-tenths of all the quarrels, and secondly, the appearance of exerting gentle pressure with the head rather than administering a rap has something

[1] Horace, *Epist. I*, XI, 29.

rather pleasant about it, something resembling the brotherly kiss to which it would surely soon lead.

The rest of the Plate hardly calls for explanation. Every reader can hear for himself the cry of 'Fire! Fire!' The Nightwatchman rushes in from the street. He lets fresh air into the stuffy room through the door, and lets out a cloud of smoke, everything physically correct and to the advantage of the gambling party, and also of the flame on the ceiling. Of the whole company, only two notice it at the time. One exactly in the posture of Hamlet when the ghost appears, had he held his right hand a little lower; this is quite natural. And then the Marqueur with the hammer and the two candles which he could now extinguish, since the sun is rising behind the cornice. The fellow's attitude is good; it is the first moment of discovery and he is still more than half in the service of the gaming-table.

In the place where a mirror should hang above the fireplace, a Mr Justian, manufacturer of playing cards, has hung his address and advertisement, and a light even burns vigil before it. To conclude from the coat-of-arms and the whole tenor of the inscription, the man is card-maker by appointment to His Majesty. Whether that was very profitable in the year 1735, I cannot say. The title still exists, but times have changed.

VII

Sɪʀ William Hamilton,[1] in his report of the last eruption of Vesuvius in the Summer of 1794, remarks that around the foot of that dangerous mountain and the neighbouring Somma, and thus within a circumference of about 30 Italian or $8\frac{1}{2}$ German miles, there lived more people than on any plot of similar area in the whole of Europe. People seemed to crowd around the volcano's mouth like gnats around a flame; even if some of them burned their wings, others always came to take their place; so little did they avoid or realize the peril. This is indeed curious, and yet far less curious than that, in a country of freedom and plenty like England, just those houses should be most crowded where everybody who enters must first make at the door his *votum obedientiae passivae et frugalitatis*. And that all the scheming and effort of a good part of that happy throng should lead to just the sort of life that would one day end in such a monastery. A plan like this rarely miscarries if one is seriously intent upon it, and of how it can be most easily effected, we have a clear example in the life of our hero.

He has just been accepted, has made his vow, and is still preoccupied with those importunities of the heart which such changes usually produce in people of the true anointing. It is not long since he left the world. His bed lies there, not yet unpacked. A grill is tied on to it. That is all he has taken with him from the secular world. If only his conscience is at peace! I am almost afraid that in Rakewell the outer man has not yet succeeded

---

[1] (1730–1803) Archaeologist and scientist. He wrote several papers on earthquakes and volcanoes. Ed.

in coming to terms with the inner one. In that case, the grid-iron tied to the bed may be, if not the model, at least the symbol of the bedstead, upon which he intends to roast himself alive at night, on his own memories.

What sort of monastery it is, the reader will already have guessed from the grated door and the Chamberlain's key which hangs from the hip of Pater Cubicularius. Rakewell is in prison, more precisely in the Fleet, also a sort of Lombard, distinguishable from the usual institutes of this sort only by its being not so much a prison for movables as for the prime movers themselves, and roughly what we call in Germany *Schuld-turm*, a 'debtors prison'.

Earlier, on page 193, there was mention of certain blessings and prophecies which might be fulfilled in our hero. And here they are. Here he is now writhing under the lash of his deserved misfortune—*tout beau!* Would it be possible to depict sorrow, misery, and awakened conscience with all the two-edged torture of fear and remorse in a debauched good-for-nothing more strongly than here? He is not yet articulate. In place of words, however, a wave of eloquent trembling runs through his emaciated limbs, from below upwards. The hand propped upon the knees is lifted with deep significance, and is followed in sympathy by the foot, just as the corrugated brow draws after it the eyelids and the shoulders; the stream flows upwards. But this is no picture of uplift, or at least it is only the sort which is inseparable from gestures expressive of a deep fall, impotence and destruction. Everything falls only the deeper, and thus he pronounces his own sentence of damnation, and through despair becomes his own hangman. What does he see now with those staring eyes? Perhaps the dancing master or the gardens or the race-horses? Or does he see absolutely nothing? Or does his ear listen to the melody of Orpheus who tamed the beasts? Oh, if only he still had the little gold snuff-box! Here the beasts are tamed more economically! We shall see how it is done. The means are drastic.

Next to him stands the little acquisition which he made in the Church of Mary-le-Bone, his dear wife, albeit somewhat changed. Her mouth, which there curved gently into a tender smile, like Luna a few days after her rebirth, could here with its full black circle indicate the new moon in some village almanack. Yet, what is more, her whole head which re-minded us of the friendly and peaceful crunching of a dainty squirrel has been transformed here into a lion's head with mane, and with jaws that

A Rake's Progress Plate VII

would crack human skulls like hazel nuts. It is quite certain that after the wedding things are rather different from what they were before. Here she is using her little fists, which have just hurriedly attended to the arrangement of her own hair, for effecting a slight alteration in that of her husband. To be exact, she probably only intends to help his memory a little over certain details concerning her dowry, which could not be achieved by that method without a disturbance of the capillary system.

To be sure, she proceeds very properly. She first applies her left fist to his shoulder, so as to shake loose his firmly embedded thoughts, and as soon as she sees that they are afloat, starts an attack with the right fist just in the place where they are swimming, to set them off in the new direction. That is how one even imparts polarity to iron. It cannot fail. But all this, troublesome though it may be in such circumstances for a man of feeling, is by no means so disagreeable to the poor devil as the terrific salvo of grape-shot which his better half's tongue shoots out of that dark thieves' kitchen into his ears and his heart. Here he indeed deserves our pity. This is too hard on him, one would be inclined to say, if it were not so natural, and if something that is natural could also be hard. All authors writing about the defensive system of the fair sex, and of its military operations in the matrimonial campaign, speak of that part of its artillery as of a sort of miracle. Fielding, one of the most illustrious, remarks[1] that the wisest men have trembled before it, and that even the most valiant who were capable of looking in cold blood into the mouth of a 24-pounder had shrunk back with pitiful face if required to look into the mouth of such a mortar. If the wisest and most valiant among men have done so, what must he now be suffering who is neither the one nor the other, and who in addition is not even in a position to slink away? And yet this is by no means all. While the woman attacks him from in front and upon the right flank, another enemy attacks his left flank, and a third his rear, while at the same time he is notified by an acquaintance in a friendly letter that his main arsenal has been blown up. Indeed under such circumstances no one but Socrates or Charles XII could sit otherwise than does Rakewell here.

A boy, or whatever sort of creature it is (for in the formation of his physiognomy insolence seems to have been working for at least a quarter of a century), has brought him the porter as requested, though

[1] In his masterly description of the battle in the Inn at Upton, *Tom Jones*, Book IX, Chapter 3.

for the time being only to look at. Without barter the poor wretch, languishing for a drink, will not have a taste of it, and there is nothing left to barter! Even the shoe buckles seem to be only mourning buckles, whose lacquer or blueing has already been mourned away. Behind him stands the executioner under-turnkey! To judge from the book which is resting on his arm, he wants to call in the garnish money, the 'welcome' from the prisoner. The face, which the fellow also offers for sale, seems to be one of the best which he is capable of producing, in the interests of the transaction. It is a pity that Rakewell does not see it, but he would not have been able to buy it in any case. The insolvency which can no longer pay for a can of beer will probably be content with such faces as insolence presents *gratis*. Does the reader notice the conclusion, *in forma iuris*, which is drawn here? A poor devil who has been put in prison because he cannot pay is required to pay for being in prison. Just like this, a few years ago, did the French deal with the good city of Worms, merely because, as they said, that city had offended the good city Worms herself.

And now for the bundle of papers and the note containing the news of the blown-up powder-magazine! This blow is one of the hardest, and acts as powerfully upon his spirit as does the fire released by his prison mate upon his heart. It is unbearable. The note reads thus: 'Sir, I have read your Play and find it will not doe. Yrs. J. R. . . . ch.'[1] The explanation is briefly as follows: this Mr Rich was then director and manager of one of the largest London theatres. Rakewell had submitted to him the MS. marked Act 4. It contains a play which he had written in his leisure hours under the auspices of the tenth Muse, who despite the decay of all the remaining nine still holds her own in England as well as in Germany, I mean *Paupertas audax*. He had hoped to bid farewell to life if not as a rich man, at least with the *splendida miseria* of a modern *bel esprit*. All these hopes are now dashed to the ground at one blow by the letter. All is over now, flown away, gone—'it will not do'. What could the theme of that play have been? *The Rake's Progress*, or *The Road to Ruin*?[2] Not

[1] Whether Hogarth intentionally made these mistakes in spelling as a satire upon Mr Rich's education, or whether it is a little *faux pas* of his own, is difficult now to decide. Since, however, the first of these views was held originally (but later the second was found more plausible), all we can say now with some certainty is that neither Hogarth nor Mr Rich can have been outstanding orthographists.

[2] *The Road to Ruin* is the title of a play which has been produced in London of recent years, with great success, some scenes from which have also been well depicted in engravings.

very likely, for it is in the nature of a bad author not to know himself, and never to write about things which he alone could write about.

What a picture this to nail up on the walls where pride of authorship draws many a bill of exchange upon the Muses, each of which is returned in the end like this one, with an insulting objection. Oh! all ye who count upon a high reward from the Muses in your old age, come over here to the torture bench of this cashiered genius; he too counted upon that reward. Such is the fate of thousands. Consider, dearest friends, that since *calamus* has other meanings in latin than 'blade' or 'reed', so *calamitas* means more than 'damage done by hail'. Since the one includes 'goose-quill' among its meanings, the number of calamities for authors, and sometimes for readers too, grows to infinity. The minor misfortune, which in the Golden and Silver ages of the world could only be inflicted upon individuals by ruined crops, now in the days of its senility is brought about with ten-fold intensity by writing quills, and inflicted upon whole generations. What, after all, was a little passing scarcity through hail compared with our present continuous indigestion from the heavy, black, sour bread of the Muses by means of which many a citizen of the world of learned beggars drags himself painfully along, on true *calami* of legs and with cheeks the colour of his laurels?

It is a thousand pities that, through a criminal misuse, one of the most powerful means for improving the human race has been rendered completely ineffective, I mean instruction by wall-posters. A group like this one, posted up in the declination-and-conjugation stable, would be of infinite advantage to the young. But I am afraid it is all over with that sort of thing, just as it will soon be all over with everything. The general endeavour of the human race to make the means the end must be regarded as a second Fall through which in the end everything will succumb. Is there not already a class of learned men called friends of books, and are they not merely insects with wing cases, but without wings? Has not the time-keeping of our wise ancestors become nowadays merely a wearing of watches? Nay, do we not hang two of them now, one opposite the other like sentries, in a region where perhaps since the fig leaf was removed from there, time and hour have never been worse kept than between those two time-keepers?

Opposite Rakewell a woman is fainting; a man in négligé strives to break her fall, or at least to keep it within the limits of decency, and two born doctoresses have loosened her stays and are trying to revive her. The resuscitative method of the one appears almost hyperphysical, at least not wholly of this world, nor is the cunning in her face. The swooning woman is the same Sarah Young who appears now for the fourth time, and the crying child is a little Miss Rakewell, who is here in visible form for the second time. Thus Sarah Young follows her faithless seducer even into jail.[1] Difficult though his complete deliverance may now be, it is easy to bring relief to one for whom a glass of porter is a boon. She must have been well aware of it. That, as is generally believed, her first sight of the dreadful decay of her former lover could by itself have effected her collapse, I do not credit. The cause was undoubtedly a moral one, but here evidently intensified rather powerfully by physico-chemical causes. For it is said that in England the air in places where people are imprisoned, who, through no fault of their own, are suffering from lack of gold, is not a whit better than in the secret kitchens where gold is made, and unfortunately this cell serves both purposes. Cold sweat over squandered gold mingles here, as we shall hear presently, with the sulphuric dew of mercury which usually accompanies the Aurora of the newly created metal-of-metals when it rises from the crucible; however, the moral cause is by far the stronger. Besides, it could not have been the mere sight of her destitute lover, since Sarah Young has walked from the door to the place where she collapsed, and it is probable that she had even been sitting there for some time. I believe, therefore, that she fell by a salvo from the thieves' kitchen at Rakewell's right wing. Probably she and her child were recognized by Madame Rakewell who, suddenly loaded with 'Bastard! Whore! and Witch!', and let fly, which of course upon a creature of Sarah Young's character must have acted like wheelwright nails and shell splinters. As she falls there occur a few circumstances which one hardly dares to notice, but which, however, undoubtedly occupy a rather high place among the sufferings which here break loose upon the sinner, Rakewell. The bared bosom of, at least, Hogarthian beauty, the position of the foot, and in general the whole collapse with the chair, which was perhaps more dangerous to certain eyes than it appears now to ours, are certainly not drawn here for nothing. For Rakewell, who sits just opposite, they must necessarily have given rise

[1] As to the morality of these traits in a character whom Hogarth meant to be innocence itself, we shall have more to say below.

to comparisons, which every reader has probably made already himself, between what he once so light-heartedly cast away, and what he now calls his own upon the right wing. Even supposing that he makes that comparison entirely upon the scales of the senses, which with him seem to be slightly out of action, yet conscience, once awakened, will always find on its own scales sufficient turning for despair. There is much more here than Mr Rich's note: all might have been well, but now it is all over; it is gone; *it will do no more!*

Thus far goes the thread of history in the picture. The rest are ornaments but of such a masterly kind that we must regret there are not more of them. Here Hogarth would have been completely in his element.

The man who watches over Sarah Young's decency we have called 'the man in négligé' and hope the reader will have nothing against the expression. The wig is, like Rakewell's and like his angel's hair, governed merely by hazard; a long time unpowdered, but the more frequently de-powdered, probably by mere forceful hitting of, and curling round, the chair back, as if upon a flax-spindle. His beard seems to keep pace with the calendar months and is fairly far advanced 'in its 'teens'. To judge from his physiognomy he must be a very low type, but his dressing-gown persuades me to recognize him as an author. The elbow has actually written its way out, and the writing sleeve suggests the meditation sleeve, which must carry the head as well. Although trousers are not of special importance where the dressing-gown is master of the house, yet one will rarely find a pair which shuns the light so utterly as these do here. They come to an end around the knee, one does not quite know how, almost with a mere etcetera. It rather looks as if they had been a pair of pantaloons of which the lower parts had been gradually used up in the service of the uppers. It is interesting to note here that at that time people already mourned for shoe buckles, at least in the London debtors' prisons. The bellows-blower position in which the prisoner appears has, apart from the purpose of supporting the fainting woman, another two-fold one. For in the first place, the hands being occupied, the trousers have evidently lost their primary support. In order to prevent their immediately taking the place of the cut-off parts, some remedy was called for, and that consisted in the thigh adopting the horizontal position. In the second place, the man had got hold somewhere of a few bundles of manuscript, which now take themselves off as well; three of them are already lying for the greater part on the ground, soon to be followed by the fourth, though this one he seems to be still trying to grip. Although none of it is breakable, this gives a bad impression, and in the end everything would have to be gathered up again. This little disorder is of extraordinary value to an inquisitive spectator. We learn here the owner of the many-cornered elbow. On one of the bundles we read the words : 'Being a new Scheme for paying ye Debts of ye Nation by T. L., now a prisoner in the Fleet.' It is thus by an author who cannot pay his own debts. The idea has become as famous as the spider's web over the Poors' Box, probably because it is, like that, as clear as it is pertinent. Also the frailties they denounce are equally common. To deny others the help one could have given without any harm to oneself is as common in human beings as it is to present them, in times of distress, with rules of conduct which have brought the donor himself to bankruptcy. Such a Mr L. is said to have really existed at that time. This does not surprise me; there are always people like that, perhaps with other initials, and with other projects! Oh there is no country and no Faculty free of them: *mutato nomine de Te*, and so on.

Back against the wall sits another, already *mutato nomine*, I mean the half-charred alchemist who has a little pot upon the fire not only for the benefit of the nation but of the whole human race. The philosophical peace in that man's face and in his whole position really has something very pleasing about it; one sees he has learned to wait, an art which in no occupation in the world is more necessary than in the making of gold. That he hears and sees nothing at all of what is going on around him he has in common with all the people who through seeing and hearing have become immortal. The friendship between the man and his furnace is indeed touching if one realizes that both have finished up here only through their connection, and that each without the other might perhaps have been something much better. Yet they cling together as if made of one piece (they almost look like it) and feed each other with hopes and coal until the day when the great problem will be solved. That day cannot possibly be far off. The flue passing through the barred window is too well designed—it *must* function; the apparatus, on the other hand, through which the rare product is to be transferred into the bottle, is not specially good—it is bound to fail. Whether Hogarth was himself an expert in these matters, or whether he followed here the instructions of an expert, or whether the inspiration of genius guided his stylus aright to an end which he himself could not have conceived, I leave undecided. It may suffice that the *circulus in destillando* cannot be mistaken; the receiver is nearer the fire than the retort, and while each vies with the other for possession of the tincture, everything goes up in smoke, and there we leave the solution of the problem; of course in a sense which nobody imagined when the question was posed, but which is an answer to that question all the same. Through the barred window something protrudes which one might almost take for an instrument with which to ask advice of the planets in complex chemical investigations, if the stand were not of all-too-limited use and altogether too uncomfortable for persons accustomed to observe with the right eye. Also the object-end of the telescope is somewhat too near the furnace chimney. Probably it is not a tube at all, but merely a rough, solid cylinder with which to push open or close the heavy window shutter. Up above on the right stand some numbered vessels; they seem to be light since they perch themselves so high up. Whether this also applies to the books of the hanging library is not so easy to decide; the title 'Philosophica' makes it at least doubtful. It is a wonder that with this library Hogarth has missed the opportunity of rendering certain contemporary works of his countrymen the two-fold favour of treating them as prisoners in the Fleet and as the secret confidants of the alchemist and universal doctor. If we consider the whole design of the stove, which is really not without elegance, and if we observe how everything fits just into that corner by the window, we can hardly avoid the idea that the Wardens of the Fleet provide chemical stoves in the cages reserved for gold-makers, just as one hangs rings in parrots' cages. If this is not so, it is at least a suggestion deserving the turnkey's attention. He could certainly count upon an annual oven-dividend. These, then, were two fanciful types in the Fleet, and there above the bedstead lies the shed skin of a third. For this one the arts of chemistry and of high finance were too low-grade; he hastened to Olympus upon the eagle pinions of an Ode, but stuck fast, as so often happened to his prototype, between the Heaven of the bedstead and the ceiling, with head pointing downwards. The apparatus is excellent; it must have roared and thundered bravely. It is a pity that it was so soon over. If the feathers themselves were so firmly fixed as are the wings on the body, then the man had nothing to fear from the proximity of the sun, in contrast with his precursor Icarus, for there are buckles and oxhide in plenty. Thus with this apparatus its inventor probably rose from the bosom of his family and above the base monotony of his official duties paralysing mind and body, up above the heaven of his bedstead in the debtors' prison.[1] If the financier T. L. had stood slightly farther back, and nearer the alchemist, and if the left wing had been spread out slightly wider, this group would be the most perfect *Sub umbra alarum tuarum* that has ever been drawn.

Lastly, I may mention that Rakewell has brought with him a rather fine cane chair, probably the last of a dozen, and that the clock on his right stocking is very noticeably shorter than on his left. Thus they are either from two different pairs, or one of them has already started, from well-known causes, to serve from above downwards, just like the trousers of the financier from below upwards.

[1] I have twice mentioned here the Heaven above the bedstead, and once even compared it with Olympus. In German one could hardly speak of it in any other way than as *Betthimmel*, and it came quite naturally. Hogarth, however, though he could, of course, always regard the height of the bedstead as a measure of the flight, could not have thought of Olympus in connection with it. This curtain carrier on English beds is called a tester.

VIII

AFTER his manifold sufferings at Pontac's, White's, in Mary-le-bone(!) and in the Fleet, our hero is here at last laid to rest. The scene is a *sepultura inter vivos*, more properly a burial among the civic dead; here in Bedlam, the London Lunatic Asylum, he is put in chains. No doubt the great fall was caused for the most part by the last heavy attack upon his conscience, carried out from the bed-and-board side. His physique might have withstood it, but his mind, which was never his strongest part, succumbed in the end. It was surmised earlier (p. 223) that Rakewell might perhaps settle outside England. This is now his *établissement*. Still in his own country then? That I would not venture to decide. Our philosophy still knows far too little about the real abode of the civiliter deceased. What after their departure are still called 'they', are indeed no more than pictures which they leave behind—to be erected as tombstones over the grave of their reason. Tombstones? Merciful Heavens! What comparisons do not spring to mind between the eloquent marble raised over the ashes of the masterpiece of creation, and the filthy, numbered stables here where his image, in greater likeness than on those marble stones, chained and lying on rotten straw, tells the passer-by still more eloquently how much lies buried there! But this is not the place for such reflections. They would put the reader out of humour for the rest of the story, if they have not already done so for the commentator, who could not entirely dispense with them.

He hopes therefore that he will be readily forgiven if he merely touches on some of the terrible scenes which are here enacted. They

263

do not call for any explanation, nor are they compatible with one.

Rakewell lies in the foreground here, naked for the most part, while a man is putting him in chains. The reason for it is that Rakewell is sinking still deeper. In the Microcosmos where he lives now, affairs are ordered very much as they are in the extended Macro-Bedlam, the world itself; not all the madmen are chained, and even the chains have their degrees. Through the long corridor, the catacomb, which we see here, the more harmless are free to walk about, at least as far as the big grating, behind which lives another class, or sect as it is called in ordinary life, having other principles, not in agreement with those on this side of the iron bars; only those of a still lower and more dangerous degree are buried in the numbered cells. Evidently Rakewell had such freedom to start with, but misused it. He began to adopt other principles and, in a mood which we might call exuberant, has given himself a dangerous stab in the region of the heart. He no longer fitted into that little Republic and now is about to be incorporated into another. It is that moment of promotion which our artist has chosen here. The expression of suffering is indescribable, and it is hard to understand how a man like Gilpin,[1] who otherwise does justice to the drawing, could have found that face empty. Mr Ireland[2] fully appreciates our artist. The late Mr Mortimer, a person of the greatest artistic talent, was, as Ireland relates, once asked to draw some of the Passions as Gray presents them successively in his poem, 'Ode on a distant prospect of Eton College'. Among them was

> Moody Madness laughing wild
> Amid severest woe.

Instantly Mr Mortimer drew from his portfolio the eighth Plate of Hogarth's 'Rake's Progress'. 'Here,' said he, pointing to the central figure, 'is everything together. Had I not seen that head I should hardly have thought it possible to express so many contending emotions in one and the same face. I could do nothing but copy it; every stroke that differed from it would represent a deviation from the character.' So much for what has been called the emptiness of that head.

[1] Author of *Essay on Prints*, where of Hogarth's prints only 'The Rake's Progress' is explained. Ed.

[2] See *Hogarth Illustrated* by John Ireland, London, 1791. Lichtenberg regarded it as the most complete interpretation of Hogarth's work, and, apart from the affected style, a very good book. Ed.

A Rake's Progress Plate VIII

Behind him kneels again Sarah Young, sympathizing with his suffering. Mr Gilpin finds this trait unnatural and the moral reprehensible. To be sure! It would perhaps have been better if after Rakewell's marriage the girl had not appeared again. I too thought so once, and Mr Gilpin, as a clergyman, is doubly deserving of forgiveness. But the notion is and remains more readily thought than experienced; it is a good instance of conduct for those who like to live by examples yet do not always have one handy. But the heart, the heart—has its own rules. True love, especially in the heart of a gentle woman but of strong feeling, can only be extinguished, if it can ever be extinguished, which I rather doubt, by a very great lapse of time, whatever else its fate may be. If this is so, is there anything unnatural here? It would be little to the honour of human nature if such love were unnatural. But what of the reprehensible aspect? This too clearly lies only in the breaking of frigid rules of conduct, of which the heart knows nothing. It would be a wicked world in which trespassing of this sort did not happen occasionally. But, of course, a still wickeder one if a sly imitation of such honourable trespassing were to find just that forgiveness or even pity to which only the original could lay claim. In this way, alas! art has made it almost hazardous for man to be natural. Besides, we must remember here that Sarah Young, a good-natured, simple creature, is not of that social standing where early enough a girl is taught a certain semblance of virtue, which stands to its true exercise in the relation of smartness on parade to courage and bravery in the field. The whole value of the former (and indeed it is very valuable) rests ultimately upon the possibility of giving support to the latter, or here and there compensating *praeter propter* for the lack of it. Without that possibility it would all be hollow machinery. If Mr Gilpin had once preached before such people on the text, 'I was sick and in prison and ye have not visited me', how would he have judged, and have had to judge a female member of his congregation who after the sermon would have been so incautious with her heart as to enter the Fleet and Bedlam like Sarah Young, without any hope of earthly reward? The answer, I think, is quite simple. One of the warders, who of course may not quite realize their relationship, seems to be touched by the girl's suffering. He tries to avert her face from Rakewell in a way that does honour to his feeling. It is pleasing to see that the man's hands, despite the hard use for which they are paid, have not unlearned such behaviour.

Of the cells, we see here only those numbered 54, 55 and 56. Number 56 is shut. We shall glance for a moment into the two open ones, and then shut them too. In number 54 lies raving religious mania, and in number 55 exaltation building castles in the air. The scenes are very accurately visualized and carried out with almost terrible realism. If 56 had contained unhappy love, then the three cells would be just those which are in greatest demand in lunatic asylums. A glance thrown into those sad corners renders all description superfluous; and for their consideration philosophy is in everybody's hands; therefore only a few words of perhaps needful explanation.

Hogarth has given to the saint *in natura*, No. 54, three more *in effigie* for company, Saint Laurence, Saint Athanasius, and Saint Clement. The idea is rather crude. Whether some special traits in the lives of these men could justify such treatment, I do not know. People like us, though we read *legenda*, rarely read *Legendas*.[1] If, however, as we are almost led to believe, the mockery was aimed at the saints of that Church in general, then the question arises whether it would not perhaps be advisable to assign to a protestantism of that kind the vacant place next to St Laurence, till the matter was settled. The good sun has, as we see, risen also above that cell and that crucifix, and we shall follow its example.

In No. 55, upon a throne of straw, and crowned with straw by his own hands, sits the political maniac. Everything around him is light, only the sceptre has full oriental weight. Before the cell stand a couple of girls in rich, pretty silks. Are they perhaps ladies of the Court? They are just being received in audience, and at the same time receive from a distance a benediction which they accept with much better grace than was intended. Each clings to the other, and through that support finds the strength to look at what by herself she would not even have dared to imagine. But seriously, what are the ladies doing here? Do they want to stay perhaps? Or like Sarah Young to clothe the naked? or merely to look at the naked and behave charmingly as if they did not see them? The girls must have great freedom, to be sure, if they can lose themselves to this extent, and much ill-breeding if they forget themselves so much. That is why Hogarth placed them in his masterly way right in the midst of those who are allowed to walk about freely. Papa and Mamma do not know a word about it; of this Papas and Mammas should take note.

[1] Lichtenberg here alludes to the *venia legendi* which he holds as university professor. Ed.

What is usually permitted to the dead in the churchyards proper only at night-time, those buried here are allowed, under certain conditions, by day as well, that is, the liberty to rise from their graves and walk. Only they must not overdo it, or, as was mentioned already, they will be put in chains, just as the others, if they do not listen to reason, are packed into sacks and thrown into the Rhine. Of these daylight spectres Hogarth gives us here, not counting the two damsels, only six. Rather few to be sure for such a ghost-seer and painter. We could hardly forgive him, had he not in his other works abundantly made good that omission, and drawn many a Bedlamite *in partibus*, or those who should more properly have been here.

On the stairs to the left hovers a sort of trio, almost like a Bedlam version of Faith, Hope and Charity. They seem to belong together and yet these three heads could well be farther away from one another than any three fixed stars, forming just such a triangle. Everything is mere appearance. Each is a world to himself and none provides light for the others, and none eclipses the other; each has its own light. If there is anyone who does not yet know that it is the head which makes the world and not the world which makes the head, he should look here. Merciful Heaven, what is man? Or rather what is the world? 'But are you aware that you are sitting in a lunatic asylum?' asked a man once in exasperation of a maniac whom he wanted to convert, upon which the latter looked at him with the greatest composure and retorted, 'But are you sure that you are not living in one?' The stranger pondered this and was silent, the maniac was silent too, but probably his capacity for pondering had vanished long ago. What became of him afterwards is not known. The stranger, however, after he had stepped out of the asylum into the world again, is said to have realized that there was between the two worlds, instead of a sharp dividing line, a sort of no-man's-land, and to have been on his guard all his life from then on against a philosophy which properly belongs only to the neutrality strip.

Faith here with his triple cross and simple crown (thus Hogarth expresses himself when he wants to indicate the Triple Crown and simple cross) sings his mass with his little bleating mouth in such a way that not a syllable of it is heard in the neighbouring systems. Hope with the music book upon his head continues fiddling, and melancholy love with his heavy theme hanging on his breast from a little ribbon continues to dream a lamento. The dog is barking at him, just as at other times it barks at the patron saint of the house, the moon, and he heeds it just as little as the moon. The stalks of straw with which madness is so fond of crowning itself form here a rope round his neck, perhaps as a first, merely poetical attempt to crown love at last. A mouth with such a look will not easily speak again; though the folded hands have this very day carved the precious name on the tree which has descended from a glade to serve here as banisters: 'Charming Betty Careless.' Of course it is sad! But how in all the world did such a mouth, such a forehead, and such a disposition to hollow-eyedness come in touch with Betty Careless?[1] and the old shepherd with such a love at all?[2] The violinist's idea to put the music book over his head so as to give the appearance of a music-stand is quite in keeping with Bedlam, and certainly provides a touch of originality. Whereas the multitude of rings on his fingers belongs among the fashions which Bedlam shares with the rest of the world, and are nothing unusual.

The wall between numbers fifty-four and fifty-five has a rather encyclopaedic appearance, at least in comparison with the cells: a three-masted ship, a crescent moon, a projection of the globe with the Antarctic circle still vacant but having most of the remainder covered by Britannia, more precisely by an English halfpenny hanging from a chain; a bomb-shell which is projected beyond all these projections, the lower part of which looking rather like a compass, and the upper part like geometrical hyphens. All this, with the exception of the medal which, as we shall hear, was daubed on it twenty-eight years later by a notorious rogue, seem to be the work of the thinker who with charcoal in hand is still occupied in prolonging one of the strokes, which, if he goes on like that, will soon reach the door of number fifty-five. Just in front of his nose we read the word 'longitude'. This is really the name of a certain *charming Betty* of another sort whose luckless lovers, alas! haunt the walls of Bedlam to this very day. The good lady demanded from her suitors neither wealth nor beauty nor possessions; there was just as little mention of family trees as of acres, and least of all youth. To possess her and her gold she merely demanded the solution of a

---

[1] It is said that Hogarth took the idea for that remarkable head and for the one opposite in No. 54 from the excellent statues above the portal leading into the courtyard of Bedlam. They are by a German sculptor, Caius Gabriel Kyber, father of the well-known poet, Colley Cibber. Pope, whose *Dunciad* that writer has unfortunately to thank for his fame, calls these statues (*Dunciad*, Book I, v. 32) 'Great Cibber's brazen brainless brothers'.

[2] The name Betty Careless is not an invention. A well-known courtesan of that name really existed in London at that time. Fielding speaks of her in his 'Amelia'.

puzzle. The affair caused an incredible sensation, and the result was for many the most melancholy in the world. Some who only wished to possess the lady proved tolerably lucky; others who wooed her only for the sake of her money puzzled themselves silly, entangled themselves in ropes and strokes and calculation and tricks, which in the end they themselves no longer understood, and so not uncommonly ended their lives in Bedlam. The strokes which our man is making here are of that sort, and the shells which he causes to be thrown all aim at the acquisition of that *Charming Longitude*.[1] The old man behind him too, who is peering through the rolled-up astronomical chart, is not really looking at the sky, but towards that same beauty, and is the rival of the bombadier. In front of him, a tailor squats upon his heels with the pattern card upon his head, like the violinist with his music book. He is almost bursting with laughter over the vain efforts of the two longitude-seekers, and his mockery is aimed especially at the old man with the scroll. 'Fool,' he seems to say, 'look, like this you must cut your paper and hold it if you want to measure length; that is how I find my longitudes, and compared with them yours are mere child's play.' Nor is he so far out, since the old man's methods for discovering longitudes are of just as little use to geography as to the art of tailoring. That one fool laughs at another is, of course, silly enough, but not uncommon, either within or without the lunatic asylum, but there is something more to it here. It is said that at that time there was in fact a tailor in Bedlam who believed that to cut out a garment for the master-piece of creation, which would fit the beautiful form as the beautiful form fitted the beautiful soul, was not only one of the most important occupations for a rational person, but also immeasurably more difficult than, say, Sir Isaac Newton's unprofitable arts. That is why the poor devil is here. The punishment is hard, especially for a tailor, a creature who as a reward for 'making' men, in *zona temperata* at least, is made fun of at every opportunity by these very people, in the manner of barbarians from

---

[1] The shells are really aimed at Whiston, who instigated that sort of experiment for finding the longitude of the sea. [William W. Whiston (1667–1752) studied mathematics at Cambridge under Newton and succeeded him as professor, lecturing on mathematics and natural philosophy. He lost the professorship by trying to combine science with theology, in which he had the sympathy of some leading divines, such as Hoadley and Samuel Clarke. He later made various attempts to devise means for measuring longitude, but without success. He drew up a survey of the coasts, the most correct at that time, and lectured on meteors, eclipses and earthquakes. Ed.]

the *zona torrida*, who have neither morals nor tailors. The medal on the wall is, as mentioned above, the reverse of an English halfpenny. It represents a seated Britannia with somewhat dishevelled hair, and bears the date 1763. If one looks a little more closely, one notices a chain which passes from under the medal on the right towards number fifty-four. There would have been more room for the chain above it. But a medal with the chain above would hang *from* the chain, and in England the words 'hang' and 'chain', even if used of medals, readily remind one of more important things than orders and child's play. Hogarth thus meant to say: in the year 1763 Britannia was, or deserved to be, in chains in Bedlam. The Glorious Peace[1] concluded at that time seemed, to some, much too peaceful; it should have been much more bellicose, they thought, and would then have been still more glorious. Britannia could have done better, said one; she ought to have been cleverer, said another; she deserves to be in a lunatic asylum, said Hogarth. *Ecce Signum.* There stands the blasphemy, and in a language, besides, which the whole world can understand, and in a Plate which the whole world will buy. Nay, what makes the crime still worse and qualifies the author if not for the block, at least to be an inmate of the Bastille for life, is that it was not a youthful escapade of his. A year before his death, in the sixty-fifth year of his life when he ought to have known better, and after that Plate had already existed for twenty-eight years, he arranged for Britannia to have a place on it. Still worse, he advertised the fact that he had only put her here in the year 1763, whereas the Plate dates from 1735. Thereby the rascal seems in addition to indicate that he dreaded far more to be accorded by posterity the venerable epithet of a new prophet, than that of a traitor by his contemporaries. That was very wicked. But are we looking at it properly? Is that really so? In such cases experience may help. What did wise Britannia do when she learnt of it? She did what might be a fair rule for every less wise and less experienced Patria. The wise and good mother smiled at the idea of a beloved child whose heart she knew, and she forgave. Thus to learn to know hearts and how to deserve their homage, that would be the thing; wit is but a feather.[2]

The painter of satires could learn something new from this Plate. The idea of adapting engravings to the times, through additions, is excellent,

[1] The Peace of Hubertusburg, which ended the Seven Years' War. Ed.
[2] 'Wit's a feather and . . .' (Pope).

and deserves imitation. Although, in our popular engravings, we already find traces of that method, for instance in the 'Game of Goose' where the version of 1756 bears little resemblance to that of 1796. We find there different customs, different inns and different geese. Oh! my good Hogarth. Had you looked into the last decade of your century, not a wall and not even the ceiling here would have remained empty! A Princess *Europa* who, in 1792, *mense Fervidor*, is about to elope with a bull for the second time; what a subject for that little space between numbers fifty-five and fifty-six![1] And for a ceiling fresco, *Brothers*[2] with his brethren on clouds of visible darkness kneeling and prophesying calamity and the Millennium.

The meaning of the little chapel carved on the post near the stairs with the letters H.S. on it, I do not understand, nor the L.E. on the wall next to number fifty-five. That syllable would be pronounced by an Englishman as Lee, and might remind one of Lee, the unhappy poet, who for some time, as we know, occupied one of these cells. The letters, however, are open to other interpretations, but I shall not venture any further. The elucidation of dark passages in the works of philosophers at liberty is already slightly disagreeable, and becomes twice as unpleasant with the *opera* of those who lie in chains, if only on account of the very doubtful credit which would be accorded to an interpreter who possessed the happy facility of succeeding in this.

So, not another word. It may be that I shall return to some Plates of this and the preceding series. Indeed, I shall have to come back to several of them. But to that eighth Plate—never again in my whole life. I cannot and will not deny that it has been a painful task for me. I know nothing with which to compare my feelings at the end of this Chapter but the indescribable sense of well-being which accompanied the first lungful of air which I drew when in October 1775 I emerged again after a short visit to that tomb into the open air of Moorfield.[3]

[1] In 1792 France declared war on Austria; Prussia declared war on France. After the successful battle of Valmy, the French armies everywhere stood on foreign soil; France became a republic. Ed.

[2] To most of our readers, this prophet born in Placentia, Newfoundland, and as far as I know now living in a lunatic asylum, will be well known from the newspapers. A certain Mr Nathaniel Halhed, M.P., declared himself on his side in a special pamphlet, and defended him in a speech in Parliament, March 31, 1795. Mr Halhed himself prophesied that the Millennium would start on November 9, 1795, when the sun rose at Jerusalem. Whether this really happened the papers have not yet reported.

[3] The London district where Bedlam lies.

The Four Times of the Day

Plate I, Morning

HOGARTH, who had a very good sense of what many a writer and artist prefers to ignore, that is, the part for which Nature had intended him, has chosen to represent this time of the day, not by any of the great soul-uplifting scenes of a spring or summer morning, but a winter one, and there again, not the funereal pomp of the frost-encrusted bushes where winter sleeps until its resurrection, or the pine forest moaning under its flaky burden of snow, but—Covent Garden vegetable market in London. That is where he feels at home. What, in fact, could his particular genius have made of a May morning in the country? No doubt a few wretched nightingale catchers with their all-too-familiar courtier faces, enticing those sweet songstresses into a trap without even noticing that the sun is rising over their noble occupation; or a few belles of doubtful reputation engaged in emptying bottles of May dew over one another's heads, with gestures and grimaces which no May dew will ever wash off. What he would make of a winter landscape, the reader will be able to surmise from what he is going to see and read here about a winter morning at the vegetable market.

It is just eight, as can be seen from the church clock, very cold, and snow has fallen. The impressions which we observe in the foreground come from the iron mounting of small wooden shoes (pattens) which were then worn by the female population, and enabled them to glide, to the advantage of shoes and feet, a few inches above the mud of the streets. These were the sort of footprints they made in the year 1738; now everything is more civilized. The clatter made by these little horse-shoes on the

London pavements is by no means disagreeable to a stranger's ear, especially if—as is mostly the case—the pedestrians are pretty. Did one not see that they were pedestrians, one might sometimes take them for cavalry approaching, at least light cavalry.

The main figure in the whole picture for which all the other splendours of the winter sky and the winter earth with its snow and riches serve only as a frame, so to speak, is the lovely pedestrian in the centre. You can see she is already beyond the first stage of a religious devotee whose double duty, towards Heaven and her neighbour, she has this morning partly fulfilled, and partly is about to fulfil. She is on her way to church, and at a time of day and year when even the decision to do so proclaims a sanctity which was never imparted to a wholly sinful heart; and how much does she not care for her neighbour! For to be sure, she would not doll herself up like that for her own benefit. She must have started already at four o'clock that morning, thus by artificial light; we cannot be surprised, therefore, if in practice everything has not turned out exactly as theory intended it should. It is a well-known principle in the building of kitchens that they should be light enough not to need any artificial light during daytime. But anything which is prepared by artificial light can, as a rule, be served to advantage only under such light; and by this token I should imagine that the lady might be acceptable by candlelight. We must also take the season into account here; the brightness of the snow as well as the cold are not at all favourable for certain little flowers; only peach blossoms thrive in the snow. But now to the subject in a more serious vein and in a manner more worthy of it. We have here, in the year 1738, a lady who would still like to look what it was already too late for at the end of the last century—charming. Beauty spots (mouches) float about her gleaming eye like midges round a candle flame, a warning to any young man whose glances would like to imitate them. On her cheek, of course, one notices something like a birth certificate in indelible writing. But it is not really that; there are wrinkles, it is true, but they spring surely from the corners of the mouth where Cupid plays his little pranks.

This gentle play communicates itself to the cheeks in tiny waves which, propagating more and more, like ripples, withdraw finally behind the ears. Even the bosom still shows its gentle undulation, although there the ice is already forming. The right arm wears its winter garment quite negligently and easily, while the hand with the fan (in winter!) succours the

Morning

lip which with that strained smile is no longer able by itself to cover the gap in the teeth. However, only two fingers are needed to look after both, fan and lip. How daintily this charming damsel handles everything! I can wager that lip grips its syllables just like the hand does its fan. The way she holds her neck is a master stroke, especially when combined with the gentle inclination of the upper part of her body. It seems as if the neck, through gentle elastic opposition, would promote the glorious waving of the pennant which flows out there from the gable into the morning air. What a pity it is that pennants have gone out of fashion! The times are not what they were, to be sure; nowadays, when Divine Service has ended, the procession looks just about as brilliant as a queue for alms; in the old days it used to look like a fleet setting sail with all the world's splendour on board. Wherever it sailed, victory attended. Everybody saluted and everybody struck—the hat; it was irresistible.

The lady is not only unmarried—but has never been married. All the interpreters agree in this, and I must confess I have no objection to raise. Whoever has long been a spinster, with all the little fineries which that state unfortunately entails, gets to like them in the end; indeed, the little bits of affectation increase since they become more and more necessary and cease only with the end of the spinsterhood, or with the spinster herself. This is as human as it can be. I should not like to decide whether even the wisest of men, were he to live for five hundred years like Cagliostro, in order to 'sell' his higher wisdom, would not also make an advertising face in the end, which would appear to our more naïve philosophers, or to the angels in Heaven, like the face of that spinster. Merely through force of habit man cannot become better on his way through life, and to get over this he must first die. I also seem to remember that somebody has called the day of death a wedding day. *Les beaux esprits se rencontrent*—just like philosophy and spinsterhood.

What may have been responsible for the definite opinion of the interpreters is perhaps the excessive dryness of the subject. Nichols even calls her 'the exhausted representative of involuntary spinsterhood'. Of course, all prolonged tending of fire is bad for the health, and none more so than that of the Vestals' fire. Just as ordinary metal smelters are subject to lead poisoning, an occupational disease of foundry work, so are the heart smelters to what one might call the Vestals' occupational disease. But— by God! the former still leave us the metal, whereas with the latter both

277

smelter and metal are lost. Have mercy on them! would I exclaim over their bosoms had I not just noticed in that saint's eye a glance at the scene in front of Tom King's Coffee House, which stifles my pity. All is not yet lost. Sounding boards are no impediment to happiness in married life. The dull murmur of reproach achieves distinctness thereby, the private sermonizing obtains more life, and the orders to the servants the needful volume upstairs and down, without all of which no household can exist. The wooden figure as it stands there has cost our good artist rather dear; it is in fact the portrait of an old spinster with whom he was, if not exactly related, at least very well acquainted. She is said to have been quite content at first with her role in the work of her friend, probably on account of its close similarity to the beloved original. A sentiment of such rare good nature, though based only upon ignorance of worldly intrigues, would have well merited Hogarth's blotting out the figure of the heroine who had expressed it. But that certain type of good friend who is never missing persuaded him to leave the magnificent figure, not without endeavouring, at the same time, to enlighten the lady as to the scandal of such a procedure, and with such good effect that in the end her portrait remained, but on account of it Hogarth was blotted out from the matron's Last Will, in which he would gladly have remained, she having rather handsomely provided for him there. Whoever hopes to inherit something from an old aunt should beware of making any satires upon women over fifty, but should be the ruder to all under forty. Readers of *Tom Jones* will remember here that Fielding, when he describes the appearance of Tom's and Blifield's mother,[1] expressly states that she looked like this lady, and Fielding, as one knows, read her character very well. *Tom Jones* is twice as entertaining to read if one knows this.

The lad, or whoever it is behind her, is her attendant. The poor devil appears to have been put not only upon half-rations, but upon half-livery too, which in addition, as a *donatio inter vivos in linea recta descendente*, seems to have been handed down from his sixth predecessor. He wears slippers only. His feet are frozen anyway. In the *Taschenkalender*[2] I have said that he has no stockings on. For this I was criticized by an Englishman of mature judgment; such a thing, he said, would be unheard of in

---

[1] *Tom Jones*, Book I, Chap. XI. Ed.

[2] As mentioned in the *Introduction*, Lichtenberg had been revising his contributions to the *Taschenkalender* before publishing them in book form. Ed.

England. The mistake is easily corrected: I have only to say that he presumably wears stockings. A more miserable, starving and frozen object would be hard to imagine; in such circumstances, of course, that inner peace cannot fail him which here plays about his eyes and lips. Under his arm he carries a voluminous prayer-book, apparently the only comfort which his mistress has vouchsafed him against all this misfortune. That is how the old, rich aunts behave, especially about the time when they are laying their Last Will; they hatch them better that way too.

On the left-hand side, as if built against St Paul's Church (St Paul's, Covent Garden—not to be confused with the famous one in the City), stands Tom King's Coffee House.[1] Hogarth has intentionally selected his viewpoint so that this den looks as if it were the sacristy of the Church. It was, strictly speaking, only a miserable shed whose chimney was lower than the epistyle of the porch in that fine church. The debaucheries which were enacted here and which not infrequently ended in murder are indescribable. After Tom King's death, the virtuous widow, who apparently stands there in the doorway, continued the evil business until at last justice roused itself. It is probable that Hogarth has by this picture contributed not a little to her awakening. A marvellous subject for the satiric artist! To get the matter talked about in public houses as well as at the dinner table of the mighty cost him only a few lines with the etching needle. The London police force is a stern, clever and order-loving lady, but it fares with her as with many another honest person: her servants are sometimes the devil of a use to her. Thus something may cry to Heaven for a long time without its being heard in the very next court of law. I say it is probable that Hogarth helped to arouse justice; for these engravings appeared towards the end of the year 1738, and in June 1739 Madame King was arrested. Her sentence was: she was to raze the 'sacristy' to the ground, pay a fine of £200, go to Newgate for three months, and if then the fine was still unpaid, she was to stay there until she had forked out the last penny; apart from all this, she was to give security with a considerable sum to be on good conduct for the next three years. This is an excellent expedient of English justice for clipping the wings of people who have

---

[1] On the original engraving everything is reversed, but wrongly, as will be clear to everybody who knows London and Lowes' famous hotel, which we see here on the right. This is again proof that Hogarth did not always take the trouble to reverse the copies of his pictures. In Ireland's version, too, this Plate is presented as in ours.

strayed into such an occupation. For should they stray again, the security will be lost, and justice will then, as a rule, cut a little deeper still, or will even hang the little bird without further clipping, according to circumstances. However, Madame King paid up and conducted herself well, and with the remaining offertory pennies from St Paul's Church built three cottages not far from Hampstead, a village near London set upon a charming hill; to this day these are still called Moll King's Row. There, in September 1747, she died, apparently in her bed. From the fine imposed on her, as well as from the offertory pennies, the reader will be able to judge for himself what may have been going on in close vicinity to the columns of that house of the Lord.

The nest has opened just now; the proceedings must have been pretty warm in there last night, for they have melted even the snow upon the roof. First to be flung out is a wig of some standing, though a false friend to its master whom it has deserted in time of trouble, leaving his bald head under a hail of blows instead of helping to ward them off. There is something very funny about the flight of that wig. Had it been a learned company which is being conducted to the door there, one might, at least in the half-light, almost take it for Minerva's bird that had presided over the night's proceedings, or for a lyre which like Spenser's harp rises to Heaven to greet the morning star. The van of the company which is spewed out here hurl themselves like liberated beasts upon a couple of innocent creatures, one of whom has come here to sell garden plants and the other, with the basket upon her arm, to shop, and who have arrived thus early. The fellow with the braided hat is said to be Irish: his wig has remained faithful to him, but it has suffered not a little in service. In any other place than upon a head it would hardly be regarded as a wig at all. Next to the fire sits a creature who would surely be much flattered if we said that she looks almost human. She seems to be dumb, or else her vocal chords have perhaps suffered in a fight, for like a medicine bottle she wears a label round her neck upon which is written what is to be found there. It is her history, though it is not this which she presents to the old spinster, but the abominable facts themselves—her face. She is a beggar; can she entertain any hopes, seeing the beggar in livery? But he addresses himself only to his mistress's love of mankind and freezes for it. And here in public something may be expected from vanity enhanced by publicity.

In the background stands the notorious French-pox doctor Rock with his notice-board and his little potions and lotions, advertising himself and his medicines, to those who have fallen for the temptations of the illness in which he deals. In spite of its being so early and cold, he already has an audience, among them a woman wearing a hood because of the cold and the onlookers. Doctor Rock is said to be a true likeness, in spite of being a portrait delineated with so few strokes. Hogarth is extraordinarily gracious towards this man; he uses every opportunity of recommending him to posterity. What can he have done for him?

In front of that group we see, quite charmingly observed, two little schoolboys who, with their satchels like snailshells on their backs, are 'creeping like snails unwillingly to school'. At the moment this is done by staying put. Their attention seems to have been caught by a lighted lantern which a very energetic and heavily laden woman, who must have started on her way before daybreak, has hung upon herself.

Between the hands of the clock and the rising smoke are the words *sic transit gloria mundi*; thus it is a choice between vapour and the moving hands of the clock; passing splendour with or without hope of return. I believe that small reminder from above is directed at the top mast with the pennant. Poor auntie! she will probably have to grasp the smoke.

In Cowper's poem (Vol. I, p. 80), there is a very good description of the old spinster and her servant in ten-syllable rhymed iambics which well deserve to be looked up.[1] I have used some of its features. But it seems to me that the verse form of Butler[2] or that used by the author of the Bath Guide[3] would have been more appropriate to a theme of this sort.

[1] 'Truth', line 131, *et seq.* Ed.

[2] Samuel Butler (1612–80), author of 'Hudibras', a comic epic in three parts, described as 'a mock-heroic poem dealing with the pretensions and hypocrisies of the Presbyterians, Independents, and the rest of the caterwauling brethren'. It is written in couplets of four stresses with comic rhymes. Ed.

[3] Christopher Anstey (1724–1805). He wrote 'The New Bath Guide', 1766, a long poem in the form of a series of letters from members of the Blunderhead family staying at Bath to relations and friends. It is in several different metres and forms a lively comment on the fashionable society of Bath, its gossip and scandal. Ed.

Plate II, Noon

ALL the interpreters agree that this Plate represents the French Chapel in Hog Lane, St Giles, London. That street, as well as part of the adjoining district, was at that time inhabited almost exclusively by French *émigrés* and their descendants. That is why the paper kite which is hanging down from the church has been interpreted as symbolizing the people who were blown across the Channel by a religious storm and found here a safe harbour. But more of the kite later. It must have been greatly to the satisfaction of our good Hogarth that fate, without any help from him, had driven the French just where he himself would certainly have put them had it been in his power—into Sow's Street. For France cannot have had a more outright enemy than Hogarth; a pig-sty and Lutetia Minor[1] were synonymous to him. Altogether, things must then have been highly Lutetic in the whole of St Giles' parish. It should be noted that the floor of a church there which had been built in the year 1625 was by 1730 eight feet lower than the street, through mere piggery. This necessitated its being built afresh.

Of Hogarth's hatred of the French there are certainly traces enough in this Plate; indeed, it is all in all a rather murderous attack upon French faces, figures and attire. When he starts on this subject he knows no moderation, and that, alas, is the case here too.

According to the tower clock in the background it is now eleven o'clock and the service has ended. The door of the French chapel stands open and the spiritual flock is streaming through, laden with the Word. Most of the members are so drawn and marked that one would think some travelling

[1] Lutèce, old Paris.

Noon

charlatan has held his healing session here and has just dismissed the walking sick. The chief male figure is evidently a dancing master, in accordance with Hogarth's conviction that the main part of the French nation consists of dancing masters. If he is not, he deserves to be one. He wears a richly gallooned coat and a waistcoat, like a heavily ornamented saddle-cloth, which almost reaches to his knees. The whole figure exhales an incredible degree of tenderness and sweetness, in temperament at least. He is posed in a *pas de minuet*; the left hand inclined slightly downwards, and bent back at the wrist, is in harmony with the unmistakable expression of submissiveness towards the lady. On the right wrist hangs a modish Spanish cane. The tip of the index finger curves daintily towards the tip of the thumb so that they form a circle far too delicately joined for even the finest pinch of tobacco, and rather as if someone were to look at uncut diamonds against the light. Very fine and expressive. He is trying with these fingers to spin the words still finer as they issue from his somewhat broad, full and altogether not very charming mouth. The gesture is not uncommon in pulpits and on platforms where they try to impart to the useless coal-dust thrown out by the mouth, while it is still in flight, the appearance of uncut diamonds, or to the yarn which they are spinning the appearance of spun silk.

The lady with the delicately though rather widely slit mouth, through the intentional contraction of her somewhat extensive speech organ, would seem to give her thoughts the appearance which her lover—or maybe even her newly-affianced—would fain give his words with thumb and finger. Though hardly two steps away from the church door, she already rests her right arm upon his shoulder. This throws some light upon various things which the crinoline is meant to obscure. Its rather queer and singular cut seems in fact to have been chosen not so much for the sake of appearances as to give relief through expansion, and to render equivocal the perhaps only-too-visible increasing natural expansion, which is not in need of further elucidation. The garment would fit any sort of waist, and again it would accord with the ebb as well as the flow. It is also possible that it was meant to cover a slight abnormality in walking, which the little heir from her first marriage cannot disguise so well. I am speaking here of that highly-decorated young person of diminutive size who, conspicuous with hair-bag, solitaire, stick and sword, struts ahead of them. Or the dancing master might be his father, who in that case could expect little assistance in his business from his son's frame. But this is the way of the world: *Heroum filii nequam*. That the dwarf, moreover, should derive so much pleasure from the silver facing of his sleeve shows a spirit in keeping with the body.

On these engravings, the fashions of 1738 deserve special attention, for Hogarth is said to have observed them very meticulously. On our lady the arrangement of the ribbon bow is specially remarkable. I do not recollect ever having seen one placed so low, especially without a trace of a sash. Is she perhaps wearing the three-coloured emblem of equality? It looks rather dark behind that bright vanguard. The old head, which together with the youthful heads of the two lovers forms a sort of blunt pyramid, is beautifully contrasted with them. The expression seems to betoken some justified righteous indignation at the behaviour of the pair so near the door of the sheep-fold together with some unrighteous indignation at her own incapacity for anything of the sort. All seven heads are true emblems of an impregnable iron dogmatism and an unction which has eaten right down into the bones. With such as these let anyone try to dispute. It would be like trying to turn back The Flood with a fan. Their faith, if it was ever a living one, is now, at least, petrified. We need only look at the face close behind the dancing master's shoulder, at the expression of the 'Dominie' at the church door, and the woman in front of him hanging her head. One would be mistaken in thinking that a hang-dog denotes a man who hangs his head. No! those are often very honest people, but it denotes the sly, rarely honest listener who carries his head on one side, with one ear pricked to overhear his unsuspecting neighbour or to hear the little angels sing.

On the right-hand side, two matrons are exchanging a loving kiss, and how fervently! Their souls seems to be quite fused with one another, and their noses would follow suit if only they were less tough and corporeal.

Immediately behind these two matrons, a saint has posted himself close to the wall. The sermon was rather a long one, and he still has not finished. The troop of cripples who move into the street there turn their backs on us, and so we will let them go. The boy or dwarf in the wig and beehive-shaped cap with his little sister are really exaggerated, and a touch like that is only tolerable if it is sparingly used and is besides accompanied by other touches which prove that one is able to do better. But this is the least reproach to be levelled against Hogarth's presentation of that community. French people are not all like that. Quite impossible! And least of all, French Protestant *émigrés* of 1738. Hogarth had certainly no knowledge of that class of people. Wherever I have seen them, I have never noticed a single trait which could have occasioned anyone to depict them *in corpore* like this. On the contrary, they were everywhere an ornament to society, and even the matrons were paragons, who taught how decent mirth befits old age, and how mirth itself could become venerable thereby. They are English people whom Hogarth has drawn here, Methodists or members of some other religious sect; English-melancholic bigots, drawn in chapel where the dark sectarian sky weighs heavily upon the earth. Here is nothing of the rosy-coloured sky of the French nation, a sky which, worthy of adoration in that colour too, as promoting a rosy-coloured view of life—yet keeps the distance necessary for brightening up a life which in itself gives little enough.

If it was a Methodist chapel just after the sermon, on which the kite is hanging, another interpretation would be possible. These religious fanatics of great spiritual mobility are lifted up by every little pulpit breeze and float upon it to the Deity, with whose essence they believe they are uniting themselves; they tremble and glow and hear inexpressible things, but no sooner does the breeze give out, than they drop down and remain stuck at the next street corner.

On the opposite side of the engraving the artist returns to his element and there we follow him with delight. First comes a house with a signboard displaying John the Baptist's head on a charger and the inscription, 'Good Eating'. The two dog-teeth of the lion or wolf which seem to serve as brackets for the motto are here not so much symbols of parenthesis as the parenthesis itself; good eating (for teeth like that, that is). In the London of that time, most of the houses had signboards, often without the slightest reference to the standing or the occupation of the inhabitants. Perhaps a restaurant keeper settled in the house when John's head was already there. Close beside it on the house of a distiller, as indicated by the jug upon the post and the wooden jars hanging round the wall, is a signboard with a headless woman, and the inscription, 'The Good Woman'. Thus, there a head without a body and here a body without a head. How in England where, as in Germany, the best women always have the best heads such a thing could have been tolerated, and still is tolerated, I fail to understand.[1] The idea is not Hogarth's invention, for in fact this type

---

[1] It cannot have escaped Lichtenberg that a woman without a head cannot nag, and so is a 'good woman'. He evidently speaks here with the tongue in his cheek. Ed.

of representation is quite common in London and, as Ireland remarks, is used especially by those who trade in paints. This I do not understand. A man without a head, on the other hand, would characterize a distillery not at all badly; for liquor puts spirit in place of the head, and spirits cannot be painted. But this is not enough for Hogarth. In that house where people eat according to the true time, he causes a little dispute about the food to arise between the man and his good woman. This is taken by her goodness in so bad part that even on a Sunday she throws a leg of mutton together with the vegetables upon the saints in the street. This is quite right. For even if the food gets no better through the transfer, still they will eat more peaceably up there. It is amusing to see how some passers-by who either hear the solid blessing coming down from above, or because they had been advised of it by the liquid blessing already upon their clothes, suddenly take refuge below in the house, either to demand damages for stains or to wait until the shower is over. One of them, happily enough, has a broom on him as if he had come to sweep up the good food.

In the foreground, to the left, just under the influence of the ominous head, there is still more of the good food on and above the pavement. A boy has planted an earthenware dish containing a baked pudding somewhat too firmly upon a wooden post. It breaks in half, and in that moment the pudding becomes good eating for a healthy English street girl, who forms an excellent contrast with the French dwarf. The figure of the poor devil who suffers this misfortune, Hogarth has taken from a picture by Poussin on the Rape of the Sabines, which is said to be in the collection of a Mr Hoare of Stourhead. Behind is a somewhat sensual coalition between Africa and Europe. The girl, whose plumpness is evidently meant to offset the flatness of the French lady, just as the vulgar sensuality of the negro the platonic whispering of the dancing master, has just fetched a pie from the bakery. Through the yielding opposition with which she meets the efforts of her coloured friend, part of the pie spills out on to the street. This, then, is good eating for the third time, and he would show a poor understanding of Hogarth's roguishness who did not see at the first glance that the kiss here is served as the fourth course. It is not for nothing that these two heads stand so directly under the motto 'Good Eating'. Quite in the foreground lies a cat that has been stoned to death—meant apparently as a cut at the filthiness of Hog Lane; perhaps also meant to symbolize good eating, for the fifth and last time.

Plate III, Evening

A SULTRY evening in September in the district of Islington, a large village near the northern outskirts of London. Among several places of public entertainment for the inhabitants of London proper, there is in that district a building known as Sadler's Wells, where in the summer plays of all kinds—comedies, tight-rope walking, acrobatics, ladder dances and gymnastics—are performed before large and hilarious audiences. The company, of course, is not brilliant, and it is not in order to be seen that the man of standing will frequent it, but more often in order to look and to find amusement, while his fine clothes remain hanging in his wardrobe and he, in his workaday coat, removed from all doing and suffering in the world of compliments, takes his ease here. There is something very refreshing about the country-side, and the interpreter of these engravings hardly ever takes up this Plate without being charmed by the memory of the few summer evenings he has spent under that sky with his friends.

The main group with which our artist has tried to animate that little paradise consists of a middle-class family, a London dyer and his wife, who neither by their physical nor—as we shall hear presently—their moral qualities are specially suited to revive in our imagination our first ancestors. They have three children with them, and our artist has raised great hopes of a fourth. In front of them slowly waddles the family dog, with strong indications of similar happy expectations. Everything is tired, lazy and heavy, and—oh, how warm![1] The housewife feels this most.

[1] Hogarth had the curious idea in the early copies of this Plate of having the man's hands blue and the face and breast of the lady red, to indicate the indigo dyer and the red glow of

She is, as one sees, nourished somewhat beyond the limits of the good and the beautiful. Bosom à la Montgolfière, happy expectations à la Montgolfière.[1] Oh my goodness! how heavy! Shakespeare once made a spring morn hang a dew pearl on every cowslip's ear.[2] With our cauliflower here, the sultry evening has essayed a similar experiment, and has hung a pearl close to the ear, beneath the hair. But this seems to have been a mere mistake, which is just about to be rectified; in a moment the pearl will be hanging on the ear lobe. In one hand she carries the hat and gloves of her dear husband, who in exchange carries the child, and even a part of the wife herself, who has been weighed out to him by Heaven with so generous a turn of the scales; for she really leans with the hand in which she holds the fan upon her husband's shoulder. On the fan we see a group from ancient times which, if we include the little urchin here in the braided hat, bears some resemblance to the present group. It is Venus and Adonis with Cupid; only there they have made themselves somewhat more comfortable. Our little city Cupid bestrides Papa's stick and expresses his indignation at his sister who, with a face already old and a temper and language even older, grudges him his little gingerbread man and wants to snatch it away from him.

What sort of children's faces these are! If it is true that early marked traits in children's faces are the precursors of ugliness in maturity, what will happen to children who were fated to be deprived already in their mother's womb of that innocent and charming vacuity of feature, so full of promise of everything good and beautiful? Cupid rides here upon the stick of Adonis and wears a cockade in his hat. The idea of giving Cupid the role of an ensign is not bad, only our young man here is a rather uncomely ensign. Briefly, the boy is not a soldier and never will be. How would he come to that so early in a country where, in addition to

---

the dyer's fire. A friend, however, dissuaded him from continuing in that manner. This has given rise to counterfeits, but since the false copies are painted over, whereas in the genuine ones only the lines are coloured and not the spaces between them, they cannot deceive a careful purchaser.

[1] A reference to the Montgolfier brothers, Joseph Michel (1740–1810) and Jacques Etienne (1745–1799), inventors of the balloon named after them. Ed.

[2] I must go seek some dew-drops here,
And hang a pearl in every cowslip's ear.
Midsummer Night's Dream
II. 1. 14

Evening

eternity. Stone monuments are not restored once they have decayed; signboards are renovated again and again and then replaced by completely new ones, till the end of time. I really think that this is a way to immortality, and since 'German' was always a synonym for 'good and cheap', a Pantheon on signboards could truly be called a German Pantheon. You may smile at this, but I am quite serious. What could be more honourable than to look down through the centuries from an inn signboard upon posterity passing in and out beneath, or to be looked up to by them? I can foresee, of course, that the idea will be ridiculed, but that is only because it is a good one. Few people can make a clever face when they look into the sun. Would it be any worse to lodge in the 'Herr von Leibniz' than in the 'King of Prussia'? Or would the place up there above the door or on the pole itself be less suited to the scholar than to the king? I should like to hear somebody tell me that, if he has the courage, and I should like to see the learned man who would feel ashamed to fill the place which up to now even the emperors and kings of the earth with their crown princes and crowns; which the golden angels; the sun, the moon and the stars; the kings of the animals and of the countryside; the eagle with single and double head, the lion with single and double tail, and the horse sometimes with none at all; which the rose and the lily of the field, as well as the French ones, in all their magnificence, have not disdained to occupy. Did they not hang up whole towns, London, Paris and Constantinople, to honour them with all their inhabitants? One should not object here that signboards also show waves, oxen, goats and Moors, who obviously belong among the apes; snakes and dragons and geese, who, even if they were made of gold, still remain geese. This is no objection for this was ever the way of the world with all marks of honour— with marble monuments and order ribbons, with letters of nobility and doctor diplomas, with titles and surrogate titles, and will ever be until the end of recorded time, who is the mother of us all. Did not the Devil himself in the shape of the last Duke of Orleans wear the Order of the Holy Ghost? Perhaps in this way the German inns will improve a little, at last. Some of them are still in a pretty bad state. What we need is a German Howard who will do for inns what the English Howard[1] has done for prisons.

A few more words about the German Pantheon in general. I would not

[1] John Howard (1726–1790), English philanthropist, pioneer of prison reform. Ed.

advise a marble one: one can foresee that eventually it would become a stony company of Germans which would not be of much more value than our papery one; even less, for it seems to me it is quite a question whether there are any other monuments at all in the world except papery ones, since tradition has ceded all her privileges to the printing presses, and now in its second childhood carries on a not quite honest traffic on the principle that one hand washes the other. I think the question must be answered in the negative. Even the eternal monuments which our fellow men have erected to themselves upon the rocks of the moon and the borders of the universe through new planets with new satellites, and on the path of the planets and comets, would be nothing without their paper certificates attached. Alexander would be forgotten like every other highway robber, had it not occurred to a writer to make him a testimonial about his commonplace exploits which, constantly renewed and embellished, continues to circulate throughout the world. On the road to the temple of eternal fame, a man may help himself along to the first few post-stations by means of gold and silver, etc., but whoever would continue his journey cannot do so without genuine paper money. Now let us keep in mind what paper signifies! A field of flax, what a prospect! What is not latent here, as a physicist would say! Oh! whoever goes past such a field, be it on horseback or on foot, he should doff his hat and ponder, not only on latent cuffs for his shirts, but on immortality too. If one wants to do something more, then I should advise signboards, for besides the publicity of marble, they possess all the imperishableness of paper. So much for the signboard of this inn, and now a few words about the inn itself.

Through the raised window we see that it is not a very brilliant company which is here, with one accord, employing Dr Johnson's remedy against suicide. The droll aspect of it is (for Hogarth does nothing without point) that these people have left a smoky town with the express intention of enjoying the country air, and have now shut themselves up in a smoky room. Those at the window have certainly the best seats here; one may reckon on a dozen others being behind them. For even at the cool window they feel so hot that they have taken off their wigs and have tied their handkerchiefs round their shaved heads. Outside the house is a man in such a position near the vine that he has drawn upon himself the attention of an inquisitive laundry girl. This class of people, the whole world over, will always poke their noses into things which have nothing to do with laundering, and which they do not understand. The meaning of the woman with the shoe in the background is, to tell the truth, not quite clear to me. The interpreters all glide over it, as if they had not noticed her, with the exception of Trusler, and he makes a remark which is not very plausible as far as I can see, namely 'that the woman behind is stretching the shoe of the girl (the elder daughter), shows that she is just as tired as the boy'. The reader will feel that there is nothing whatever to this. But there is surely something behind it. The English speak of a horseshoe, and, if a horse has already been mentioned, of just a shoe. If now, in addition, they had a certain saying, very common in German, about the horseshoe and its loss, then this female shoe may well have been lost, and such a thing could easily happen at Sadler's Wells, especially if one is accustomed to wear one's shoes somewhat lightly.

Plate IV, Night

HOGARTH has thought fit to present us here with a night scene which deserves the name only by the position of the sun, for we can see into the distance here just as well as at the three other times of the day, and can even read the smallest writing on signboards, mail coaches, and so on. In the first place, a bonfire is blazing in the foreground; secondly, there is a hand-lantern hard by; thirdly, fireworks are being let off, one of which is lighting the passengers in the coach the way to the grave; fourthly, these squibs are being let off by a boy with a torch which sends its light into a deep recess and brings something to the notice of the police; fifthly, a fellow operating at a barrel has stood on it his own candle-end in an earthenware candlestick;[1] sixthly, several houses are lit up; seventhly,

[1] It has been thought that this man was one of those useful citizens who devote themselves to the dirtiest business in the community, and who in English are sometimes jokingly called 'gold-finders'. Usually they are called night-men, and their carts night-carts. Their names and the time of day devoted to their business might have induced a man like Hogarth to put something of the sort into this picture. We find a similar lack of delicacy in him sometimes, and really even in this Plate, but this surely has a different meaning: the considerable size of the barrel and the fact that there is absolutely no trace of a cart point to something cleaner. Mr Ireland is quite right on this point; a distribution is to be made to the people on this (as we shall presently hear) festive evening of a barrel of strong beer, and that is what is being filled here. Thus, the interpreters could not well contradict one another more flatly, and the author is not entirely without blame: one knows the rogue and does not expect too much good of him, especially in the dark.

[A third interpretation, and one more in the spirit of Hogarth than either of the others, is that the man is pouring water into the barrel of beer, and thus uses the water in the wrong place; instead of quenching the real fire he only quenches the alcohol. His action would thus repeat in a modified way what happens a little in front of him, where the pisse-vache is cooling the spirit of the Freemason. Ed.]

the moon is shining; and eighthly, there is at the far end of the scene, just behind the bonfire, a great mal-fire, that is to say, a house ablaze. Perhaps a useful lesson on the consequences of bonfires. Thus Nature, art and chance have combined here to lend the artist their light. Boursault,[1] if he had sought to explain this picture to his Babette, would probably have said: 'Nothing is lacking here, but the lustre of your eyes to make day complete.'

It is the night of May 29th, when the restoration of the monarchy and of King Charles II is celebrated by the supporters of that great event (and who would not be among them?) with bonfires and illuminations. That is why we see oak leaves on the houses here and on the hats, in memory of the famous Charles' Oak which has become immortal. With that in mind, the artist has chosen the scene really well, and with a degree of feeling, traces of which are none too frequent in this work. For we must know that this is the district of Charing Cross in London, where stands that masterpiece in the art of bronze casting, the statue of the unhappy King Charles I, which is seen here in the background, and which our artist thus, in a way, causes to take part in the festivities. Who among our readers will not feel a longing for some future statue of the equally unhappy Louis XVI being a witness to similar joyful celebrations? We must not allow the impression which the artist's idea must make upon every person of feeling to be obliterated by the pranks which he has put into the foreground. It could not be otherwise at the public celebrations of a great and healthy people. Every creature enjoys himself according to his taste; the butcher boys, some of whom we see here, differently from the chamberlain, and the boon companion, who is here too, differently from the archbishop; and in such an event the artist who wants to represent all these pleasures will surely deal with them most wisely if he selects only those which he can himself appreciate.

The old man in the foreground is a heavily drunk and wounded Freemason still in full regalia with the square and apron. His forehead drips with blood as his mouth with wine. He glows all over and would burst into flames had he not fortunately crossed the stream of an artificial *pisse-vache*[2] from the upper storey. He is being led home by the Lodge porter

---

[1] (1638–1701) A French dramatist, well known in the seventeenth century. Among his works are also *Lettres de respect, d'obligation et d'amour*, also known as *Lettres à Babette*, 1666. Ed.

[2] The honourable name of a famous natural cascade in Switzerland.

Night

and candle-snuffer of the society, who has taken charge of his sword, but left him the stick. Such marked and re-marked skulls and brows as his are not afraid of a stick, but against the sword wisdom itself would not prevail. The old man is supposed to be the portrait of a certain Sir Thomas de Vale. Sir John Hawkins, who had known Sir Thomas, assured Mr Nichols that there was no resemblance whatsoever. On the other hand, Mr Ireland affirms that he very much resembles a portrait of that nobleman, which he had seen. *Grammatici certant.* Enough that we see here a drunken Freemason under the *Pisse-vache*—but this certainly is not satire upon the Order, at least not upon the true Order. It seems rather to be aimed at the drinking bouts and gaming clubs which called themselves Lodges, and with which London is inundated at every corner. Probably the cut here is even aimed at that notorious house 'The Rummer Tavern', the 'Roman Inn' where sessions of the Lodge were formerly held, but the new signboard which it bears, 'The New Bagnio', makes it clear what sort of sessions those were.

The house on the left-hand side contains a barber's shop with a signboard showing a head from which a hand is just about gently to extract a tooth, if the tooth does not devour the hand first, and the inscription: 'Shaving, Bleeding, and Teeth drawn with a Touch.' *Ecce Signum.* Through the raised window we look into the shop itself where, in fact, two of the operations which the signboard advertises are being executed upon an old head, namely shaving and bleeding, with one and the same touch. The teeth are not being extracted, it is true, but the nose of the poor sufferer is almost torn out. The barber's assistant who carries out the execution is, as one can see from the comb, a hairdresser at the same time. Comparing the fellow's dripping mouth and his razor opened at a right-angle with Sir Thomas's mouth and his Freemason's square, we are almost inclined to believe that he too belongs to the Lodge in the Rummer Tavern and has only been called away for a moment to minister to the old gentleman. And why should the old gentleman at that hour of the night find it necessary to dispose of his beard? Under the barber's display shelf a public dormitory is revealed, many of which could at one time have been found in London; a true Thieves' Caravanserai where young and old of both sexes with hen-equality and cock-prerogative publicly slept together. Thus a 'Bagnio' here, too, and a third over the way.

295

On the left is the Salisbury Flying Coach,[1] just about to rest from its flight and to collapse upon the pavement, so that even the slowest and heaviest German Diligence (sometimes it should more appropriately be termed a Negligence) would have time to crawl past it. On the side where it has come to rest is the gutter, and on the other the bonfire, which already seems to have caught one of the wheels. The unhappy passengers had reckoned more upon some gentle sleep than upon this dilemma, which calls for a quick decision, whether it is preferable to be drowned or burned. The little rascal beside the dormitory has evidently thrown a squib among the horses, and is now blowing with bursting impatience at another. The boys in front of the coach are butcher boys who are tending the bonfire. They appear to take a very cheerful interest in the happy arrival of the travellers, and to welcome them to the gutter. One of them holds the sort of mop with which one first swabs down and then dries the floor, probably to swab down and dry the passengers with it. This instrument forms a good contrast with the firework, like the gutter and the bonfire.

Anyone would think that with this the satire in the scene was complete. But it is not even half done; it is only just beginning. Up above there hangs upon a signboard the portrait of a somewhat broad, proud and pompous-looking gentleman, and beneath we read his name, the Earl of Cardigan. This is the inventor of the Flying Coach, who hangs here for the purpose of witnessing the execution of his idea down below, and as it were to write the epitaph over the grave of his own work. Others interpret it as merely a cut aimed at his lordship's fast and sometimes incautious driving. But whatever it may be, the lesson he gets is splendid. In a marble Pantheon his effigy would never have had the opportunity of witnessing a thing like that.

To finish with, a feature which is not easily noticeable but, once it is noticed, strikes one as one of the finest touches in the whole picture. In front of the statue there we see a cart with furniture. These are people who want to shake the dust of their residence off their feet unobserved, and move therefore at night; they are, however, unlucky enough, plan and

[1] If the English speak of 'flying' on the door of their mail coach, then they mean flying. This is no *cito, citissime* on an envelope; they keep their word. Only one must not mind from time to time a little halt, like the one in the picture. The Spaniards have improved upon this; they put on their mail coaches which are drawn by mules, *seguridad y celeridad*—safe and speedy—and also keep their word. The German post-chaise is the cleverest—it promises nothing and can therefore do what it likes.

details having probably been determined some time in advance, not only to have hit upon a night of celebration, and therefore illumination, but also to have come just between these two fires, so that, as if by the fire-balls of a besieged garrison, the silhouettes of their beds and chairs and their whole machinations become visible some hundred yards away. Should they be discovered by their creditors, they would not escape their 'Restoration'.

Of the original paintings, 'Morning' and 'Noon' were bought by the Duke of Lancaster for fifty-seven guineas, and 'Evening' and 'Night' by Sir William Heathcote for sixty-four guineas.